Handbook of
Emergency Management

Handbook of
Emergency Management

*Programs and Policies
Dealing with Major Hazards
and Disasters*

Edited by
WILLIAM L. WAUGH, JR.
and
RONALD JOHN HY

GREENWOOD PRESS
New York • Westport, Connecticut • London

Library of Congress Cataloging-in-Publication Data

Handbook of emergency management : programs and policies dealing with
   major hazards and disasters / edited by William L. Waugh, Jr., and
   Ronald John Hy.
      p.   cm.
   Includes bibliographical references.
   ISBN 0-313-25691-8 (lib. bdg. : alk. paper)
   1. Disaster relief—United States—Management.   I. Waugh, William
L.   II. Hy, Ronald J. (Ronald John)
   HV555.U6H35   1990
   363.3'48'068—dc20   90-2744

British Library Cataloguing in Publication Data is available.

Library of Congress Catalog Card Number: 90-2744
ISBN: 0-313-25691-8

First published in 1990

Greenwood Press, 88 Post Road West, Westport, CT 06881
An imprint of Greenwood Publishing Group, Inc.

Printed in the United States of America

The paper used in this book complies with the
Permanent Paper Standard issued by the National
Information Standards Organization (Z39.48-1984).

10 9 8 7 6 5 4 3 2 1

Copyright Acknowledgment

Material from S. C. Reznikoff, *Specifications for Commercial Interiors:
Professional Liabilities, Regulations, and Performance Criteria,*
copyright © 1979, is used with permission from Watson-Guptill.

Contents

Figures and Tables

Preface

The incremental nature of public policymaking in
response to major societal problems is very evident in
the analysis of governmental responses to hazards and
disasters. Policies and programs address small aspects
of larger problems and, in some few cases, small
portions of several problems. Emergency management
policies and programs in the United States, in other
words, overlap in some cases and fail to address other
important concerns. As a result, examining such
policies and programs as they address specific
disasters and hazards results in some unavoidable
redundancy.

Notwithstanding that problem, these chapters do
offer a needed focus on specific kinds of hazards and
disasters and indicate major facets of emergency
management that have not yet been addressed by
policymakers. It is hoped that the focus on specific
hazards and disasters will clarify a muddled arena of
policymaking for those readers seeking an overview of
the policies and programs currently in place and will
tie the issues together better for others. In a field
characterized by case studies and technical reports,
there is a need for broad, integrating analyses.

The chapters also suggest that concerns about
natural and man-made hazards and the potential for
catastrophic disasters are changing the field of
emergency management. State and local government
capacities to address complex issues are clearly
expanding. Demands for federal government programs to
provide technical assistance and financial support for
emergency management programs are increasing. The
demand for technical expertise is also increasingly

involving the private sector in everything from disaster response training to software development. Moreover, legal liability for failure to prepare reasonably for disasters and the expense of public and private insurance when adequate regulation has not been implemented are also forcing greater attention to emergency management as an aspect of risk management.

The field of emergency management is a relatively new one for students of public administration, political science, and public policy. Some of the credit for stimulating that interest in emergency management has to be given to the Federal Emergency Management Agency and the National Association of Schools of Public Affairs and Administration for sponsoring a faculty workshop at the National Emergency Training Center in Emmitsburg, Maryland, during the summer of 1984. This book is just one of products of that investment.

Emergency management has become so popular recently that it is now being taught in an inchoate form to students in the aforementioned disciplines. This text is designed to introduce the complexities of emergency management policies and programs to such students and furnish them with enough information to give them a firm grasp of the subject.

This text stresses the utility and applicability of emergency management policies and programs and is peppered with illustrations explicitly related to the most frequently occurring emergencies in the United States. In addition, the material unambiguously demonstrates the generalizability of policies and programs from one disaster to another.

Many persons have helped us prepare this book. Although it is impossible to cite each person individually, a few deserve special thanks. We are particularly indebted to Dr. Marvin Health of Washburn University and Mr. Monte Venhaus of the University of Arkansas at Little Rock. We are also grateful to our students at Georgia State University and the University of Arkansas at Little Rock whose blank stares and illuminated faces pointed us in the right direction. Finally, this book is dedicated to our families as a way of thanking them for their understanding, patience, help, and love.

Needless to say, we bear the responsibility (but not the blame) for all errors and omissions.

William L. Waugh, Jr.
Atlanta, Georgia

Ronald John Hy
Little Rock, Arkansas

Handbook of
Emergency Management

1

Introduction to
Emergency Management

William L. Waugh, Jr., and Ronald John Hy

One of the more telling applications of the
fundamental values of a society can be found in how
that society responds to risk, particularly risk that
may result in major losses of human life and/or
property. How society prepares for and invests in
programs to prevent or lessen the effects of such
disasters demonstrates the values placed on safety and
security, the capacity of its political and
administrative structures, the dominant political and
economic interests in the decision making process, and
the technical expertise that can be brought to bear on
problems. While all risks cannot be eliminated, many
can be minimized once they are identified.

During the 1980s Americans experienced the
tragedy of dozens of major catastrophes, from volcanic
eruptions to air crashes. Nonetheless, although the
decade closed with the devastating Exxon Valdez oil
spill, Hurricane Hugo, and the Loma Prieta earthquake,
it is too early to tell whether policy changes will be
made to change significantly how we deal with such
disasters. It is not too early to see, however, that
the threat of technological and natural disaster has
become very real for many Americans. The objective of
this volume is to examine how we have addressed some
of the major hazards and, in some measure, to assess
the adequacy of those efforts.

To some extent, the development of policies and
programs to deal with potential disasters in the
United States does point out the value that we place
on security, that is, the levels of risk with which we
are willing to live. The assessment of that risk, in
itself, is a political process influenced by the

personal and professional interests of the assessors, the level of public attention (or inattention), the economic interests that may be affected by programs to eliminate or lessen the risk, and the reality that many social and economic interests have little influence on the policy process.

For example, exposure to radiation beyond certain levels is harmful to humans. Radiation can be detected and levels of radiation can be monitored, usually in terms of the number of roentgens of exposure per hour. However, the minimum number of roentgens per hour to which humans can be safely exposed is not really known, but is set by scientists who are influenced by their professional judgment, the level of public attention, and various social and economic factors.

In the area of environmental hazards local governments are key actors in policy development and implementation. They make land-use decisions, enact construction codes, and frequently act as primary administrators in disaster management. When formulating such policies and programs government officials almost always defer to "political feasibility," even at the expense of technical knowledge.

In general terms, emergency management policies can be divided into four categories: mitigation, preparedness, response, and recovery. Mitigation policies and programs are those involved with the decision of how to respond to a risk and the implementation of programs to reduce or eliminate that risk (Petak, 1985: 3). Scientific assessments of risk generally represent a consensus derived from a large number of competing interests rather than a simple, objective assessment (Johnson, 1987). Risk reduction programs, too, can be intensely political when they involve land-use decisions, building codes, and other forms of regulation. Preparedness policies and programs are those involved with the development of response plans, identification of resources, and the training of emergency services personnel (Petak, 1985; Waugh, 1988). Response policies and programs are those that become operational once a disaster occurs, including emergency medical services, housing and food assistance, evacuations, and search and rescue operations (Petak, 1985; Drabek, 1985). Recovery programs address the immediate problems of stabilizing the affected community and assuring that life-support systems are operational (Petak, 1985).

There is some overlap in these four functions, but the categorization is useful in identifying the appropriate timing for various activities. Efforts to restore the community to its original condition or to some degree of "normalcy" are generally beyond the scope of emergency management, although there is considerable interest in the long-term effects of major disasters. These four functions will be examined more closely in chapter 2, but the terms are important to a full and complete understanding of emergency management policy.

As this volume will illustrate, there are numerous considerations that have generally determined how we define specific hazards and respond to potential disasters. Generally speaking, the major determinants of emergency management policies are issue salience, political and administrative responsibility, and technical expertise. These factors have profound implications for the effective design and implementation of emergency management policies and programs.

ISSUE SALIENCE

Issue salience is a critical variable in the policy making process. Many disasters result in large numbers of casualties and/or considerable loss of property. In that regard policies and programs to identify risk and prevent or lessen its potential effects, to prepare for the actuality of disaster, to respond to its occurrance, and to recover from its effects are imperative and should be recognized as such by policy makers. Many if not most disasters, however, occur so infrequently, as a result their effects are very difficult to anticipate. It is difficult to justify the expenditure of scarce public monies to prepare for events that may not happen (Waugh, 1988, 1990). In short, disaster preparedness efforts generally have very low salience among public officials, as well as among the general public itself, and that is a major impediment to effective policy making.

For example, when one warns about "one hundred year" floods, it is hard to generate public concern. When the odds are that the most severe floods will only occur once every century, the public and government officials are not as willing to allocate scarce resources to address the risk of flooding. Nonetheless, even though the odds are extremely low, there may be several "one hundred year" floods in the same year.

By the same token, the infrequency of major earthquakes militates against serious public preparation for their occurrence. The frequency of earthquakes in California tends to increase public awareness of seismic risk, but the infrequency of major quakes makes that risk abstract. Recent major earthquakes in Mexico have caused California authorities to reassess their understanding of the risks to their constituents and to reevaluate their emergency management programs. While seismic risk is recognized, albeit only abstractly, by residents of California, public awareness of the earthquake potential along the New Madrid fault in the central United States and around the Charleston, South Carolina, area is minimal.

Much the same can be said of the hurricane threat along the Florida coast. The history of major hurricanes is not well documented because of the relatively short time that records have been kept on storms along the North American Gulf coast. Experts have noted a general trend in the landfalls of major hurricanes from the south Florida coast toward Texas, but that trend is only a very general one and not one that suggests laxity in preparedness efforts in Florida. Increased development and the long periods between major events mean that there is a very large population in south Florida who have had little or no experience with major hurricanes, a significant percentage of which are elderly and may require special assistance in responding to a hurricane threat. Increased development also means more vulnerable property, despite building codes and zoning regulations designed with hurricane risks in mind.

Similar examples can be drawn from our experience with tornadoes, hazardous waste spills, structural failures, volcanoes, mudslides, tsunami, fires, droughts, nuclear accidents, air and train crashes, and other disasters. The infrequency of events lessens the competitiveness of emergency management programs for public funds and political support.

FRAGMENTED GOVERNMENT RESPONSIBILITY

The second major impediment to effective action is the fragmented government responsibility for emergency management programs. The U.S. federal system fragments policy making vertically between national and state governments with relatively little real autonomy at the local level, and horizontally among a multitude of competing agencies with overlapping jurisdictional prerogatives (Mushkatel and Weschler, 1985). Effective decision making and program coordination is difficult at best, particularly in the absence of a strong "lead government."

Most disasters do not result in mass casualties or high levels of property damage. Consequently, local authorities generally have to assume full responsibility for disaster preparedness and mitigation efforts despite limited technical expertise, fiscal resources, and administrative capacity. The net effect is that many communities find that it is much easier to secure funding to rebuild after a disaster than it is to find funding for disaster planning and preresponse efforts (Waugh, 1988).

When disasters are more frequent, the risk of casualties and/or property loss is very great, and the hazard crosses state boundaries, there is greater likelihood of a prominent federal role in policy making and program administration. In general, federal attention to hazards means greater technical and fiscal resources for emergency management programs. Nonetheless, local governments still tend to be the first responders to disasters. Many types of disasters, such as floods, fires, and tornadoes, produce very localized damage. Only when such damage is very great is there an expectation of federal assistance in responding to and recovering from the disaster. Presidential disaster declarations are intended to provide assistance in such cases. Similarly, state government assistance may be triggered by the severity of disaster with local authorities and individuals expected to assume sole responsibility for lesser events. Such expectations would appear to need little explanation; however, the determination of whether a disaster declaration will be made is not necessarily a purely technical one. Economic, social, and political considerations influence the willingness of federal and state agencies to intervene in largely local disasters. As will be evident in the analyses to follow, there are many reasons for federal or state involvement (or its lack) in emergency management programs.

The most visible institutional response to emergency management concerns nationally is the Federal Emergency Management Agency (FEMA), which was created in 1979 by Executive Order 12148. The constituent programs were transferred from several departments to FEMA. The Defense Civil Preparedness Agency was transferred from the Department of Defense; the Federal Disaster Assistance Administration and the Flood Insurance Administration were transferred from the Department of Housing and Urban Development; the U.S. Fire Administration was transferred from the Department of Commerce; and the Federal Preparedness Administration, largely a product of the 1973 oil embargo, was transferred from the General Services Administration. The merger was designed to bring most of the disaster preparedness efforts under one roof. Administratively, the merger caused some difficulties because of differences in organizational structure and process and differentiation by disaster type caused by the separate program mandates. More importantly, politically, the merger resulted in the dominance of a civil defense perspective among the senior FEMA administrators. As will become clearer in the chapters to follow, the political and administrative context of FEMA's development has had a profound impact on the federal emergency management effort and, in turn, on state and local efforts.

In the 1980s, the Reagan administration proclaimed a strong commitment to state and local self-reliance. In terms of most emergency management programs, that commitment manifested itself as a reluctance to assume responsibility for disaster preparedness. The exception to that predilection was in the area of civil defense. The Reagan administration demonstrated a willingness to commit federal dollars to programs designed to increase the "survivability" of nuclear war, both in terms of relocating and protecting people and in terms of assuring the continuance of economic and political institutions. To the extent that crisis relocation or evacuation programs and other emergency management programs may contribute to civil defense objectives, the administration was willing to provide more federal funding and support. An outgrowth of this merger of agencies and the Reagan administration's professed commitment to state and local self-reliance was the development of the Integrated Emergency Management System (IEMS). The premise behind FEMA's IEMS model was the promotion of generic disaster programs. Indeed, as the legislative history reveals, the creation of FEMA itself was based on the view that disaster-related programs may be useful adjuncts to U.S. civil defense efforts (GAO, 1980; GAO, 1984). Unfortunately, that close connection between federal emergency management efforts and civil defense has had a "contamination effect" on many state and local efforts (May, 1985). Dozens of communities have chosen not to have mass evacuation plans because to do so might increase the likelihood of nuclear war or, at minimum, more risk taking by nuclear strategists. Notwithstanding that perspective on the connection between crisis relocation and civil defense, the field of emergency management has suffered from the tendency to liken emergency managers to the air raid wardens so familiar during the 1940s and 1950s. The fact that the officials and offices to which many states and localities assign emergency management responsibilities still have titles denoting their "civil defense" origins does little to help the situation.

Apart from the concerns raised by the civil defense applications of some emergency management programs, there have been problems more clearly related to the partisan and philosophical orientations of the Reagan administration. The General Accounting Office (GAO) has expressed its concern that many FEMA programs have been poorly implemented, specifically programs in hurricane preparedness, earthquake mitigation and preparedness, and civil defense. GAO has concluded that FEMA has failed to provide adequate leadership and direction to those programs, despite its role as the "lead agency" for most federal disaster programs (May, 1985). Interagency coordination has been lacking in the hurricane preparedness program, resulting in considerable duplication of efforts by FEMA, the National Weather Service (National Oceanic and Atmospheric Administration), and the U.S. Army Corps of Engineers. Similar problems were found in the earthquake hazards reduction programs, with overlapping programs sponsored by the National Science Foundation, the U.S. Geological Survey, and the National Bureau of Standards. In both programs, there has been uncertainty concerning FEMA's responsibilities as lead agency, staffing problems (largely related to high turnover), and limited technical expertise. Often competing agencies have had far more expertise in the program areas than has FEMA (Waugh, 1988).

Quite apart from these difficulties, the reticence of FEMA to assume a more proactive role in the programs is more likely due to the Reagan administration's (and now the Bush administration's) preference for federal agencies to adopt supplementary roles, providing technical assistance to state and local governments but little funding and coordination of programs. Federal policy making has also lacked consistency and coherence--program emphases have changed frequently (May and Williams, 1986: 168; Waugh, 1988). The result has been uneven state and local efforts because of the lack of consistent federal leadership.

The barriers to effective action raised by political and administrative conflicts and distrust among emergency management-related agencies even within the same governments are also critical. The conflicting perspectives and jurisdictions of police and fire service agencies are common problems at the local level. Moreover, "turf" concerns and mandate prerogatives may even exist within agencies, such as among the constituent programs of FEMA. Without a higher authority responsible for coordinating emergency management efforts, jurisdictional conflicts can exacerbate already serious challenges raised by hazards and disasters. Concerns about legal liability for failure to respond to disaster effectively have prompted many communities to move the emergency management function into the city hall or county courthouse, rather than entrusting it to one of the public safety agencies or an independent office lacking a strong administrative mandate and sufficient authority to coordinate programs and disaster responses effectively.

TECHNICAL EXPERTISE QUESTIONS

The third major impediment to effective emergency management policies and programs is the lack of technical expertise to identify and assess hazards adequately, predict the occurrence of disasters, and provide the requisite technical information for the design and implementation of effective programs. In many instances, there is no clear causal relationship between possible precipitants and disasters, particularly for technological or man-made ones. Even when the hazards have been identified, it is unclear just how much risk is involved. Science provides considerable information on the precipitant conditions for many disasters, from earthquakes to droughts and tornadoes, but that knowledge is inadequate to the task of effective response. The timely prediction of major earthquakes, volcanic eruptions, and hurricane landfalls is crucial to the implementation of mass evacuation plans. Predicting flood and drought conditions accurately can facilitate the design of mitigation programs. The dilemma of emergency managers is that there is political risk in sounding alarms and putting emergency response plans into operation before disaster strikes, yet a few hours of extra time can mean saving lives that otherwise might be lost and reducing property losses.

THE PURPOSE OF THIS BOOK

The purpose of this book is to provide an overview of various hazards or risks in the United States. To the extent possible, each chapter will examine the following aspects of a given disaster type:

1. The level of risk in terms of frequency of the disaster, amount of public exposure, predictability of events, and history of property loss and casualties

2. The historical development of emergency management efforts by local, state, and federal governments to mitigate the effects of, prepare for, respond to, and recover from the disaster

3. The major policy problems in responding to the risk or hazard, including low levels of issue salience, inadequate funding of programs, unclear causal relationships, lack of technical expertise, and intergovernment and interagency conflicts

4. The options for alternative policies and programs to address the hazard

5. The status of current emergency management programs in terms of the levels of funding, capacities to respond to potential events, experience with disasters, levels of public support, and available technical expertise

6. The adequacy of present emergency management policies and programs

Disaster types can be divided into two categories: (1) natural, including earthquakes, volcanoes, hurricanes, floods, fires, and droughts; and (2) man-made or technological, including hazardous materials incidents, nuclear accidents, structural failures, aircraft disasters, public health disasters, and nuclear wars.

The objective is to provide the reader with an overview of the risk presented by each kind of disaster and the efforts that have been and are being made to reduce that risk. Treating the policies and programs that address the risks presented by each of the different types of disasters as discrete complexes, however, is not an easy task. There is a tremendous amount of overlap among the policies, programs, and agencies involved. To the extent possible, overlap has been avoided here. The reader should be aware, however, that program descriptions may fit several disaster types. For example, the assessment of FEMA disaster responses in the chapter on tornadoes will also be applicable to the chapters on hurricanes.

The question of whether emergency management policies, programs, and agencies are effective is also not easy to answer. For severe disasters, no amount of preparation is likely to be adequate. Those caveats will be examined in the final chapter, particularly as they relate to the current efforts to design and implement generic emergency management programs, such as FEMA's Integrated Emergency Management System and so-called comprehensive emergency management systems. The first task, however, will be to examine the four emergency management functions in greater depth.

REFERENCES

Drabek, Thomas E. (1985). "Managing the Emergency Response," Public Administration Review (January): 85-92.

Johnson, Branden B. (1987). "Political Interests in Risk Assessment," paper presented at the annual meeting of the American Political Science Association, Chicago, Illinois, September 3-6.

May, Peter (1985). "FEMA's Role in Emergency Management: Examining Recent Experience," Public Administration Review (January): 40-48.

____ and Walter Williams (1986). Disaster Policy Implementation: Managing Programs under Shared Governance (New York: Plenum).

Petak, William J. (1985). "Emergency Management: A Challenge for Public Administration," Public Administration Review (January): 3-7.

U.S. General Accounting Office (GAO)(1980). States Can Be Better Prepared to Respond to Disasters (Washington, D.C.: U.S. General Accounting Office, CED-80-60, March 31).

____ (1984). The Federal Emergency Management Agency's Plan for Revitalizing U.S. Civil Defense: A Review of Three Major Plan Components (Washington, D.C.: U.S. General Accounting Office, GAO/NSIAD-84-11, April 16).

Waugh, William L., Jr. (1988). "Current Policy and Implementation Issues in Disaster Preparedness," pp. 111-25 in Managing Disaster: Strategies and Policy Perspectives, ed. Louise Comfort (Durham, N.C.: Duke University Press).

____ (1990). "Emergency Management and the Capacities of State and Local Governments," in Cities and Disaster: North American Studies in Emergency Management, eds. Richard T. Sylves and William L. Waugh, Jr. (Springfield, Ill.: Charles C. Thomas).

2

The Function of
Emergency Management

Ronald John Hy and William L. Waugh, Jr.

Emergency management exists within a complex
political, economic, and social environment which
explains the lack of a coherent, coordinated policy
framework. Designing and implementing comprehensive
emergency management procedures is easier said than
done, principally because of the obstacles to
effective action created by the low salience of
disaster issues, the vertical and horizontal
fragmentation of our government system, and the
technical problems involved in identifying disasters,
defining risk, designing and implementing mitigation
and preparedness programs, and responding to and
recovering from the disasters themselves.

The unwillingness of federal and state
authorities to assume the lead role in the development
of emergency management procedures and to furnish
state and local governments with sufficient resources
to design, implement, and maintain effective emergency
management programs has become more apparent in recent
years. Inasmuch as disasters are geographically
localized, county and municipal authorities are most
often required to assume primary responsibility for
emergency management. However, the policy-making,
administrative, and fiscal capacities of local
governments to design, implement, and support
effective programs is very problematic (Waugh, 1988a;
Waugh and Hy, 1988).

As noted earlier, horizontal fragmentation is the
result of the multiplicity of state and local
jurisdictions that might be involved in an emergency.
Mutual assistance agreements may alleviate some of the
jurisdictional confusion, but emergency responses

normally create unanticipated intra- and interjurisdictional conflicts (vertical fragmentation) that may interfere with emergency management (Waugh, 1988b, 1989). Peter May and Walter Williams (1986) have suggested that a vertical and horizontal fragmentation--which they refer to as "shared governance"--is something with which emergency managers must learn to deal. Such fragmentation will not disappear, despite the fact that shared governance normally constrains the development of effective emergency management. Vertical and horizontal fragmentation, they contend, almost assures a lack of technical expertise, a scarcity of fiscal resources, and confusion concerning legislative mandates.

Emergency management is also constrained by a fundamental public distrust of government planning efforts, strong resistance to land-use and construction regulation, and a tendency--especially at state and local levels--to focus only on recent disasters. Then, too, levels of risk generally are difficult to measure and consequently are at best rough estimates. Cause-and-effect relationships are elusive and the levels of intensity of events may purely be matters of conjecture. As a matter of fact, it is often easier for government officials to wait for emergencies to happen and then deal with them than it is to attempt to prepare for and mitigate their effects; relief assistance is popular while mitigation and preparedness efforts are not.

Emergency management suffers from a lack of strong centralized direction and leadership. In large measure, the federal system's division of powers gives state governments, and their subunits, the lead role in responding to most types of hazards and disasters. A "facilitating role" has been adopted by the federal government, through the Federal Emergency Management Agency, leaving it up to state and local governments to develop emergency management procedures (Waugh, 1988b). Hence, we have a highly decentralized and largely uncoordinated set of emergency management procedures designed for and developed by each local government for some types of disasters. For other types, most notably civil defense and nuclear accidents, the federal role in policy-making and program administration is clearly dominant. In a few cases, such as terrorism-related events, the lead role is less easily determined unless law defines the responsibilities very clearly and the nature of the event is unambiguous (Waugh, 1990). As the following chapters will demonstrate, the lack of clarity in law, regulation, and historical practice and the differences in perceptions and interpretations of risk and disasters certainly complicate the assigning of jurisdictional responsibility.

DIMENSIONS OF EMERGENCY MANAGEMENT

Such decentralized procedures are not necessarily bad; in fact, decentralization, though not a lack of coordination, is essential given the complex array of dimensions and factors that must be incorporated into emergency management if it is to be successful. Also, because most emergency management procedures are implemented by local government to meet local needs, it is hardly reasonable to assume that one set of procedures is applicable to all localities regardless of the type of emergency.

Though certainly not an exhaustive list, figure 2.1 schematically illustrates the primary dimensions and factors that are discussed in the literature as being essential to emergency management. To be sure, the extent to which one dimension or factor is stressed over others depends upon the needs of each locality and the type of disaster.

The first dimension of emergency management mentioned in the literature is the need for strong cooperation and coordination among and within local, state, and federal governments. Almost all the evidence indicates that local government is the first responder, and thus its agencies are the primary managers of an emergency--even though the federal government may furnish most of the resources and technical expertise. According to Roger Kemp (1985: 42), most citizens expect their local government to:

1. Alert citizens of an impending emergency

2. Assess the magnitude of an emergency

3. Keep citizens properly informed of the situation

4. Evaluate the safety of dangerous areas

5. Relocate citizens from dangerous areas

6. Provide for rapid restoration of services

7. Assist in recovery services

8. Mitigate the impact of future emergencies

9. Protect life and property

Translated into its simplest terms, citizens expect local governments to prevent, respond to, and manage emergencies effectively. But, without inter- and intragovernment cooperation and coordination local government officials cannot implement emergency management procedures very well.

The second dimension found in the literature is the need for strong cooperation and coordination among public, nonprofit, and private sectors. Inasmuch as emergency management normally is conducted in a very ambiguous and fluid (even chaotic) environment, government--especially local government--faces implementation difficulties if it has to interact with other government jurisdictions and/or private and nonprofit sector agencies. In the areas of mitigation, preparedness, response, and recovery, local government needs help not only from other government agencies but also from the private and nonprofit sectors. For instance, construction companies implement building codes and chemical companies help detoxify hazardous products. Without help from the private sector in some cases, emergency management efforts are doomed to failure.

The third dimension specified in the emergency management literature recognizes the need to consider the type of disaster. When it comes to emergency management, this dimension is perhaps the most complex. The debate concerning the utility and effectiveness of so-called generic emergency management programs will be dealt with in the final chapter. Certainly we cannot anticipate all the possible types of disasters that might occur, although we hope to have identified the most common, major types of disasters in this volume. The risk presented by AIDS, for example, is something new for public health officials and, in many respects, is quite unlike other health threats that we have dealt with in the past. We are just beginning to recognize and respond to the risks presented by acid rain, the depleted ozone layer, subsidence and its effects on coastal areas, and other "emerging" hazards. In other words, there are many types of disasters that could be included in this volume but are not. There are also many types of disasters that may occur in the future. The potentially devastating effects of, say, a large meteor strike are difficult to anticipate in the absence of historical experience with such events.

For purposes of ease, the disasters with which we will deal here can be characterized as either natural or man-made. But, more complex typologies and categorizations are used, too.

CATEGORIES OF DISASTERS

Before proceeding further, a brief review of the different categories of disasters (see figure 2.1) is in order, especially since the literature indicates that different emergency management procedures are developed and utilized for different types of disasters.

Natural disasters are those caused by environmental phenomena. In many instances, natural disasters are associated with particular locales (e.g., hurricanes along the East coast; volcanoes in the Pacific Northwest and Hawaii) and appropriate emergency management procedures need only be implemented in the threatened communities. Certainly some locales are at greater risk for certain natural disasters.

Man-made disasters, on the other hand, are emergencies resulting from human activity, usually due to technological hazards not being properly addressed or "normal accidents" caused by factors such as imperfect hazard reduction systems, ignorance of the hazard or proper action, and/or human error (Perrow, 1985). Other factors resulting from intentional human action, as in the cases of arson, terrorism, intentional dumping of hazardous wastes, and war also contribute to man-made disasters. Normally, such disasters are not so locale-specific as they are industry-specific (e.g., hazards associated with the nuclear and chemical industries). To the extent that some hazardous materials are transported, there may be risks to communities not geographically close to the industrial plants that make, store, or use such materials. Disasters may also spread to distant communities when hazardous materials are carried by rivers, lakes, and the air. Nonetheless, it may be easier to judge the levels of risk that a man-made hazard presents to a community than it is to judge the risk presented by natural phenomena. The obvious exceptions are floods and mudslides for which there are data on past disaster events and clear patterns on which estimations of probability and intensity may be based and risks can be assessed.

Beyond describing disasters as either natural or man-made, the emergency management literature classifies them according to the degree of failure, and often concentrates on those disasters in which a high degree of failure occurs. In this context, disasters are grouped as either collapse or functional. A collapse occurs when all or part of a structure comes apart or undergoes large, permanent deformation and loses its capacity to perform all intended functions. A functional failure, on the other hand, occurs when, because of a natural or human activity, a structure lacks the capacity to perform one or more of its intended functions. Examples are leaking roofs and deteriorating parking structures. Normally, functional failures do not constitute a hazard or problem to human life and until recently were not considered to be part of emergency management. Now, however, there is increasing concern over various infrastructure problems occuring all over the country. Still, the bulk of emergency management continues to focus on collapses.

Figure 2.1

Dimensions of Emergency Management Policy

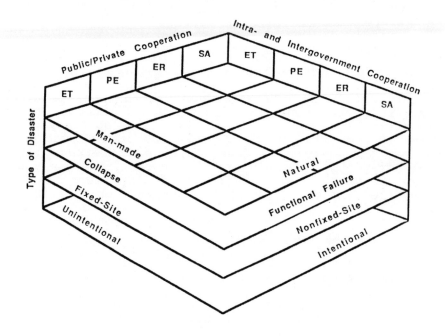

ET = engineering technology

PE = public education

ER = emergency response

SA = systematic assessment

Emergency management procedures also tend to differentiate between fixed-site and nonfixed-site emergencies. Fixed-site emergencies are those that occur at a specific location (e.g., nuclear contamination at a power generating plant), while nonfixed-site emergencies are those that occur at somewhat unpredictable locales (e.g., hazardous materials spills during the transportation of dangerous chemicals). The literature suggests that fixed-site emergencies are dealt with more quickly and easily than nonfixed-site disasters. For instance, when a chemical spill occurs in an industrial plant, managers are more likely to have expertise readily available to respond to the emergency. However, when a chemical spill occurs in a small town while that chemical is being transported from one site to another, communities may have more difficulty marshaling the necessary expertise to respond to the emergency. Federal and state regulations govern the transportation of dangerous materials and identification of threatening chemicals may not be a problem if regulations are complied with, but the lack of experience with such hazards can confound emergency management efforts. The professionalization of public safety agencies and development of state and local special response teams can increase the effectiveness of emergency management efforts, but the capacities of communities to respond to such threats still are very uneven.

Most emergencies are unintentional occurrences, although there has been a rapid increase in the number of intentional emergencies with which local governments must deal. That increase is largely a reflection of the impact of technology and population growth. Communities have become more fragile as they have modernized. Our complex "life-support" systems are more vulnerable to disruption (Waugh, 1982, 1990). The risks to life and property have multiplied as the potential for creating mass destruction and mass casualty events has increased. Individuals and small groups can create great havoc by intentionally disrupting transportation and communication networks, setting fire to large high-rise complexes, and so on, whether their intentions are political or simply criminal.

EMERGENCY MANAGEMENT FRAMEWORKS

There are a number of ways of structuring emergency management, including the mitigation-preparedness-response-recovery model mentioned earlier. The model chosen, however, may have a profound impact on the design of policies and the implementation of programs. From the language of the analyses to follow, it will be apparent that the aforementioned model is the dominant one, but it is also instructive to examine at least one other model.

According to the Merchant model (1986: 234), there are at least four major methods used in emergency management to deal with actual and potential problems created within each of these three dimensions: (1) engineering technology to reduce risks; (2) public education to address the potentiality of disasters; (3) emergency responses to coordinate efforts to reduce loss of life and property; and (4) systematic assessment to look at the effects of a disaster to prepare for similar future occurrences.

1. <u>Engineering technology</u> is used not only to forecast events but also to prevent undesirable reactions. Properly engineered systems and adequate maintenance furnish the best assurance of mitigation and to some extent preparedness.

2. <u>Public education</u> alerts persons to probable imminent dangers and keeps them informed as to potential risks and measures to take to reduce loss of life and/or property.

3. <u>Emergency responses</u> may reduce the loss of life through rescue and rapid medical treatment. Since in many instances the earliest and most crucial responses must come from the private and nonprofit sectors, coordination is essential.

4. <u>Systematic assessment</u> investigates the impact of a disaster on the affected community. A coordinated and collaborative effort involving inter- and intragovernment agencies as well as the private and nonprofit sectors is needed to furnish definitive data on long-term and short-term effects.

The Federal Emergency Management Agency (FEMA) classifies these four ways of dealing with emergencies into four categories: mitigation, preparedness, response, and recovery (McLoughlin, 1985: 166). In brief, the four functions can be described as follows:

1. <u>Mitigation</u>--activities that reduce the degree of long-term risk to human life and property from natural and man-made hazards (e.g., building codes, disaster insurance, land-use management, risk mapping, safety codes, and tax incentives and disincentives)

2. <u>Preparedness</u>--activities that develop operational capabilities for responding to an emergency (e.g., emergency operations plans, warning systems, emergency operation centers, emergency communications networks, emergency public information, mutual agreements, resource management plans, and training and exercises for emergency personnel)

3. <u>Response</u>--activities taken immediately before, during, or directly after an emergency that save lives, minimize property damage, or improve recovery (e.g., emergency plan activation, emergency instructions to the public, emergency medical assistance, manning operations centers, reception and care, shelter and evacuation, and search and rescue).

4. <u>Recovery</u>--activities that restore vital life-support systems to minimum operating standards and long-term activities that return life to normal (e.g., debris clearance, contamination control, disaster unemployment assistance, temporary housing, and facility restoration)

As a result, emergency management requires that governments possess the capability

> to understand (1) the total system, (2) the uses to which the products of the efforts of various professionals will be put, (3) the potential linkages between the activities of various professional specialists, and (4) the specifications for output and language which are compatible with the needs and understanding of others within the total system (Petak, 1985: 6).

EMERGENCY MANAGEMENT PROCEDURES

As indicated by this analysis, emergency management procedures are not only decentralized, but they are also differentiated enough to address the various types of emergencies--and are locale-specific and industry-specific enough to be useful to local officials who implement the procedures.

Figure 2.2

THE INTEGRATED EMERGENCY MANAGEMENT SYSTEM

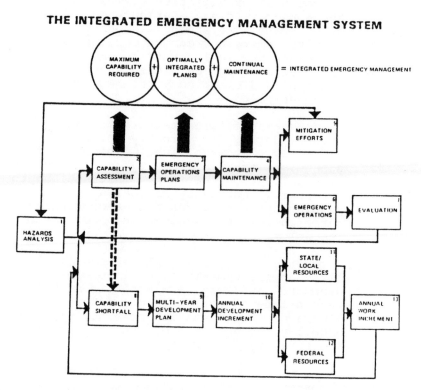

Source: Federal Emergency Management Agency

At the same time, FEMA is promoting an Integrated Emergency Management System (IEMS) based on the belief that there are elements common to most disaster emergencies and that increasing local governments' capabilities to deal with these elements will improve their abilities to handle any type of emergency. Among these common elements are provision of shelter, delivery of food and medical supplies, communications, continuity of law and order, and movement of people away from the danger zone (Giuffrida, 1984: 32). Such a position suggests that FEMA views emergency management as centered on response and recovery rather than on mitigation and preparedness, although it does not ignore the latter two elements. While such a focus is conducive to certain types of emergencies, it is not useful to other types. Intentional or not, FEMA's focus favors natural, collapse, fixed-site, and unintentional disasters and deemphasizes other types of emergencies.

Nevertheless, as previously mentioned, the literature indicates that emergency management stresses cooperation and coordination among public, private, and nonprofit agencies. Cooperation and coordination are essential in the areas of evacuation, declaration of emergency, medical care, public information, public safety, use of private property, record-keeping, and use of shelters.

Roles and Responsibilities

Citizens rely first and foremost on their local government for timely, coordinated, and comprehensive responses during an emergency. Furthermore, government officials may be held responsible if known potential hazards are not included in the emergency management plans. In its simplest terms, officials may be legally liable if they are not prepared to respond properly to emergencies. Consequently, local officials, whether elected or appointed, are obligated to have adequate procedures in place to avoid litigation (Kemp, 1985: 42). Notwithstanding the legal imperative to respond, however, emergency management programs do not compete well for scarce local resources (Waugh, 1988b). As a result, the level of preparedness among communities is quite uneven. Some communities, simply put, are grossly ill-prepared for disaster. In such communities, roles and responsibilities remain undefined and underdeveloped.

To establish clearly the roles and responsibilities of local officials responding to an emergency, the literature suggests various mechanisms that need to be incorporated into emergency management. Kemp's suggestions (1985: 43) are quite typical:

1. <u>Mitigation and Prevention</u>. Actions designed to prevent emergency situations or their consequences should be taken whenever possible.

2. <u>Role of Elected Officials</u>. Such officials should serve as public liaisons among their constituents, emergency workers, and media. They should officially declare an emergency,

request assistance from state or federal authorities, and guide policy-making.

3. <u>Chain of Command</u>. Lines of authority for all operational personnel through all phases of the emergency operation should be delineated, especially since a number of agencies from differing levels of government and the private sector will be involved. Ideally, operational personnel should know the chain of command and their precise duties during each phase of the operation.

4. <u>Organizational Structure</u>. Such a structure should be an extension of the routine organization, with additional functions added as needed. Existing lines of authority should be used whenever possible to avoid confusion.

5. <u>Emergency Management Procedures</u>. Such actions should be as nearly as possible integrated into normal operations. They should be part of routine activities. All operating personnel should be acquainted with each other. Procedures should be geared to deal with the types of emergencies most likely to occur.

6. <u>Employee Involvement</u>. The existing organization should require employee participation in emergency situations as part of their normal job description, requiring assessment and evaluation. Employees should know their roles and be able to carry them out competently.

7. <u>Coordination</u>. Plans must identify those agencies within the community that can lend support. Staff should be designated to serve as liaisons to facilitate cooperation among organizations in the public, private, and quasi-public sectors.

Randy Adams (1985: 52) points out that these roles and responsibilities need to be complemented by an operational plan which could include:

1. Specific information on the deployment of assigned personnel and their responsibilities

2. Needed background information, including potential problems as well as problems encountered during similar types of emergencies

3. Necessary logistic information about equipment, communication, health care, and safety needs

4. Instruction on tactical moves and strategies that will be employed during an emergency

Emergency Management Prescriptions

It has been suggested that the formulation of emergency management procedures follow several prescriptions (Michelson, 1984: 47). In the first place, emergency management is a continuous process. To be practical, therefore, it should not be formulated on the basis of a single emergency, but rather on several past emergencies, while at the same time allowing for the constant incorporation of new findings from new disasters.

Second, emergency management should attempt to reduce uncertainty in crisis situations by anticipating problems and projecting possible solutions. In this context, it is important to remember that the appropriateness of a response is better than the speed of that response, if the two cannot complement each other.

Third, emergency management always needs to be based on what will probably happen. Procedures should address what persons are likely to do in emergencies rather than be based on the expectations of their behavior patterns. In other words, procedures must be founded on factual knowledge and not on myths. There is a strong temptation to rely on such myths as persons will panic and be unable to cope or that local organizations will be overwhelmed and unable to perform effectively.

Fourth, emergency management is an educational activity which suggests that involved persons must first be aware that procedures exist and then understand them. Such information customarily has to be relayed to potential workers so that they know what to expect as well as what is expected of them. Simultaneously, many officials and community leaders resist formulating emergency procedures because they believe it to be unnecessary. Consequently, emergency management has to be "sold" effectively to each community or it will not be taken seriously.

Finally, emergency management ought to include exercises, especially for the response and recovery phases. The absence of actual practice will largely negate even the best plans. This, too, is sold to each locality since emergencies are not likely to happen frequently, and thus the community seldom takes such procedures seriously.

One other point needs to be made. According to the Trend Analysis Program of the American Council of Life Insurance, many emergencies, especially man-made ones, do not occur randomly or without warning. They are preceded by forces that can be identified well in advance (e.g., functional failures such as decaying physical infrastructures). Thus, policies ought to depend on forecasting.

EMERGENCY MANAGEMENT IMPLEMENTATION

Even after procedures are formulated and established, breakdowns may occur in the implementation phase. As an illustration, Congress passed the Resource Conservation and Recovery Act (RCRA) of 1976, a fairly comprehensive law designed to regulate and control the manufacturing, use, handling, and disposal of toxic materials. But, as Larry Swanson (1984: 260) has pointed out, the variety of materials are too complex and too numerous to be feasibly articulated in one set of procedures. He suggests that one set of procedures designed to address a vast number of situations is doomed to failure in the implementation phase. According to Swanson, while the listing by the Environmental Protection Agency of wastes considered hazardous is the backbone of RCRA, it is also the act's Achilles' heel. In attempting to apply the act to literally thousands of different types and subtypes of hazardous materials being generated in the United States, EPA could be expected to leave a few off the list that perhaps ought to be included. However, under the methods selected by EPA to identify hazardous wastes, many of the most toxic waste materials being generated are not listed and only a fraction of all hazardous materials are covered. For example, most dioxins were not listed as hazardous by the agency until after the dioxin episode in Missouri that required eventual evacuation and a multimillion-dollar buyout of property at Times Beach.

To be effective, therefore, emergency management has to be concerned with implementation as well as mitigation, preparedness, response, and recovery. This means that procedures to address regulatory compliance, enforcement, and training, particularly in the area of man-made disasters, are crucial. Whether they are implemented is another matter that will be dealt with in this book. For instance, more than 100 million shipments made up of over 2,400 substances of hazardous materials are made annually within the United States. It is estimated that these materials comprise more than 4 billion tons annually (Scanlon, 1986: 3). The vulnerability of any locality to the release of hazardous materials during manufacturing, transferring, storing, or transporting has to be an essential part of emergency management.

CONCLUSION

The following chapters attempt to deal with the various dimensions and factors summarized in this chapter. The authors, needless to say, differ as to which set of dimensions are central to emergency management, depending primarily on the type of hazard being addressed. Hence, the reader is treated to a variety of perspectives, promoting a rich diversity of emergency management procedures. Alternative procedures and strategies are explored, not prescribed.

But, it is important to remember that regardless of each author's preferences, the dimensions and factors set forth in this chapter are addressed in some fashion in the succeeding chapters. Improvement in procedures depends on a sound understanding of the nature and complexity of emergency management.

REFERENCES

Adams, Randy (1985). "Special Events Planning," Police Chief 52 (June).

Chartrand, Robert (1985). "Preparing for Emergencies," Futurist 19 (December).

Giuffrida, Louis (1984). "An All-Hazards Approach to Emergency Management," Police Chief 51 (May).

Kemp, Roger (1985). "The Public Official's Role in Emergency Management," Police Chief 52 (June).

Kowalchyk, John (1986). "Hazardous Waste Generators: How Much of a Hazard Is a Small User?" Public Management 68 (March).

May, Peter, and Walter Williams (1986). Disaster Policy Implementation: Managing Programs under Shared Governance (New York: Plenum).

McLoughlin, David (1985). "A Framework for Integrated Emergency Management," Public Administration Review 45 (January).

Merchant, James (1986). "Preparing for Disaster," American Journal of Public Health 76 (March).

Michelson, Rick (1984). "Emergency Planning Principles," Police Chief 51 (May).

Petak, William J. (1985). "Emergency Management: A Challenge for Public Administration," Public Administration Review 45 (January).

Quarantelli, E. L., and Jane Gray (1986). "Research Findings on Community and Organizational Preparations for and Responses to Acute Chemical Emergencies," Public Management 68 (March).

Scanlon, Raymond (1986). "Hazardous Materials---A Community Strategy," Public Management 68 (March).

Swanson, Larry (1984). "Shifting the Burden of Environmental Protection," Journal of Economic Issues 18 (March).

Waugh, William L., Jr. (1982). International Terrorism: How Nations Respond to Terrorists (Chapel Hill, N.C.: Documentary Publications).

____ (1988a). "States, Counties, and the Questions of Trust and Capacity," Publius 18 (Winter): 189-98.

____ (1988b). "Current Policy and Implementation Issues in Disaster Preparedness," pp. 111-23 in Managing Disaster: Strategies and Policy Perspectives, ed. Louise Comfort (Durham, N.C.: Duke University Press).

____ (1990a). "Emergency Management and the Capacities of State and Local Governments," in Cities and Disaster: North American Studies in Emergency Management, eds. Richard T. Sylves and William L. Waugh, Jr. (Springfield, Ill.: Charles C. Thomas).

____ (1990b). Terrorism and Emergency Management: Policy and Administration (New York and Basel: Marcel Dekker).

Waugh, William L., Jr., and Ronald John Hy (1988). "The Policymaking, Administrative, and Fiscal Capacities of County Government," State and Local Government Review 20 (Winter): 28-31.

3

Earthquakes

Richard T. Sylves

This chapter examines various aspects of preparedness for, response to, and recovery from earthquake devastation in the United States. It demonstrates how and why earthquakes pose a serious public policy problem. It furnishes an overview of national laws, agencies, and programs directed to earthquake mitigation, preparedness, response, and recovery. In assessing the politics surrounding earthquake damage recovery, the presidential declaration process will be inspected as will the problem of America's under-insurance against earthquake casualty and property loss.

A little after 5:00 the night of the 17th, San Franciscans felt the earth rumble beneath their feet. Suddenly the ground "vibrated, heaved, and pitched, wobbling in a demonic dance." In two distinct stages lasting a minute and five seconds, the quake stunned the populace. Showering plaster, scattering bric-a-brac, breaking dishes, shifting furniture, toppling walls, and collapsing roofs sent people scurrying. Waterfront houses lurched and fell apart. Streets developed gaping fissures. Many well-built structures survived with minor damage. But, fires broke out from severed gas lines and overturned stoves. Wood frame structures were soon ablaze as brave city fire fighters found their work stymied by broken water mains. Ultimately, about 250,000 San Franciscans were made homeless as a result of the quake and its consequences (Trippett, 1989).

Is this a description of the 7.1 Richter scale earthquake that struck the San Francisco Bay area at 5:04 p.m. on October 17, 1989? It is not. Rather, it is an encapsulated account of the great San Francisco quake, an estimated 8.3 Richter scale magnitude phenonenon that occurred at 5:12 a.m., before dawn, April 18th, 1906. While there are parallels between these two seismic disasters, the separation of eighty-three years makes each very different. Today, San Francisco, and California in general, is measurably better prepared for earthquakes than turn-of-the-century San Francisco. Yet, there are those who believe that the October 1989 earthquake is merely a prelude to one that is even more powerful and destructive. One California newspaper correspondent comments,

> The nightmare the state lives with is of an earthquake so disruptive it will disable the emergency services so critical in such an event. What everyone will want to know in the wake of such mind boggling tragedy is whether enough had been done to teach, test, equip, design, construct, and otherwise prepare for such an epochal event (Harris, 1987).

Whether the government had done enough to teach, test, equip, design, build, and otherwise prepare for a catastrophic quake was certainly a question raised by many Soviet Armenians in the aftermath of their December 1988 earthquake. Soviet officials report that the quake killed 25,000 people. About 15,000 people had to be extricated from the rubble, some 112,000 were evacuated from the area, and an estimated half-million were left homeless after the quake. Infrastructure loss covered an eighty kilometer area (NCCEM Bulletin, May 1989).

In following media coverage of the Armenian disaster, many Americans must have asked themselves whether the United States is open to such earthquake devastation and when the day of reckoning might come. A partial answer may have come in San Francisco's October 1989 quake, a seismic event of **greater** magnitude than the one that struck Spitak, Armenia. The epicenter of the 1989 quake was ten miles northeast of Santa Cruz and sixty miles southeast of San Francisco near Loma Prieta Mountain. The San Francisco/Loma Prieta quake was the third most powerful U.S. quake this century. Only Alaska's, 9.2 Richter scale Anchorage quake in 1964 and the "great" San Francisco quake of 1906 were more powerful. The 1989 quake affected eight counties covering 15,000 square miles and inhabited by more than 7 million people. Yet, there were only sixty-three confirmed casualties and 2400 reported injuries. Property losses were estimated in excess of $7 billion and 100,000 homes were destroyed or damaged leaving about 7000 people displaced in the weeks and months after the event (Klem, 1989).

No American state is more prone to earthquake activity than California. Having experienced so many seismic events of both small and large magnitude, no state is better prepared for an earthquake than California. The state's earthquake politics and policies have been carried forward in national earthquake policy. The state has a U.S. House of Representatives delegation numbering forty-five, more than ten percent of the chamber. It is expected to grow even larger after 1990 Census-triggered reapportionment. California obviously has enough political clout to influence national policy. As the nation's most populous state, it is often a trend-setter for the nation as a whole. Public opinion surveys of California disclose "a concern about earthquakes and show that a large percentage of the public wants strong governmental action to mitigate earthquake risk" (Turner, 1979).

Yet, in the early 1980s, one authoritative source observed,

> . . . .research in California, Washington, Missouri, and a score of other states has made it clear that seismic safety is not an important issue to public officials. Likewise, officials report that their constituents do not express any significant interest in this area. Seismic safety has not been an issue of importance in state and local elections (National Research Council, 1982).

Yet, since 1982, citizens and their political leaders have paid more attention to seismic safety, although much of this attention has been educational or symbolic. There are vocal and active political and administrative officials who are worried about seismic safety. However, these leaders are scattered thinly across the nation and are understandably most evident in areas that have already experienced earthquake destruction. The U.S. seismic safety constituency is not strong politically or economically.

Moreover, there are those who claim little has been, or can be, done to protect against earthquake destruction in the United States,

. . .some geographical areas have higher
risk profiles than others, and presumably
would want to be more cautious. So one of
the high-priority tasks is to develop a
spectrum of policy options, with cost
estimates for various areas, so that
informed debate can occur on the "How safe
is safe enough?" issue.

If, however, the goal is to help
society protect itself against the
financial, social, and psychological damage
cased by earthquakes, it is questionable
whether much has been accomplished in the
past two decades (Woodhouse, 1989).

This said, it is fair to ask how Americans perceive
risk in general and whether their political leaders
are responding in a way that the citizenry might
expect.

THE POLICY PROBLEM

An elemental step in the evolution of the U.S. policy
process is an understanding of the problem deserving
public attention. "Problems result from events that
affect people differently. Now all problems become
public; not all public problems become issues; and not
all issues are acted on in government" (Jones, 1984).
How do Americans perceive earthquakes? Do they
understand and appreciate what an earthquake is and
what it can do? Do they dismiss earthquakes as
regionally localized, low probability events with few
national consequences? Do they understand that seismic
mapping has revealed that a great many areas of the
United States, besides California and Alaska, are
subject to highly destructive earthquakes?

How does an earthquake hazard create a "public"
problem? What is it about the earthquake issue that
justifies creating government policies, programs, and
organizations to address it? Does national government
have a responsibility to respond to earthquake-damaged
state and local areas? If so, what should be the
character and extent of response? Should the federal
government assume responsibility in mitigating or
abating the destructiveness of earthquakes before they
occur and, if so, to what extent? How is reducing
vulnerability to seismic damage serving the public
interest? Are government efforts to promote this
purpose cost effective given the probability of
catastrophic earthquake and given pressures to use
dwindling budgetary resources to meet more immediate
political and social demands? In spite of a variety of

federal laws, agencies, and programs that exist to address earthquake disaster, many of the questions posed above have not been answered clearly in policy.

In simple terms, earthquakes, like other disasters, could overwhelm the emergency response and recovery capacity of individuals, businesses, and state and local governments. The human and economic loss inflicted by an earthquake and its consequences may be so great that tremendous help must be provided by people, businesses, and governments outside the damage zone.

This being the case, the problem of earthquake threat and destruction has been manifested in national policy and federal law. The federal government is expected to step in to provide basic humanitarian aid to the devastated areas. Many existing federal programs in place to serve purposes unrelated to disaster have emergency provisions and disaster response capabilities that can be marshalled and coordinated to address earthquake aftermath. Also, the president can independently issue a major disaster declaration or can grant a declaration once a state governor (or governors) petitions for one. Clearly, earthquakes are a legitimized public policy problem in the United States, but there remains tremendous variability in levels of earthquake mitigation and preparedness across the nation.

FEDERAL EARTHQUAKE LAWS AND AGENCIES

Federal authority to respond to disasters of any type can be traced back to the Disaster Relief Act of 1950. The act was intended to provide for a modest federal role by supplementing state and local efforts and in limiting federal aid to funds for temporary repair of local public facilities (May, 1986). The federal role was later expanded so that by the time the 1974 Disaster Relief Act was passed, federal relief programs included grants to states and localities for reconstruction of public facilities and to individuals for emergency needs, unemployment assistance, and mental health care. Low interest federal loans with extremely generous repayment provisions were made available to businesses, farmers, and individuals sustaining property losses.

Under a presidential disaster declaration in the aftermath of an earthquake, a wide variety of federal assistance is made available to the public. Temporary housing may be provided, but direct payments to individuals to secure their own temporary housing is more likely. Certain individual and family grant assistance is extended. This can be used for home restoration, medical and dental costs, and funeral expenses. Home restoration funds are intended only to help make one's home minimally habitable with the bulk of repair expenses to be covered by private homeowner insurance or from other sources. Post-quake unemployment assistance goes to migrant workers, the self-employed, and others not covered by unemployment compensation programs. Federal money can be provided to help quake victims even pay for legal services. Federal agencies can assist in search and rescue, debris clearance, repair of roads and damaged facilities, all in coordination with state and local agencies. Home and personal loans can be approved in post-quake circumstances.

The U.S. Federal Emergency Management Agency (FEMA) has lead authority to direct federal disaster response to a variety of emergencies and disasters, including earthquakes. As the smallest independent non-regulatory agency of the federal government, FEMA assumes the role of coordinator of assistance, some of which is provided by the agency itself but most is provided through the labor, budget authority, and resources of other federal agencies. It is important to remember that FEMA is not really a first responder to earthquake disaster. Instead, it is mainly in the business of earthquake disaster recovery.

While FEMA has authority to issue checks directly to the general public from its disaster field offices, there is still a general six- to eight-week waiting period attributable to the need to verify assistance claims (Cruickshank, 1990). Individuals, as well as local and state governments, may also find help from the federal departments of Transportation, Housing and Urban Development (HUD), Labor, Commerce, Agriculture, and others.

Communities can apply for federal disaster loans in the period of long-term recovery. The cost share under a presidential disaster declaration is 75 percent federal and 25 percent state, with states expected to reimburse the federal government for 25 percent of the total federal disaster relief and recovery cost. In FEMA organizational terms, the State and Local Programs and Support Directorate, through the offices of Natural and Technological Hazards Programs and of Disaster Assistance Programs, plays a central role in directing U.S. earthquake disaster response and recovery.

PREPARING FOR EARTHQUAKES

Today, federal policy directed toward the reduction of life and property loss in earthquakes is embodied in the Earthquake Hazards Reduction Act of 1977 (Public Law 96-124). The main objectives of the act are:

1. Development of earthquake resistant construction and design methods for public and high occupancy buildings in areas of seismic risk.

2. Development of procedures for identifying seismic hazards and predicting damaging earthquakes.

3. Coordination of information about seismic risk with land-use policy decisions and building activity.

4. Development of improved methods for controlling the risks from earthquakes and planning to mitigate such risks; also planning for reconstruction and redevelopment after an earthquake.

5. Education regarding earthquakes and ways to reduce the adverse consequences should an earthquake occur.

6. Development of research on utilization of scientific and engineering knowledge to mitigate earthquake hazards. Including the social, economic, legal, and political consequencies of earthquake prediction and ways to assure the availability of earthquake insurance or some functional substitute.

7. Development of research applied to control or alteration of seismic phenonema.

Under the law, the Geological Survey, the National Science Foundation, and the Bureau of Standards were furnished budget authority to research earthquakes. Some of this research was to be devoted to improved methods of earthquake prediction, but these agencies were also to conduct seismic risk analyses for emergency planning, set out zoning guidelines, and develop earthquake mitigation techniques for engineered structures.

The 1977 law called for preparation of an implementation plan and the start up of a program based on the plan by 1985. Land-use, building design, public information, insurance, warning, and relief activities were to be undertaken by federal, state, and local agencies. It was assumed that the greatest earthquake hazards result from inadequacies in building construction. A House Committee on Science and Technology report prepared collaterally with the 1977 measure concluded, "of all potential mechanisms to avoid earthquake hazards, the simplest and most direct would be zoning" (Petak and Atkisson, 1982). The report called for "risk zoning" critical parts of already developed areas, turning them into park land or maintaining them for purposes that do not make them a threat to public health and safety in quake conditions. High-risk undeveloped areas would be guarded against future earthquake-vulnerable development. Moreover, microzoning, that is zoning of small areas, was advocated along with revised building codes manifesting higher levels of earthquake resistance. Existing structures determined to be designed inadequately for earthquake were to be strengthened or replaced. New construction was to meet seismic design criteria intended to reduce earthquake hazards (Petak and Atkisson, 1982).

In compliance with the Earthquake Hazards Reduction Act, a five-year earthquake plan was submitted to Congress in 1984 under the earthquake program. The plan sets out the activities undertaken by the federal government to support the program and to address the U.S. earthquake hazard. The Comprehensive Emergency Preparedness Planning budget of FEMA for fiscal year 1987 was $5.778 million. The proposed fiscal year 1988 request was for $5.313 million with state and local governments sharing half of the cost in all natural hazard preparedness planning grants and including earthquake hazard reduction (FEMA Newsletter, May/June 1987).

PROBABILITY AND PREDICTION

Earthquakes are defined as high consequence, low probability events. Seismologic research shows that the possibility of earthquake is unevenly distributed over the United States. For example, geologic researchers tell us that the occurrence of major earthquakes along the San Andreas fault and its associated fault zones follows a general 80-year cycle. California was due for another major earthquake when the San Francisco/Loma Prieta earthquake struck in October 1989; however, scientists are uncertain whether this quake continues the 80-year cycle or is merely the precursor of an even more powerful earthquake to come soon.

Before the October 1989 quake, the U.S. Geological Survey reported a 50 percent probability of a magnitude 7.0 earthquake on the San Andreas or Hayward faults in the San Francisco Bay area during the next thirty years. The same study estimated that, "there is a 60 percent probability of a magnitude 7.5 or larger earthquake occurring along the San Andreas fault system in Southern California during the next 30 years." A 50 percent probability of 6.5-7.0 magnitude quake exists for the next 30 year interval along Southern California's San Jacinto fault, according to the study (FEMA Newsletter, September-October 1988). Consequently, many California officials are saying that the next catastrophic quake is not a question of "if" but a question of "when."

Most Americans know about California's vulnerability to earthquake, but many fail to recognize that Alaska and Hawaii are also states with high earthquake potential. Even fewer understand that a risk of major earthquake exists for the central United States owing to the New Madrid fault zone of southeastern Missouri and northeastern Arkansas.

> The probability that an M6 or greater earthquake will occur in the New Madrid region by the year 2000 has been estimated at 40-63%; by the year 2035 the probability increases to 86-97%. Depending on its actual intensity, location, and time of occurrence, such a quake could cause considerable damage, injury, death, and social disruption (Natural Hazards Observer, July 1989).

Seismic threat also exists for areas along the Carolina coast, for northern New York State, for much of New England, for Utah, and for seismically active, sometimes volcanic areas of Washington State and Oregon.

The ability to predict earthquakes is still a developing science. Japan spends more than $30 million per year on earthquake prediction research, but the United States dedicates much less public money to this purpose (Natural Hazards Observer, March 1983). However, no expert or technology can yet reliably provide an advance warning of major earthquake in the day or hour before it occurs. But, advances in seismographic, laser, and other technologies may soon make possible accurate prediction of earthquakes in some limited areas.

PUBLIC AND EXPERT EDUCATION ABOUT EARTHQUAKES

There is some consolation in that public education about U.S. earthquake threats is being advanced through the efforts of FEMA and the U.S. Geological Survey, both of which direct a variety of workshops, earthquake education centers, and community outreach programs. The agencies also circulate earthquake education brochures, maps, homeowner handbooks, and press releases. Several years ago the federally supported National Center for Earthquake Engineering Research (NCEER) in Buffalo, New York, began operation. NCEER disseminates state-of-the-art research results and information from a variety of earthquake research fields and heightens public awareness of the earthquake hazard (<u>Natural Hazards Observer</u>, November 1987).

FEMA has supported efforts of the Building Seismic Safety Council (BSSC), a private sector organization, to set out recommended provisions for the development of seismic regulations for new buildings. These are to be used by design professionals as well as by state and local standard-setting and building regulatory authorities. Completed in 1985, the BSSC document is an up-to-date set of design standards devoted exclusively to the improvement of seismic resistance in new buildings (<u>FEMA Newsletter</u>, November-December 1985).

ENGINEERING FOR EARTHQUAKES

The matter of abatement or mitigation of seismic hazards is, in policy language, a problem of "technocratic politics." It involves active participation of technical experts in policy making. Technocrats are usually highly specialized, can be found working at several levels in the policy process, work on projects requiring their expertise, promote the values of their professional training or discipline, and behave as rationalists who display confidence within limits (Jones, 1984).

The problem of seismic vulnerability is inherently technical in nature. But, if local governments are serious about abating seismic hazards in their community, structural engineers, geologists, architects, and other technocratic officials responsible for formulating and implementing such a program must agree on the scope and magnitude of the corrective action necessary. If they cannot agree on the technical means for reinforcement of buildings or facilities against seismic threats, there is little hope that the average citizen can be educated and convinced to support a program of seismic hazard abatement. Owing to long and relatively frequent experience with earthquakes, California's state government and many of its local governments have had considerable success in regulating new construction in a way that controls against seismic shocks. Reinforcement of old existing structures has proven to be more difficult. Petak and Alesch claim that there are tens of thousands of unreinforced masonry buildings in California, many built between 1900 and 1930, that are vulnerable to structural failure in an earthquake. After Long Beach and neighboring communities were rocked by a 6.8 Richter scale quake in 1933, 86 percent of such structures in the primary damage zone experienced structural failure (Petak and Alesch, 1988). These investigators reveal that while Long Beach and many other California cities adopted tough ordinances and codes for new buildings, it proved extremely difficult to force property owners to reinforce existing buildings. Add to this better reinforcement of utilities or infrastructure against seismic forces has been technically feasible, but has been resisted by public and private authorities who claim it is too expensive, unnecessary, or both.

It is essential to remember that structural mitigation of earthquake damage is not the complete answer to earthquake preparedness. Nonstructural approaches can be used, such as building and land-use regulations, construction standards, development restrictions, and zoning. Nevertheless, promotion of both structural and nonstructural approaches to earthquake mitigation involves the active participation of technocratic experts and officials.

RESPONDING TO EARTHQUAKE DISASTER: SEARCH, RESCUE, SECURITY, EMS, AND FIRE SUPPRESSION

National policy extends to either leading or augmenting post-quake search and rescue operations. The armed forces, reserve military organizations, and National Guard units can be mobilized, especially when an earthquake disaster assumes the dimensions of a national emergency. People in these organizations can conduct search and rescue operations, as well as serve security functions. Also, Forest Service, Park Service, Bureau of Land Management, and other federal agencies have some fire fighting capacity, although there is no formal national fire fighting organization. FEMA can be called out to assist other organizations fighting active fires. Local governments inside and outside the damage zone provide fire fighting capability, but firefighting elements of federal agencies can be lent to assist state and local fire fighting units. There is evidence that fire fighters working to extinguish massive southern California forest fires on federal lands were for a period detached to areas of Los Angeles to aid in mopping up fires in the aftermath of the Whittier quake of October 1987 (Passerello, 1987).

There is no formal national police force but instead special mission police-type units: the Federal Bureau of Investigation agents; Bureau of Alcohol, Tobacco, and Firearms agents, Treasury agents, Immigration and Naturalization Service border police, military police, and so on. In various ways these law enforcement agencies can supplement state and local law enforcement in post-earthquake circumstances.

The national government can augment post-quake emergency medical services where there are Veterans Administration hospitals and other federal medical facilities. The National Institutes of Health and Centers for Disease Control can also make contributions to protecting public health in periods of post-earthquake recovery. Military hospitals and staff may be used, as well.

What is most notable here is that federal offices and facilities are dispersed across the country. Therefore, many federal agency resources can be used in the response to earthquake disaster. It is the job of FEMA to help coordinate this response and to call in additional public and private resources if necessary. Under the Stafford Act, "In any major disaster the president may direct any federal agency, with or without reimbursement, to utilize the resources granted to it under federal law . . . in support of state and local assistance efforts" (CQ Weekly Reports, October 28, 1989).

According to the "Digest of Federal Disaster Assistance Programs," there are well over one hundred programs administered by about twenty agencies that can contribute to earthquake disaster response. Many of these programs are run by FEMA, but forty programs run by HUD and Agriculture comprise the bulk of the federal government's urban and rural housing efforts. Federal disaster relief law gives disaster areas priority in applying for assistance under several laws authorizing federal aid for housing, public works projects, water pollution control, and rural, community and economic development efforts. The scope of available aid ranges from major reconstruction help to many smaller benefits. States, for example, can get FEMA grants to provide mental health counseling to victims. The Internal Revenue Service can help disaster victims file tax returns that reflect losses, in effect helping them search for loopholes to cut their tax bills. The FBI can help identify fatalities by their fingerprints. In addition, the Department of Agriculture can provide food for the mass feeding of disaster victims, as well as distribute extra food stamps. It can also lend up to $500,000 to replace or repay damaged farm property or pay off debts. The Department of Labor can provide unemployment benefits for up to twenty-six weeks to disaster victims. In the event an earthquake demolishes dams or other flood control facilities, the Army Corps of Engineers can help repair the projects, as well as design and build projects to prevent erosion damage to highways. The Department of Education can even provide grants to repair or replace public schools, build new ones to replace destroyed private institutions, and furnish funds for operating expenses (CQ Weekly Reports, October 28, 1989).

PRESIDENTIAL DECLARATIONS AND EARTHQUAKES

Earthquakes of even moderate magnitude have triggered presidential disaster declarations. In 1983 Coalinga, California, experienced a moderate quake that caused extensive property damage but no loss of life. Owing to national media attention, the mayor of Coalinga was successful in convincing Governor Deukmejian and in turn President Reagan to grant Coalinga both a state and a presidential disaster declaration. Each presidential disaster declaration is determined subjectively, that is to say, largely politically. Not long ago when FEMA proposed regulations that would better define the criteria under which a presidential disaster could be issued, Congress forced it to withdraw the proposed rules (Settle, 1990).

Nevertheless, there have been regular efforts at the national level to rationalize the process under which a presidential disaster declaration can be granted. There exists a Federal Earthquake Response Plan which applies to twenty-five federal agencies. The plan covers the entire nation and emphasizes area specific planning and emergency requirements. There is also extensive regional planning applied to high probability earthquake vulnerable states. As recently as January 1988, President Reagan approved a "National System for Emergency Coordination" under which FEMA assumed the lead federal agency role in natural disaster, this including earthquakes of course (Meese, 1988).

The Robert T. Stafford Disaster Relief and Emergency Assistance Amendments of 1988 streamlined the declaration process so as to make federal aid to state and local governments more timely. The law contains few provisions specifically targeted to earthquake disaster, however, many of the assistance rules would apply in the aftermath of earthquake as they would for other types of disasters. One key passage gives FEMA new authority to participate with states in approved cost-effective mitigation projects on a 50-50 matching grant basis with total funding capped at 10 percent of the grants for all public facility restoration in a disaster. The limits on disaster preparedness improvement grants for each state were raised from $25,000 to $50,000 a year. The new law gives the president authority to call on the Department of Defense (DOD) before a disaster declaration is issued, if he or she judges that this is needed to save lives and protect property. This aid is limited to ten days and provides only 75 percent federal subsidization of DOD costs (FEMA Newsletter, November-December 1988). Many sections of the new law seek to provide more and faster individual and family assistance, particularly for temporary housing assistance. The Stafford Act, however, does little to remove the subjectivity of presidential disaster declaration issuance.

THE EARTHQUAKE INSURANCE ISSUE

A chronic problem of earthquake policy has been what to do about residential earthquake insurance. To date, the thrust of national earthquake policy has been to reduce the destructive power of earthquakes through the hazards reduction program discussed above and to administer disaster aid in the aftermath of an earthquake when a presidential disaster declaration has been issued. However, the federal government has not yet addressed private earthquake insurance or the reinsurance of private firms that sell earthquake insurance. Nevertheless, the Federal Insurance Administration (FIA), an arm of FEMA, has sold $165 billion worth of flood insurance to the public. Why does Uncle Sam help insure us against floods but not earthquakes?

In the United States, floods have occurred more often than destructive earthquakes; floods are generally more predictable than earthquakes; almost every region of the nation has experienced flooding over the years while earthquake experience has usually been region-specific; and assessment and validation of flood-caused damage is considerably easier than that of earthquake-caused damage. The frequency of flooding and the nationwide scope of the flood problem have helped build a strong coalition of political support within Congress for federal flood insurance. More than 18,000 communities follow the requirements of the flood insurance program. Collecting on a flood insurance claim is generally simpler than collecting on an earthquake insurance claim because water damage, more so than seismic damage, is likely to be observable and causality is therefore easier to establish. Insurance adjusters inspecting alleged seismic damage may argue that the settling of structures on their foundations, undermining by underground water flow, minor ground movement unrelated to earthquake, or shoddy construction caused the damage, not an earthquake, and they might then disallow the claim.

Moreover, the public and private insurance industry had had much more experience in marketing and managing flood insurance policies. Few private insurers are willing or able to sell a massive amount of homeowner earthquake insurance. Those that do sell residential earthquake insurance usually charge high premiums and make conditions of claim pay-outs extremely stringent. The Wiggens Report commissioned by FIA in 1980-81 concluded that many "large businesses in all parts of the country have earthquake insurance" (FEMA Newsletter, September-October 1987). But a later report by the California Insurance Department says few homeowners are insured against earthquakes. A secondary consequence of a major earthquake is fire and many homeowners in seismically active areas believe that their fire insurance will cover their losses should a quake trigger fires that envelop their homes. Some have even argued that homeowners without earthquake insurance may be tempted to set fire to what remains of their property in the aftermath of a quake so they can try to collect on the fire insurance portion of their homeowner policies.

An administrator of the FIA, Harold T. Duryee, believes that the federal government may soon provide an insurance mechanism to financial losses caused by an earthquake. Duryee has stated,

> FIA's position has been that action to establish a Federal Earthquake Insurance Program would be premature until the private insurance industry develops a consensus on the need and form of such a program. And even then, to the extent that federal involvement is required, it should be kept to a minimum, with as little burden as possible on the federal taxpayer (FEMA Newsletter, September- October 1987).

Duryee said that Congress, knowing that the private insurance industry now bears 100 percent of the risk of insuring earthquake losses, will not agree to any arrangement under which 100 percent of the risk is transferred to the federal government. Federal involvement in earthquake insurance would have to include, if it is agreed to at all, some risk-bearing share by the private sector (<u>FEMA Newsletter</u>, September-October 1987).

Since 1985, an Ad Hoc Industry Group on Earthquake and Related Natural Disaster Insurance Issues has been holding regular meetings. Composed of representatives from major private insurance companies, the group has proposed that private insurance companies be permitted to issue earthquake policies to owners of residential dwellings under the Write-Your-Own concept used by FIA for flood insurance. Under the National Flood Insurance Program's Write-Your-Own program, private insurance companies sell and service flood insurance under their own names, but through arrangements with FIA they are assured that they will not lose money as a result of their flood business. If applied in the realm of earthquake damage, a company could sell residential earthquake insurance in its own name what would protect against the "shake" damage of earthquakes and volcanic eruptions. "The premiums, less expenses of issuing and servicing the policies, would be remitted to the federal government, which would use the balance of the premiums and such additional federal funds as were needed for the payment of claims" (<u>FEMA Newsletter</u>, September-October 1987). Duryee said that if such a mechanism were approved in law it should permit reserves to be earmarked and accumulated against eventual earthquake catastrophe rather than require funneling of premium monies into the general fund of the U.S. Treasury.

Regarding commercial earthquake insurance, the industry group would like the federal government to serve as a final back-stop in the event of a catastrophic earthquake. At present, potential losses to the industry from commercial earthquake policy claims far exceeds potential losses from residential claims. Most private commercial earthquake policy insurers are reinsured by other private insurance companies, however, a congressional report says that a single earthquake could potentially kill tens of thousands of people and cause more than $60 billion in property damage. Such a level of devastation would financially overwhelm both primary and secondary insurers. Therefore, the group advocates creation of a federal back-up program of reinsurance to provide coverage against losses at a high level after a major earthquake.

The ad hoc industry group hopes to prepare legislation to be submitted to Congress that would address the twin problems of residential earthquake insurance availability and insurance industry solvency in the wake of a great quake (FEMA Newsletter, September-October 1987). But, at this writing, the federal government is not in the business of underwriting residential earthquake insurance coverage nor is it yet prepared to serve as the reinsurer of private commercial earthquake insurance companies.

BUILDING EARTHQUAKE PROGRAM SUPPORT

If "events" are defined as natural acts perceived to have social consequences and if those social consequences create human needs for which relief is sought, a "problem" is said to exist. However, not all "problems" deserve to become "public problems;" that is, problems that governments are obligated to address. When the human needs produced by the social consequences of an earthquake event cannot be met by private sources, a "public problem" results. Moreover, the fact that one level of government does not mitigate earthquake hazards has consequences for other levels of government. Vertical and horizontal information exchange about the problem of earthquake mitigation, as well as selected demonstration projects funded by joint federal-state arrangements, would go far in getting earthquake reinforcement on the policy agendas of each level of government.

If it is technically feasible to reinforce public and private facilities against seismic threats, then reinforcement must be cost effective for the state, the municipality, the special district government, or the private property owner. Advocates of a program to build or reinforce more earthquake-resistant structures must prove to political executives and to regulatory overseers that past and present methods used in design and construction engender significant earthquake vulnerabilities. More than this, they must prescribe appropriate corrective measures and estimate the costs of these measures to the government in question.

One way to advance this purpose is to advocate use of the Uniform Building Code (UBC). The 1988 UBC contains the most significant changes in seismic design provisions since 1973, among them a new base-shear formula, a new seismic zone map, new definitions for regular and irregular structures, new rules for dynamic analysis, and special design and detailing for masonry, wood, concrete, and steel. Engineers, architects, planning officials, and building inspectors making use of the new UBC now have a better basis for building new structures and reinforcing old ones against earthquake forces (<u>Natural Hazards Observer</u>, May 1989).

Obviously, assessing the seismic vulnerability of existing structures must be supplied by utility or public works officials. The costs of collecting, organizing, and analyzing this information is likely to be high and so there may be resistance to the effort. If this resistance occurs, it may be necessary for state authorities to mandate that local seismic vulnerability assessments be conducted.

There are cost-effective ways to improve seismic resistance in existing structures even in the absence of a complete vulnerability assessment. Areas of low seismic probability, but high damage consequence, should incorporate mitigation techniques and technology as routine inspection and building maintenance is performed. For example, utility workers doing routine inspection and maintenance could tie transformers down with cabling to protect them from being toppled and knocked out of operation during an earthquake. Natural gas utilities could replace each damaged or deteriorated pipe joint with an earthquake-resistant flexible connector, as part of standard repair and maintenance practice.

State and local officials must have some estimate of the earthquake magnitude for which they should prepare. This involves measures of both frequency and intensity of previous seismic events and it entails probabilistic studies of the frequency, location, and intensity of anticipated seismic events. If the consequences of failure are severe, one should should design for the worst-case earthquake regardless of its probability of occurrence. Where failure has only economic consequences and an owner wishes to accept some risk in the interest of reduced construction cost, it is appropriate to accept some less conservative design (Scott, 1979). Government must, however, limit damage and maintain its capacity to rebuild in the aftermath of a major earthquake.

If these studies and calculations can be made, it then becomes necessary to identify the most highly vulnerable areas of the community. Low cost reinforcement measures will obviously be better received by public and private officials than will high cost measures. However, high cost measures such as reinforcement of major public facilities, or relocation of existing or planned buildings, is likely to meet strong resistance.

In determining the seismic hazard abatement actions to be taken, costs imposed on the taxpayer and the private property owner must be considered. Obviously, municipal officials can be expected to oppose the abatement program if it threatens to consume too much financial capital and labor relative to the benefits it provides in seismic safety, in more rapid recovery of services when seismic disruptions occur, and in minimizing harm to the public.

Another matter involves <u>public</u> benefits versus <u>private</u> benefits. Seismic hazard abatement carries with it both private and public benefits. A store owner who reinforces the brick masonry on the front of his or her building helps reduce damage and repair costs to the building in an earthquake, yielding a private benefit in terms of damage costs avoided. At the same time, such reinforcement is a public benefit to sidewalk pedestrians who may be passing in front of the store at the time of an earthquake. Consequently, tolerating high vulnerability to earthquake damage carries with it, in many cases, social costs that are higher than individual private costs.

In the case of an electric utility, if the financial cost of a hazard abatement program is perceived only in terms of the utility's internal costs and benefits, the program may be adjudged inefficient, or cost ineffective, at too low a threshold. The failure of the utility to abate seismic damage carries with it social costs. If, for example, the full social costs of electric power loss are considered by the utility and its regulators, a program of seismic hazard abatement may be warranted even if it appears uneconomic in terms of the utility's internal accounting.

An important constituency for earthquake mitigation, preparedness, and response should be the emergency management community itself. Those who conduct search and rescue operations, provide emergency medical care, maintain public safety, and suppress fires should press for stronger seismic hazard abatement programs.

Private industry has a vested interest in seismic hazard abatement. The accelerating use of high technology in commerce and industry and the deemphasis of physical human labor or human-powered machinery (including even the manual typewriter and paper files) have made business extremely dependent on the continuous availability of electric energy. Businesses such as banks have converted their records from paper to bits of data stored on computer tapes and disks. Many firms conduct virtually millions of electronic and telecommunications transactions each day through a system abjectly dependent on uninterrupted electric power. A prolonged power loss, for example, could create corporate disasters so serious that loss or unretrievability of computer-stored information may be more costly than all the firm's facility losses from an earthquake. Moreover, many businesses would not be able to operate on any level after a major earthquake. Even firms with auxiliary power generation capabilities might find that they cannot resume operation satisfactorily in the absence of utility-supplied electric power.

The public is more than simply inconvenienced by a widespread power outage. Because today even the most routine banking transactions require availability of computer information processing, and therefore electric power, people would soon discover that a power outage prevents them from withdrawing cash from their bank accounts. Retail stores would be unable to process even cash purchases if registers became inoperative. Credit verification of purchases would be impossible in the absence of electric and telephone services. The effect of prolonged power loss on residential, retail, and wholesale refrigeration facilities would be dramatic. Thousands of tons of perishable food would gradually become inedible, posing yet another threat to public health. Households without electric power lose use of cooking and washing appliances, lighting, television, air conditioning, and sometimes heating, to a name a few effects.

When Mexico City suffered its twin devastating earthquakes in September 1985, the loss of electric power closed the city's subway and trolley system. Four million daily commuters were left to find alternate means of transport. Hundreds of subway passengers had to be led through unlit tunnels back to the street. Traffic control devices went dead and center city traffic came to a complete halt, impeding the passage of emergency vehicles (The New York Times, September 20, 1985). Television and most radio communications were knocked off the air by the quake. Communications facilities unable to generate their own electricity did not function.

Electric power was cut in large sections of the capital by the first quake (estimated 7.8 Richter scale). Within two days of the first quake, an "aftershock" measuring 7.3 rocked the city, knocking out much of the power restored after the first quake. Because other utilities depend in varying degrees on electric utility-supplied power, communications, water, and sanitation services were impeded by the power outages.

The Mexico City quake may prove that the consequences of power loss are serious enough to justify electric system reinforcement even in low seismic activity areas. Concrete proof of the technical feasibility of a seismic hazard abatement program would go far in securing its advocacy and endorsement by national, state, and local government officials. The recent rise of corporate emergency management and planning should be an indicator of corporate executives' growing fear of the consequences of disaster.

People from areas that may never experience major earthquake must be persuaded that the loss prevention benefits of a seismic hazard abatement program carries political, social, and economic benefits to their area and to the nation as a whole. This is because of the interconnectedness and interdependency of all sectors and regions of the national economy. Consequently, these people must concede that they are obligated to absorb a portion of the costs of the abatement program commensurate with their share of the benefits. Distributing the costs of preventive and remedial measures and apportioning cost shares of post-earthquake rehabilitation and recovery programs among governmental jurisdictions will be a necessary task (Scott, 1979).

CONCLUSION

The October 1989 San Francisco/Loma Prieta earthquake captured the nation's attention and, perhaps for a time, sensitized Americans to the threat of major earthquake. This quake also helped Americans appreciate the national consequences of earthquake loss. U.S. House Speaker Thomas S. Foley remarked only days after the quake,

> It is obvious to me that we are not going to
> resolve this problem by letting California
> or other areas of disaster go without
> federal funds. That is not going to happen.
> If we have to take funds from other sources,
> we will have to do that . . . . If we have
> to regrettably increase the deficit, we will
> have to do that, but we will not have to say
> to one part of the country or another, "You
> have to bear this disaster alone" (CQ Weekly
> Reports, October 21, 1989).

Yet, most national, state, and local seismic safety and earthquake preparedness programs can be said to have been fashioned and implemented in the absence of experience with catastrophic earthquake. The San Francisco/Loma Prieta quake will certainly not be the last U.S. earthquake, nor will it likely remain the third most powerful U.S. quake in this century. Thus, it is fair to ask whether earthquake programs are adequate and whether they have yet been sufficiently tested by earthquake experience. Just as in national defense against nuclear attack, the proof of success in earthquake mitigation and preparedness will only come on some future day of reckoning. U.S. earthquake mitigation and preparedness programs must continue as policy based on "attainable consensus" of political and administrative officials, rather than on a "substantive conviction" of program participants. Widespread disagreement about the location, destructive power, and timing of earthquakes, combined with the expense and oft-times questionable engineering feasibility of reinforcement measures, make even "attainable consensus" difficult to achieve and sustain.

The adoption of seismic hazard abatement measures in the United States will probably be event-driven, much as federal air and water pollution control programs have been. A temperature-inversion air pollution tragedy in Donora, Pennsylvania, in 1948 helped initiate state and federal air pollution control laws and programs. Similarly, the Santa Barbara oil spill of 1969 helped launch tougher state and federal water pollution control statutes and programs.

Earthquake preparedness demands research, public safety resources, specialized expertise, and drills or practice exercises. For example, detailed seismic maps of the United States should be made available to state and local officials, particularly those responsible for public works and for emergency management functions. Earthquake preparedness needs to be better integrated into the work of utility and public works officials. Seismic vulnerability studies of municipal structures need to be undertaken in areas of even modest earthquake potential. Municipal officials should conduct thorough cost assessments of the facilities they own and operate, under an accepted accounting system, before they suffer earthquake damage. Past experience has revealed that municipal officials frequently fail to secure all the federal assistance they deserve because they cannot document the value of what they owned and operated before the quake disaster (Settle, 1990).

Private businesses and corporations of all types would do well to meet with public works and utility authorities so that common strategies and contingency plans can be drawn up to help abate seismic hazards. Such mutual planning efforts help protect expensive, delicate, and vital computer facilities and systems that are so necessary to public health, safety, and commerce after a great earthquake.

Media people and the public need more and better information about seismic risk and how it relates to land-use planning. Much could be gained by studying the earthquake mitigation and preparedness efforts of other nations, most particularly Japan and the Peoples Republic of China. Japan spends more than $2.2 billion a year on earthquake preparedness. California and the U.S. federal government together spend only a minute fraction of this sum on earthquake preparedness (Blakeslee, 1985).

Major American cities should examine their capacity to undertake large-scale rescue operations. New York City, for example, regularly must respond to the collapse of buildings. For this purpose, the city maintains an inventory of construction equipment and can, on short notice, call in private construction people and equipment to aid in extricating people from the rubble (Sylves and Pavlak, 1990).

American insurance firms and the federal government must work together to promote ways that make residential earthquake insurance more widely available, more affordable, and better serviced. It is unreasonable and foolish to think that private insurance companies individually or collectively could absorb the costs of catastrophic earthquake damage, even if they do not sell or service residential or commercial earthquake insurance. This is because a catastrophic quake would produce a colossal amount of claims by those with fire, auto, homeowner, life, and other types of policies. The question is, how under-insured is the United States for a major earthquake? Is it reasonable to expect a national government with a $2 trillion-plus debt and self-imposed, Gramm-Rudman policed annual budget deficit ceilings to swallow the bulk of catastrophic earthquake response and recovery costs? Is American earthquake mitigation and preparedness adequate to address catastrophic earthquake? Those questions are highly debatable.

REFERENCES

Blakeslee, S. (1985). "California at the Ready, It Hopes, for Big Quake," The New York Times (April 14), p. I1.

Congressional Quarterly Weekly Report (1989). "Help for Quake Victims," (October 21): 2797.

___ (1989). "President, Agencies Have Wide Latitude in Providing Aid in Wake of Disasters," (October 28): 2854-2855.

Cruickschank, J. (1990). Presentation at FEMA Headquarters, Washington, D.C., for Office of Training, January 25.

FEMA Newsletter (1987). "A Role for FEMA in Earthquake Insurance?," (September-October): 4-5.

___ (1987). "Federal Emergency Management Agency Proposed FY '88 Budget," (May-June): 8-9.

___ (1988). "New Disaster Legislation is Passed," (November-December): 1, 7-8.

___ (1988). "Probability of Earthquakes Cited," (September-October): 11.

___ (1988). "Seismic Safety of Existing Buildings," (September-October): 9-10.

Harris, T. (1987). "Are We Really Prepared for the Inevitable Great Quake?," The Sacramento Bee (October 11), Editorials Section 4, pp. 1, 6.

Jones, Charles O. (1984). An Introduction to the Study of Public Policy, 3rd Edition (Monterey, Calif.: Brooks/Cole).

Klem, T. (1989). "Earthquake Tests Disaster Response," Fire Command (December): 19-22.

May, Peter J. (1986). Disaster Policy Implementation: Managing Programs Under Shared Governance (New York: Plenum Press).

Meese, Edwin (1988). "National System for Emergency Coordination," Memorandum for the Domestic Policy Council (19 January).

National Research Council (1982). Earthquake Engineering Research - 1982 (Washington, D.C.: National Academy Press).

Natural Hazards Observer (1983). "Japanese Earthquake Preparedness," Vol. VII, No. 4 (March): 6.

___ (1987). "NCEER Seminars on Earthquakes," Vol. XII, No. 2 (November): 6.

___ (1989). "The Last and Next New Madrid Earthquake," Vol. XIII, No. 5 (May): 11.

___ (1989). "Earthquakes and Building Codes," Vol. XIII, No. 5 (May): 5.

NCEEM Bulletin (1989). "Speakers Focused on Implications of Earthquake in Armenia," Vol. 6, No. 5 (May): 5.

The New York Times (1985). "Mexico Quake," (September 20): 6.

Passerello, J. (1987). "Reader Response to October Whittier Earthquake Inquiry," Emergency Management Dispatch 4 (October-December): 1-3.

Petak, W., and D. Alesch (1988). "Earthquake Hazard Mitigation in Long Beach and Los Angeles," in Crisis Management: A Casebook, eds. Michael Charles and John Choon Kim, pp. 231-47 (Springfield, Ill.: Charles C. Thomas).

Petak, W., A. Atkisson (1982). Natural Hazard Risk Assessment and Public Policy (New York: Springer-Verlag).

Scott, S. (1979). Policies for Seismic Safety: Elements of a State Governmental Program (Berkeley, Calif.: Institute of Governmental Studies, University of California, Berkeley).

Settle, A. (1990). "Disaster Assistance: Securing Presidential Declarations," in Cities and Disaster: North American Studies in Emergency Management, eds. Richard T. Sylves and William L. Waugh, Jr., pp. 33-56 (Springfield, Ill.: Charles C. Thomas).

Sylves, Richard, and Thomas Pavlak (1990). "The Big Apple and Disaster Planning: How New York City Manages Major Emergencies," eds. Richard T. Sylves and William L. Waugh, Jr., pp. 185-219 (Springfield, Ill.: Charles C. Thomas).

Trippett, F. (1989). "First the Shaking, Then the Flames," Time 134 (October 30): 50-1.

Turner, R.H., et al. (1979). Earthquake Threat: The Human Response in Southern California (Los Angeles: Institute for Social Science Research, University of California).

Woodhouse, E. (1989). "Earthquake Hazards: A Political Perspective," Annals of the New York Academy of Sciences (January): 72-80.

4

Volcanic Hazards

William L. Waugh, Jr.

Prior to the spectacular eruption of Mount St. Helens in Washington State in 1980 there was relatively little attention in terms of either emergency management programs or research paid to volcanic hazards in the United States. The U.S. Geological Survey (USGS) was responsible for issuing warnings of volcanic activity under the Disaster Relief Act of 1974 (PL 93-288). But, volcano-related programs were spread among several divisions within USGS, including the geologic, water resources, and national mapping divisions, with no designated lead unit. USGS has operated a monitoring station, the Hawaiian Volcano Observatory, near the Kilauea volcano since 1948 (established in 1912), but monitoring of potentially hazardous volcanoes in the continental United States was less systematic, largely limited to some seismic monitoring (Perry and Hirose, 1985; U.S. House, 1987). The May 18, 1980, eruption of Mount St. Helens focused attention on volcanic hazards in the United States and there is now greater awareness of the potentially hazardous effects of volcanic activity. But, there is still no comprehensive set of programs to address volcanic hazards.

Most of the world's volcanic activity has been centered in what is known as the "ring of fire" around the Pacific basin. Eighty percent (221) of the volcanoes considered potentially active, including those located in Alaska and along the West Coast of the continental United States, are located along the "ring" (Bernstein, Baxter, and Buist, 1986: 6). Between 1600 and 1980 over 250,000 people have been killed by volcanoes with the largest numbers of deaths occurring in Indonesia, the Caribbean, Japan, and Iceland. While the older statistics are questionable, the destructive potential of volcanic activity has been amply demonstrated in more recent years. The eruption of the Nevada del Ruiz volcano in Colombia in 1985, for example, caused approximately 28,000 deaths (Bernstein, Baxter, and Buist, 1986), mostly due to flooding and mudslides.

The experience in the United States has been much more limited. While Kilauea in Hawaii is one of the world's most active volcanoes, having been in continuous eruption since 1983 (reaching the sea in 1986), its lava flows have caused only minimal property damage (destroying over one hundred homes since the eruptions began). Most U.S. volcanoes have been characterized by effusive activity rather than explosive and most are located in very sparsely populated areas. The eruption of Mt. Redoubt in Alaska which began in late 1989, for example, has been characterized largely by clouds of ash and gases. The impact of the Mt. Redoubt eruption is only now being assessed.

There is tremendous variance in the explosiveness of volcanoes and the kinds of hazards produced by that kind of volcanic activity. The potential activity ranges from effusive phenomena such as lava flows, gas releases (some highly toxic and others not), and the venting of steam as molten rock rises to meet ground water, to explosive reactions such as pyroclastic flows and major ashfalls, as well as combinations of the two (Baxter, Bernstein, and Buist, 1986: 85). Volcanic activity may also be accompanied by major seismic activity, including ground fractures and subsidence. Such activity may also precipitate debris avalanches, mudflows, floods, glacier bursts, tsunami, and other phenomena. Lava flows seldom are the most destructive results of volcanism, however, as they are generally very slow-moving and only a danger to property located very close to the volcano. Pyroclastic flows and surges, fast moving air and/or gases carrying debris and possibly lava particles, are very dangerous and can present risks to people miles from a volcano (United Nations, 1985).

The most recent explosive eruption on the North American continent, prior to Mount St. Helens, occurred at Lassen Peak, California, between 1914 and 1917. Mount Hood in Oregon erupted ash in 1906. Between 1831 and 1880 ash and lava were produced by eruptions of Mounts Baker, Rainer, and St. Helens in Washington State and Mount Hood in Oregon. No deaths from volcanic activity were recorded in the United States until the May 1980 eruption of Mount St. Helens

(Bernstein, Baxter, and Buist, 1986) which killed fifty-seven people (May, 1985) (the numbers are as high as sixty-eight in some accounts, e.g., Bradford, Passerello, and Passerello, 1988).

THE MOUNT ST. HELENS EXPERIENCE

Despite the history of volcanic activity along the U.S. West Coast and a prediction of significant activity at Mount St. Helens specifically which was published in USGS reports in 1978 (Crandall and Mullineaux), virtually nothing was done to prepare for an explosive eruption. A USGS warning was issued in December 1978 describing the hazard and even the likely impact of an explosive eruption and plans were developed by the Washington Department of Emergency Services to respond to the threat. Plans were made for an evacuation of the immediate area around the volcano, but the inability to predict the likely time of the eruption mitigated against such an action (Bradford, Passerello, and Passerello, 1988: 153-55).

On March 20, 1980, an earthquake drew attention to increasing risk and scientists began closely monitoring seismic activity in the area. On March 27 Mount St. Helens vented steam and ash and, by April 3, monitors were indicating the movement of molten rock near the volcano (Bernstein et al., 1986: 25). A bulge appeared in the volcano's crater and after consulting volcano experts, the Mount St. Helens Watch Group, the governor of Washington ordered the evacuation of residents in the immediate area surrounding the volcano on April 4 (Perry and Hirose, 1985: 27).

Lead roles were taken by the U.S. Forest Service (USFS), which was responsible for managing the Gifford Pinchot National Forest around the volcano (United Nations, 1985), and the Cowlitz County Department of Emergency Services, which assumed responsibility for coordinating the warning and evacuation systems (Perry and Hirose, 1985: 33). The procedures for responding to forest fires were adapted to the newly recognized hazard (United Nations, 1985: 83). Access to the volcano area was restricted with roadblocks operated by National Guardsmen. No public access was permitted within a "red zone" close to the volcano and limited access, during daylight hours and only by permit, was permitted in a broader "blue zone" (Bernstein et al., 1986: 29). A media center was jointly operated by the U.S. Forest Service and the U.S. Geological Survey to provide information to the public and to public officials (United Nations, 1985: 83). Despite warnings, there was increasing public pressure to reopen the area in late April and early May.

At 8:32 on the morning of May 18, 1980, an earthquake measuring 5.1 on the Richter Scale precipitated an avalanche on the side of the volcano. An explosion of tremendous force reduced the cone of Mount St. Helens from 9,677 feet to approximately 4,400 feet. The explosion was followed by hurricane-force winds that left destruction as far as twenty kilometers from the summit of the volcano. Mudflows and floods resulted as the heat and lava reached Spirit Lake and surrounding waters, and a debris dam threatened further flooding. Approximately 150 square miles of forest and 300 homes were destroyed and fifty-seven people were killed. The economic damage from this and subsequent eruptions has been estimated at $1.86 billion. Lesser eruptions followed on May 25, June 12, July 22, August 7, and October 16 (Perry and Hirose, 1985: 24, 27, 29, 32).

One day after the eruption, state officials contacted the Center for Environmental Health (CEH) of the federal Centers for Disease Control (CDC) for information concerning possible health risks from ash and other effluents. On May 20, scientists from the CEH and the National Institute for Occupational Safety and Health met with representatives of the involved federal agencies, including the Federal Emergency Management Agency, Environmental Protection Agency, USGS, USFS, National Oceanic and Atmospheric Administration (NOAA), and the National Weather Service to assess the health risk.

On the following day, the president declared Washington State and part of Idaho, which was subjected to heavy ashfall, disaster areas and made available disaster assistance. FEMA opened an interagency center in Vancouver, Washington, to coordinate efforts and to disseminate information. FEMA and CDC began publication of technical reports, the Mount St. Helens Technical Information Network Bulletins and the Mount St. Helens Volcano Health Reports, and provided daily briefings for public officials and the news media. Health and environmental agencies began monitoring air quality, conducting epidemiological studies of high-risk population groups, and analyzing the toxicity of the ash. A supplemental appropriation of $946 million by Congress in July provided more relief aid, although relatively little was provided for the study of the hazard by health and geological agencies and not all was spent on the Mount St. Helens disaster. The largest portion of the funding, $430 million, was provided to the Small Business Administration to respond to the economic problems created by the eruption and other emergencies (Bernstein et al., 1986: 26, 34; May, 1985).

THE LESSON OF MOUNT ST. HELENS:
CURRENT POLICY

As a result of the Mount St. Helens eruption and the lack of preparation in terms of hazard assessment and the design and implementation of emergency management procedures, USGS has focused more of its efforts on North American volcanic hazards. On the second anniversary of the May 18 eruption, the David A. Johnston Cascades Volcano Observatory was established near Mount St. Helens to monitor that and nearby volcanoes, to test scientific instruments, and to provide scientific training. On August 27, 1982, President Reagan signed legislation creating the Mount St. Helens National Volcanic Monument, offering some control over development near the volcano. More attention has also been given to the Alaskan and Hawaiian volcanoes. The program has four primary objectives: assessment of volcanic hazards, monitoring of known hazards, fundamental research on volcanism, and the planning of emergency responses and public education.

The assessment of volcanic hazards has begun with the classification of the over thirty-five U.S. volcanoes into three groups:

1. Those with short-term eruption cycles (two hundred years or less) and those which have erupted in the last three hundred years

2. Those with eruption cycles less frequent than every thousand years and those which last erupted over one thousand years ago

3. Those which last erupted over ten thousand years ago but which overlie large magma chambers.

Mount St. Helens, the Mono-Inyo Craters, Lassen Peak, Mount Shasta, Mount Rainer, Mount Baker, and Mount Hood are all in the first group, carrying the greatest potential for eruption in the near future, along with ten other volcanoes. Ten volcanoes are in the second group and three in the third. The assessment of hazards presented by each volcano included determining the periodicity or frequency of eruptions and other related phenomena, the magnitude of past activities, and the predominant forms of activity at each site (Bailey et al., 1983; Bernstein,

Baxter, and Buist, 1986: 7-8; Perry and Hirose, 1985: 11-12).

In terms of the monitoring of known hazards, USGS created a second volcano monitoring center, the Cascades Volcano Observatory, in Vancouver, Washington, near Mount St. Helens, Mount Rainer, and Mount Hood, as well as stepping up monitoring of other volcanic sites. Volcanologists are looking for the signs of increased activity such as volcanic seismicity, swelling of the earth, increased surface temperature, and gas emissions. Samples are taken of volcanic products, such as ash and gas. Scientists are also looking for unrest in other volcanoes that might indicate regional stresses (Newhall and Fruchter, 1986). Increased seismic activity and ground deformation in and around the Mono-Inyo Craters in California has focused attention on that area since 1980 and similar kinds of activity at the Yellowstone National Park in Wyoming have prompted increased monitoring since 1983 (U.S. House, 1987).

Similarly basic research on volcanic processes has been increased under the agency's sponsorship and with funding provided by the National Science Foundation (NSF) and other agencies. USGS has also become more involved in providing advice to government agencies for the development of emergency responses and the provision of public education programs. Technical assistance is provided to state and local authorities by both USGS and FEMA (Perry and Hirose, 1985: 12).

The primary responsibility for volcanic hazard reduction programs and emergency response, however, resides with state and local governments. Technical expertise, including monitoring of hazards, is provided by state agencies, such as the California and Alaska Geological Surveys and the office of the Oregon State Geologist, with research and technical assistance provided by university scientists (United Nations, 1985), as well as through USGS, FEMA, CEH, and other federal agencies.

The implementation of programs to deal with volcanic hazards has been relatively recent. The long experience with effusive activity in Hawaii and outside the United States and the recent experience with explosive activity at Mount St. Helens provide a limited number of tools to emergency managers. The principal responses to volcanic hazards are through land-use planning, such as restricting development in hazardous areas, and preparing to evacuate threatened populations. Restricting access to hazardous areas, particularly during periods of strong activity, may be the only way to reduce the threat of pyroclastic flows and toxic ash and gas releases (Bernstein, Baxter, and Buist, 1986: 8).

Lava flows present little danger to human life, although property may be threatened when development has been permitted too close to the volcano or major flows occur. To some extent lava flows can be diverted by constructing earthen walls, bombing the flows, and/or cooling them with water. The damage caused by major ashfalls can be lessened by removing ash from roofs to prevent collapses and enforcing building standards so that roofs can withstand heavy ash (Perry and Hirose, 1985: 41). Other measures to mitigate, prepare for, respond to, and recover from the effects of volcanism are much the same as for other natural hazards, including assessing health risks, providing adequate emergency medical response capacity, training emergency response personnel, and testing disaster plans.

CONCLUSION

Some action has been taken since the Mount St. Helens disaster to develop effective programs to deal with volcanic hazards, but much still needs to be done. The principal responsibility still resides with state and local officials and, thus, the task is to provide adequate technical assistance for them to design and implement effective emergency management programs. Critical to the effectiveness of such programs are the assessment of the threats posed by volcanism, both in terms of the immediate threats around volcanoes themselves and in terms of the broader impact of ashfalls and the public's sensitivity to the risk (Perry and Hirose, 1985: 41).

Volcanism is particularly problematic for emergency managers because of the infrequency of activity and the technical problems involved in the prediction of such activity. While the capacities of USGS and its state counterparts to predict eruptions and related phenomena has improved since the Mount St. Helens disaster in 1980, better predictive capabilities would certainly facilitate effective responses, particularly since evacuation is a principal concern.

While some research has been done on the epidemiological effects of volcanism, major questions are still unanswered concerning possible pulmonary and other problems caused by ash and vented gases. There are indications that chronic health problems, including cancer, may be endemic to populations exposed to volcanic products, quite apart from the risks to health posed by explosive episodes

(Bernstein, Baxter, and Buist, 1986: 5). The effects of such long-term exposure may pose a more serious threat to human life than the infrequent eruptions.

The major recommendations concerning volcanic hazards must center on the need for basic research on volcanism and the long-term health effects of volcanic activity, as well as the effects of more spectacular volcanic disasters. The key to responding effectively to the kinds of activity that occurred at Mount St. Helens is the timely prediction of effusive and explosive eruptions and related seismic and other phenomena.

REFERENCES

* Special thanks are due to Peter J. May of the University of Washington, on leave during 1987/88 at the Office of Policy Analysis of the U.S. Department of Interior, for reviewing an early draft of this chapter and offering suggestions and corrections.

Bailey, R. A., et al. (1983). The Volcano Hazards Program: Objectives and Long-Range Plans (Reston, Va.: USGS Open File Report 83-400).

Baxter, Peter J., Robert S. Bernstein, and A. Sonia Buist (1986). "Preventive Health Measures in Volcanic Eruptions," American Journal of Public Health 76 (March): 84-90.

Bernstein, Robert S., Peter J. Baxter, and A. Sonia Buist (1986). "Introduction to the Epidemiological Aspects of Explosive Volcanism," American Journal of Public Health 76 (March): 3-9.

Bernstein, Robert S., et al. (1986). "Immediate Public Health Concerns and Actions in Volcanic Eruptions: Lessons from the Mount St. Helens Eruptions, May 18-October 18, 1980," American Journal of Public Health 76 (March): 25-37.

Bradford, Janet K., Bev Passerello, and John Passerello (1988). "The Eruption of Mount St. Helens," pp. 151-177 in Crisis Management, eds. Michael Charles and John Choon Kim (Springfield, Ill.: Charles C. Thomas).

Buist, A. Sonia, and Robert S. Bernstein (1986). "Health Effects of Volcanoes: An Approach to Evaluating the Health Effects of an Environmental Hazard," American Journal of Public Health 76 (March): 1-2.

Congressional Research Service, Library of Congress (1984). Information Technology for Emergency

Management, Report prepared for the Subcommittee on Investigations and Oversight, Committee on Science and Technology, U.S. House of Representatives, 98th Congress, 2d Session, October 9.

Crandell, Dwight R., and D. R. Mullineaux (1978). Potential Hazards from Future Eruptions of Mount St. Helens (Washington, D.C.: U.S. Geological Survey, GS Bulletin 1383-C).

Crandell, Dwight R., and Donald R. Nichols (1987). Volcanic Hazards at Mount Shasta, California (Washington, D.C.: U.S. Geological Survey/U.S. Department of the Interior).

May, Peter J. (1985). Recovering from Catastrophes: Federal Disaster Relief Policy and Politics (Westport, Conn.: Greenwood).

Newhall, Christopher G., and Jonathan S. Fruchter (1986). "Volcanic Activity: A Review for Health Professionals," American Journal of Public Health 76 (March): 10-24.

Perry, Ronald W., and Hirotada Hirose (1985). Social Responses to Volcanism in Japan and the United States, Research Paper Series, School of Public Affairs, Arizona State University, Tempe.

Saarinen, Thomas F., and James Sell (1985). Warning and Response to the Mount St. Helens Eruption (Albany: State University of New York Press).

United Nations, Office of Disaster Relief Co-Ordinator (1985). Volcanic Emergency Management (Geneva and New York: United Nations).

U.S. House of Representatives (1987). Hearings before a Subcommittee of the Committee on Appropriations, Department of the Interior and Related Agencies Appropriations for 1988, 100th Congress, 1st Session, U.S. Government Printing Office.

Warrick, Richard A. (1975). Volcano Hazard in the United States: A Research Assessment (Boulder, Colo.: University of Colorado, Institute of Behavioral Science).

5

Hurricanes

William L. Waugh, Jr.

Severe tropical cyclones threaten approximately 15 percent of the world's population. With wind speeds of as much as two hundred miles per hour, accompanying tornadoes, heavy rains, and storm surges of up to twenty-five feet, hurricanes (called typhoons in the western Pacific and cyclones in the Indian Ocean) can devastate hundreds of square miles of coastline and cause wind and flood damage far inland. For example, in 1972, Hurricane Agnes caused approximately $2 billion in property losses along the U.S. coast (National Research Council, 1987). In 1988, Hurricane Gilbert, the most powerful North Atlantic storm of the century, caused approximately $800 million in property losses in Jamaica alone and killed almost three hundred people in the Caribbean and Mexico (McDonald and Boulle, 1988). Fears of a large storm hitting a major U.S. coastal city were realized with Hurricane Hugo's landfall near Charleston in September 1989. Damage estimates are as high as $12 billion, but generally in the $7-9 billion range.

Hurricanes are relatively common threats along the southeastern U.S. coast, as well as lesser threats along the Pacific coast and in Hawaii and other American Pacific locales. While the United States has experienced relatively little loss of life from hurricanes in recent decades, the potential for catastrophic events remains and may in fact be increasing. A 1900 storm caused approximately 6,000 deaths in and around Galveston, Texas, and a 1928 storm caused 1,836 deaths in southern Florida. While those statistics do not compare with the 300,000 killed in 1970 or the 10,000 killed in May 1985 by tropical cyclones in Bangladesh, there is a real and growing potential for massive loss of life along American coasts. That increased risk can be attributed to a number of factors. Despite improved weather surveillance and warning systems and greater land-use and building regulation, tremendous population growth and low issue salience have increased the risks associated with a major hurricane, particularly around New Orleans, southern and southwestern Florida, Texas, Ocean City (Maryland), and the New Jersey barrier islands, but including communities all along the Eastern seaboard (Leavenworth, 1986). Complicating factors include the size of the populations to be moved and the willingness of residents unfamiliar with hurricanes to respond quickly to warnings and to accept regulatory efforts to mitigate the effects of severe storms. As the Hurricane Hugo experience illustrated lax land-use regulations and building codes in those communities can increase property loss.

The consensus among experts generally is that the U.S. has been lucky thus far. The four strongest (force 5) hurricanes of the century (the 1935 hurricane and Hurricanes Camille in 1969, Allen in 1980, and Gilbert in 1988) did not hit the most heavily populated coastal areas. Hurricane Allen cut a destructive path through the Caribbean islands before making landfall in Texas and Hurricane Gilbert with its 125 mph winds devastated parts of the Caribbean, particularly Jamaica, before coming ashore in Mexico (See Table 5.1). While Gilbert did not hit the U.S. with its full force, the destruction wrought by flood waters in Monterrey, Mexico, which resulted in the deaths of nearly 200 persons being evacuated from the path of the storm (McDonald and Boulle, 1988), is warning of the potential danger to the U.S. Hurricane Hugo in late 1989 was a category 4 storm with 135 mph winds and its impact on the South Carolina barrier islands and small communities in the lowlands close to the coast, as well as in Charleston itself, has yet to be fully assessed. While the number of deaths attributable to the storm was small, property losses were quite high.

When the 1980s began, it was estimated that approximately 40 million Americans may potentially be threatened by hurricanes with 80 percent of them having no experience with the storms. For example, the last major hurricane to hit Tampa, Florida, was in 1921 when the population of the city was about 20,000 (Funk, 1980). Tampa currently has a population of about 300,000 and is in a metropolitan area with millions more residents.

Table 5.1

MAJOR U.S. HURRICANES
(Estimated Deaths and
Property Loss in Billions of Dollars)

Year	Hurricane and Location	Deaths	Property Loss
1989	Hugo, U.S. Virgin Islands, Puerto Rico, S.C., N.C.		$7-9.0
1983	Alicia, southern Texas	21	$2.0
1980	Allen, Caribbean, Texas	272	
1979	David, Caribbean, Eastern U.S.	1100	
1979	Frederic, Alabama, Miss., Florida	16	$2.3
1975	Eloise, Caribbean, N.E. U.S.	71	
1972	Agnes, Fla., Va., Md., Penn.	122	$2.1
1969	Camille, La., Miss., Va.	256	$1.4
1965	Betsy, Fla., La.	75	$1.4
1961	Carla, Texas	46	$ .4
1960	Donna, Fla., N.Y., New England	50	$ .4
1957	Audrey, La.	390	$ .15
1938	New England Hurricane	600	$ .3
1935	Florida Keys Hurricane	408	$ .06
1928	Palm Beach, Okeechobee, Florida Hurricane	1,836	$ .25
1919	Florida Keys; Corpus Christi, Hurricane	600	$ .2
1900	Galveston, Texas, Hurricane	6,000	$ .3

Figures compiled from: Congressional Research Service, 1984; and, Simpson and Riehl, 1981.

The threat of hurricanes has raised a number of critical issues concerning the responsibilities of federal, state, and local governments and the technical problems of evacuating large areas of coastline. The experience in South Carolina with Hurricane Hugo demonstrated that those issues have not yet been addressed effectively.

Until rather recent years, hurricane warnings were dependent upon ship observations. Now satellite surveillance, supplemented by aircraft observation, is becoming more sophisticated as the technologies of nuclear defense are made available to investigate tropical low pressure areas. Scientists are having some success predicting increased hurricane activity. Professor William Gray at Colorado State University, for example, is finding correlations between the absence of El Nino (warm currents in the Pacific along the coast of South America), westerly equatorial stratospheric winds, and spring barometric pressures in the Caribbean and increased numbers of hurricanes. Significant improvements in the capacity to predict landfalls, however, are not likely in the near future.

Table 5.2

SAFFIR-SIMPSON DAMAGE-POTENTIAL SCALE RANGE

Scale Number	Central Pressure Inches	Winds (mph)	Surge (Ft)	Damage
1	Over 28.94	74-95	4-5	Minimal
2	28.50 - 28.91	96-110	6-8	Moderate
3	27.91 - 28.47	111-130	9-12	Extensive
4	27.17 - 27.88	131-155	13-18	Extreme
5	Under 27.17	Over 155	Over 18	Catastrophic

Adapted from Simpson, 1981: 368.

THE COMPLEXITY OF HAZARD REDUCTION: THE GALVESTON EXAMPLE

The Galveston situation is somewhat more problemmatic than most other coastal communities, but can serve as an example of the complexity of the issues. Galveston Island on which the community is located is 32 miles long with a population that expands to as many as 120,000 during the summer months. There is one effective escape route, a causeway connecting the Island to the mainland. A bridge and ferry (on the west and east, respectively) connect the island to low-lying peninsulas and another bridge has been proposed. An 11-mile, 16- to 17-foot seawall protects the more populous parts of the island from most storm threats. The seawall was built and the town was literally raised so that the island could be elevated with landfill following a 1900 hurricane that destroyed 3600 buildings and killed 6000 people along the Texas coast (Walker, 1984; Leavenworth, 1986). The wall was not effective in dealing with 21-foot waves during a 1915 hurricane and the downtown was flooded, but subsequent storms in 1932, 1941, 1943, 1949, 1957, 1961, 1983, 1986, and 1989 produced only minimal damage. In June of 1983, the then mayor of Galveston announced that the seawall provided enough protection to make evacuation in the face of a major storm unnecessary. Two months later, in August, Hurricane Alicia hit the community during the night and residents found that they could not evacuate had they wanted to do so. Major efforts have been made by the State of Texas, through the Governor's Division of Emergency Management and with the assistance of the Texas Insurance Advisory Association, to provide better hurricane preparedness and mitigation programs (Walker, 1984). Those preparations, as well as the weakness of the storm, may account for the minimal effects of Hurricane Jerry in late 1989.

The complexity of major evacuations can be seen in the Galveston case. The limited access to the Island increases the time needed for evacuation. Evacuees using the causeway would find themselves having to contend with Houston traffic and a simultaneous evacuation of Houston itself might greatly increase the time necessary to evacuate Galveston Island and other communities along the coast. Moreover, evacuees using the ferry or bridge might well find themselves moving from one dangerous low-lying area to another (Leavenworth, 1986).

The Galveston case is doubly illustrative because of state encouragement of development along the coast. Communities had difficulty getting insurance following Hurricane Celia which hit Corpus Christi in the early 1970s. To alleviate the insurance problem, the state helped create an insurance pool, the "catpool" named after the Texas Catastrophe Property Insurance Association, with the state pledging to provide tax credits when property losses exceed $100 million per year. Property claims in the Galveston area following Hurricane Alicia in 1983 totalled $155 million and the "catpool" had only collected $87.5 million. In 1985, the state added a surcharge to the premiums to increase the reserve (Leavenworth, 1986), but it is likely that the damage caused by a major (force 4 or 5) hurricane could cause a financial crisis in the state and the threat from Hurricane Gilbert in 1988 caused considerable concern among coastal residents.

HURRICANE HAZARD REDUCTION PROGRAMS

There are a number of options available to communities to reduce the threats of major hurricanes, but none can entirely eliminate the risk. With millions of Americans living in low-lying coastal areas, including many in communities along the 2700 miles of barrier islands from Maine to Texas (Leavenworth, 1986), and the inability of authorities to predict hurricane landfalls with sufficient lead time to effect evacuations of all threatened, the risk of major losses of life and property will continue.

Mitigation Programs

Mitigation efforts generally fall into four categories: "hard" engineering or structural responses; "soft" engineering or environmental responses; "passive" or nonstructural responses (Miller and Bachman, 1984); and meteorological responses. The "hard" engineering approaches are usually the most expensive and, it can be argued, are not necessarily the most effective because they attempt to control rather than reduce exposure to damaging tidal surges. These approaches include building:

1. Offshore breakwaters to reduce the force of tidal surges before they reach land

2. Seawalls to reduce flooding inland, including the initial surges

3. Earthen levees to direct flood waters away from populated areas

4. Floodwalls, usually concrete, to direct flood waters away from populated areas

5. Bulkheads, vertical structures, to hold landfill in place

6. Revetments, usually large stones, on relatively flat slopes to slow flooding

7. Groins, built from shorelines into the water, to keep sand from migrating down the beach (to stabilize the beach)

8. "Perched" beaches or artificial beaches created by using structures to hold sand on a beach area

The "soft" engineering approach is to use beach and other shoreline areas as "buffers" between tidal surges and populated areas. These approaches include using:

1. Sand fill to build up beach areas, i.e., to increase beach slope to deflect surges

2. Snow or sand fences to inhibit the natural migration of sand dunes along the coastline

3. Beach grasses and other vegetation to reduce the movement of sand and to maintain natural slope

4. Walkways and other structures to reduce the size and number of "cuts" created by pedestrian and vehicle traffic to and from the beach (which provide channels for flood waters, reducing the effectiveness of beach barriers)

5. Salt marshes to dissipate the strength of tidal surges and other flooding before they reach populated areas.

The "passive" or nonstructural approaches are principally regulatory, involving land use. Some of these approaches might include:

1. Controlling traffic, pedestrian and vehicle, along the beach to reduce damage to dunes

2. Creating setback lines (usually using 100-year surge levels, maximum wave runup, erosion trends, vegetation lines and/or other factors) to prevent development in risk areas

3. Using zoning regulations to limit development close to the shoreline, particularly in high risk areas

4. Purchasing high risk areas by governments to prevent development

5. Using building codes to harden (reinforce) or elevate buildings and other structures to reduce damage from flooding and winds.

Some communities have been creative with the use of land-use regulations. Warrick, Rhode Island, has "graduated use" zones based on the level of risk along the coast. Portsmouth, Virginia, does not permit developers to subdivide land without adequate protective measures. Sanibel Island, Florida, has placed a lid on population growth, based on the number of people who can be evacuated safely. But the adequacy of regulatory and planning efforts by states and communities is questionable at best (Clary, 1985: 22).

The difficulty in implementing mitigation programs at the local level can be seen in the experience of Gulf Shores, Alabama, following Hurricane Frederic (a category 3 storm) in September of 1979. The city had passed its first building code in 1971 and its flood control ordinance in 1978 in response to requirements of the National Flood Insurance Program. The devastation wrought by the storm has been called "hurricane renewal." In the absence of building codes and zoning for risk, much of the older building was destroyed. When the recovery and reconstruction processes began in earnest, recommendations to make the city's sewer and utility lines more resistant to storms, to move the state highway to safer ground further from the beach, and to force compliance with new building codes for new construction and major reconstruction were disregarded or circumvented. Controversy and conflict erupted in the city government over the implementation of more stringent standards and those opposing the new regulations (including the mayor, all but one of the city council, city clerk, and head building inspector) were voted out of office.

The mitigation efforts that followed under the new administration included beach setbacks based on the primary dune crest (the natural barrier to storm surges), side setbacks to prevent the development of a solid line of structures along the beach which will be particularly vulnerable to wind and flood, and public purchase of high risk areas. The Federal Emergency Management Agency provided funding for a professional planner and for the purchase of several tracts of hazardous real estate. In short, local officials were very much resistant to the implementation of mitigation programs until public pressure and state and federal requirements forced action. However, it is likely that those efforts are inadequate given the increase in population and development since Hurricane Frederick (Godschalk, 1988).

A number of meteorological approaches to reduce the strength of hurricanes have been suggested, but only cloud seeding has been experimented with seriously. Project Cirrus in 1947 was the first attempt to use cloud seeding to reduce the threat of a hurricane. In the early 1960s, Project STORMFURY attempted to "moderate" the "destructive potential" of hurricanes, beginning with Hurricane Esther in 1961, continuing through Hurricanes Beulah in 1963, Debbie in 1969, and Ginger in 1971. It is uncertain whether the apparent reductions in the wind speed achieved through seeding the eyewall also reduced the destructive force of those storms, particularly storm surges and flooding. Part of the focus on Project STORMFURY was on encouraging maximum wind speeds in the outer eyewall and surrounding clouds, i.e., increasing the size of the eye and diluting the effects of the concentrated low pressure funnel that determines the height of the storm-surge. In short, in theory, the seeding should reduce the storm surge and resultant flooding (Simpson, 1981: 340-347). The findings of the experiments remain inconclusive although they have been encouraging. The meteorological approaches that have been suggested include cooling the surface of the ocean by pulling colder deep waters to the surface, towing icebergs to the areas through which tropical storms will pass, reducing evaporation from the ocean around the storm to reduce the circulation of winds by applying a thin chemical coating to the water, or, as suggested by W. M. Gray, using carbon dust seeding to alter a storm's wind flow. Funding for Project STORMFURY and other proposed experiments has been sporatic and limited, however (Simpson, 1981: 348-353). Scientists are still somewhat hesitant to attempt major alterations in the weather patterns precipitating or resulting from hurricanes because of potential disruption of natural climatic patterns. Hurricanes are important influences on rainfall and temperature transference.

With the exception of the meteorological experiments and similar proposals, most of these mitigation techniques are the responsibility of state and local governments and subject to economic and political review, as well as technical assessments of utility in reducing risk (Clary, 1985; Waugh, 1989).

Preparedness Programs

The most effective way to reduce the threat to human life is to evacuate coastal areas that may be subject to storm surge and secondary flooding, high winds (including tornadoes spawned by the storm), and secondary threats (including fires and structural failures). Evacuation, under the best of circumstances, is costly and dangerous. Unnecessary evacuations may, for example, lead to law suits brought by businesses suffering economic loss, persons suffering physical injury, and persons suffering losses from looters and other nondisaster-related causes.

Responsibility for hurricane preparedness belongs largely to local governments, with most state governments requiring local preparedness plans to reduce threats to human life. Most of those plans focus on the evacuation and/or sheltering of populations threatened by the initial tidal surges along the beachfronts and flooding that may extend well inland along rivers, creeks, and other low-lying areas. Given population increases along many of the coasts, hundreds of thousands of people might have to be moved to safer areas. While the time required to effect such evacuations can be a full day or more, decisions concerning evacuation generally have to be made with very little lead time, e.g., 12 to 16 hours. For example, the Florida Keys may take more than 30 hours for evacuation along the two-lane Overseas Highway and the Galveston/Houston area in Texas may take as many as 26 hours for complete evacuation. The lack of experience with severe storms among the current populations of some of the most vulnerable communities may well have a negative impact of the speed of evacuation, particularly as some residents may choose to disregard warnings. Moreover, evacuations of the residents of many Florida communities, the Caribbean islands (including the Florida Keys), and Hawaii could create problems because evacuees may be moved into hazardous areas, even into the path of a storm, rather than to safety.

Increasing lead times for evacuations may permit local authorities to move the most vulnerable populations, e.g., persons requiring medical treatment and the nonambulatory elderly and infirm, as well as implementing the marine evacuation, so that the remaining population can be moved much more quickly, according to Robert S. Wilkerson, Director of Public Safety for the State of Florida (Congressional Research Service, 1984: 370). The "phasing" of the evacuation, including voluntary evacuations, can significantly reduce the costs of unnecessary evacuations. The value of "phasing" has been one of the more persuasive arguments in favor of early warning of potential landfalls, instead of waiting until the storm pathes can be more accurately predicted. Probability estimates of landfalls were added to advisories in 1983 to increase the reaction time (GAO, 1983). The difficulty in predicting landfalls was illustrated in 1985 when some communities along the northwestern coast of Florida were evacuated several times as Hurricane Elena threatened to come ashore in Florida, moved toward the mouth of the Mississippi River and New Orleans, and ultimately made landfall in Mississippi.

One of the foci of research now is the potential for "vertical evacuation." As stricter building codes and zoning regulations "harden" some structures, particularly hotels and large apartment buildings, increasing their likely survivability, authorities are considering evacuating residents to those structures rather than inland. Given the logistics and politics of mass evacuations of any distance, the alternative of leaving people in their communities is a compelling one. Also, the advantages of such a strategy are several. Elderly and infirm residents not easily evacuated large distances might be accommodated in secure buildings, densely populated areas may not have to be evacuated at all, and an emphasis on developing survivable properties may sensitize the public to the danger of hurricanes.

FEDERAL POLICIES AND PROGRAMS

Federal responsibilities for hurricane hazard reduction and management are generally spelled out in legislation, most of which has been in response to specific disasters (oft-times having little impact beyond the immediate disaster recovery efforts)(May, 1988). Much the same can be said of state programs (Mittler, 1988), but the result is that the aftermath of disaster is a poor time for the development of comprehensive, integrated programs because interest in the disaster usually focuses on recovery rather than mitigation or preparedness and begins to wane quickly. The loans and grants provided by PL 92-385 to aid recovery after Hurricane Agnes in 1972 is a case in point. Because of mudslides in California, the legislative response to Hurricane Camille was much broader in scope. The Disaster Relief Act of 1969 (PL 91-79) brought together disaster recovery programs including monies for debris removal, food stamps, unemployment compensation, Small Business Administration loans, Federal Home Administration loans, and Veterans Administration loans. The following year the Disaster Assistance Act (PL 91-606) provided monies to individuals for such needs as temporary housing, relocation, and legal services and revised some of the federal loan provisions (May, 1988).

The National Flood Insurance Act of 1968 (PL 90-448) was at least partially in response to the major flood damage caused Hurricane Betsy in 1966. Expansion of coverage under that act followed with the Flood Disaster Protection Act of 1973 (PL 93-234) due to both the hurricane experience and flooding in Rapid City, South Dakota, and the perceived need for sanctions against communities not participating in the flood insurance program (May, 1988).

Federal responsibilities are generally in the areas of hurricane forecasting, technical assistance, and financial assistance. The principal federal agencies involved are the National Oceanic and Atmospheric Administration (NOAA), the Federal Emergency Management Agency (FEMA), and the U.S. Army Corps of Engineers.

The National Weather Service (NWS) within NOAA is charged with issuing advisories to threatened communities and conducting public awareness programs. The NWS program is centered in the National Hurricane Center in Miami, the Eastern Pacific Hurricane Center in San Francisco, and the Central Pacific Hurricane Center in Honolulu and uses satellite surveillance and aircraft reconnaissance to gather storm information (GAO, 1983b), although the most sophisticated meteorological technologies have not yet been made available to NWS.

NWS uses two computer simulation models to provide information on possible flooding: the SPLASH (Special Program to List the Amplitude of Surges from Hurricanes) model and the more sophisticated SLOSH (Sea, Lake, and Overland Surges from Hurricanes) model. The models permit planners to estimate the probable effects of flooding and to plan evacuations, as well as mitigation programs. A topographical "fit" is made so that the model reflects the characteristics of the terrain and an average of 250 simulations are conducted based on possible storm intensities and other characteristics. At the time of the GAO review in 1983 (b), NWS had scheduled 22 locales for SLOSH modelling but simulations had only been completed for five locales. Funding for the simulations was the major obstacle.

The Federal Emergency Management Agency is the lead agency for federal programs under the Disaster Relief Act of 1974. Through the Hurricane Preparedness Planning Program FEMA provides financial assistance to improve state and local programs in high-risk areas. 22 such areas were targetted initially (see Table 5.3) with the completion date for the entire program expected in Fiscal Year 1988. The FEMA preparedness studies include a vulnerability analysis and appropriate mitigation, evacuation, response, and recovery plans.

In a series of reports in the early to mid 1980s the General Accounting Office examined FEMA's role in developing state and local hurricane preparedness programs and found that the agency had failed to provide leadership in the development of workable plans, criteria for the review of planning proposals to determine levels of funding, and coordination of hurricane-related programs. The lack of coordination of federal activities was resulting in duplication of efforts. For example, the NWS and FEMA lists of high risk areas overlapped somewhat, but were different, which confused the process of identifying priorities and responding accordingly. Part of the dilemma was the fact that FEMA was assigned responsibility for coordinating efforts, but NWS and the Corps of Engineers were the agencies with the technical expertise (GAO, 1980, 1983a, 1983b; Waugh, 1988). Indeed, the success of some of the FEMA studies, most notably for Tampa Bay, Georgia, Galveston, and southeast Florida, was attributed to competent local analysis and, at least in the Tampa Bay case, funding from the Corps of Engineers. Priority was given to the development and application of the SLOSH and SPLASH computer simulation models with appropriate technical assistance to bring state and local disaster plans up to standard. The GAO also suggested that FEMA have the Corps of Engineers and offices of NOAA review state and local proposals to determine their technical feasibility (GAO, 1983b).

The Corps of Engineers was responsible for developing evacuation plans for Lee County, Florida; Tampa Bay; and, southeast Florida, which laid the groundwork for integrated preparedness plans. Corps hurricane-related programs have been largely curtailed, however. The Office of Sea Grant and the Office of Ocean and Coastal Resource Management (both in the NOAA) have also provided funds for major studies. The Office of Sea Grant funded much of the development of the SLOSH model and some area studies and the Office of Ocean and Coastal Resource Management has provided some monies for studies under the Coastal Zone Management Act.

THE REALITY OF RESPONSE:
THE 1985 FLORIDA AND 1989 SOUTH CAROLINA EXPERIENCES

The effectiveness of hurricane preparedness and mitigation programs can only be measured as they affect the outcomes of actual disasters, i.e., in the response of communities. In 1985 authorities in the State of Florida were forced to respond to four serious storms between July and November. Tropical storm Bob crossed south Florida from the Gulf to the Atlantic in late July reaching hurricane force shortly before his second landfall (in South Carolina).

Hurricane Elena sat off the northwestern coast from August 29 to September 1 before making landfall near Biloxi, Mississippi, on September 2. Tropical Storm Juan passed further west making landfall near Pensacola in October. Finally, Hurricane Kate made landfall at Mexico Beach, on November 21. Bob and Juan caused minimal damage, but Elena and Kate were more destructive (Stokes, 1986).

Table 5.3

HURRICANE RISK AREAS - FEMA HURRICANE PROGRAM

Tampa Bay, Florida
Georgia Coast
Galveston/Houston, Texas
New Orleans, Louisiana
South Florida
Tri-State: Florida, Mississippi, Alabama
Hawaii
New Jersey
Long Island, New York
Puerto Rico/Virgin Islands
Beaumont/Port Arthur, Texas
Charleston, South Carolina
Corpus Christi, Texas
Pamlico Sound, North Carolina
Brownsville/Rio Grande, Texas
Norfolk/Virginia Beach/Newport News, Virginia
Guam/Samoa/Trust Territories
Rehoboth/Delaware Coast
Ocean City/Maryland Coast
Connecticut Coast
Boston Bay/Cape Cod, Massachusetts
Narragansett Bay, S. Rhode Island

Source: GAO, 1983b.

Approximately 1.25 million residents were evacuated in the face of Hurricane Elena as nineteen counties were subject to mandatory evacuation and thousands of residents of other counties also moved inland seeking shelter. The Florida Department of Health and Rehabilitative Services (DHRS) was responsible for providing emergency shelter, emergency medical care, emergency food and clothing, and other services, including administering food coupon, individual and family grant, and other social programs. Most of the evacuation programs were contracted out to the American Red Cross with the proviso that DHRS would provide sufficient personnel to man the programs if needed. The Red Cross took care of approximately 300,000 evacuees in 494 shelters, suggesting that almost a million evacuees found shelter on their own. Pinellas County alone had to evacuate nineteen nursing homes and three hospitals (Stokes, 1986).

Uninsured losses, according to Governor Graham, reached $15.9 million ($7.5 million to private residences and $8.4 million to businesses) and insured losses, according to the Insurance Information Institute, amounted to $46.8 million (Stokes, 1986). Costs to the state for delivery of services and personnel and equipment costs were also significant. Damage to the oyster industry in Apalachicola Bay will take years to repair, costing the state economy and local businesses millions of dollars per year. Seven counties were declared disaster areas and, thus, eligible for federal assistance (Stokes, 1986).

Hurricane Kate's arrival precipitated the evacuation of over 58,000 residents in the Mexico Beach area. Again, the American Red Cross opened shelters for thousands. Again, seven counties were declared disaster areas, two of which were so declared following Hurricane Elena (Stokes, 1986).

Herman O. Stokes, Jr., Disaster Preparedness Coordinator for DHRS, has concluded that there were a number of problems with the responses to the four storms that should be addressed. During the evacuations, it was found that many left their homes without necessary medication, clothing, and bedding. Although having mandated evacuation plans when Hurricane Elena threatened, some of the nursing homes in Pinellas County had contracted with the same firms for evacuation. The evacuation of special needs populations raised a number of issues concerning the need for staff to accompany them, the expense of transportation and shelter when they are moved to other facilities, and the high demand for ambulance service to move those unable to move themselves. Problems with drinking water and electrical power were also noted (Stokes, 1986).

The State of Florida acted in the aftermath of Elena and Kate to improve evacuation planning. Some concern was expressed, however, that the moderate severity of the storms might make some residents so complacent that they will not respond quickly when a major (force 4 or 5) storm threatens. Public safety agencies, too, might find themselves understaffed if military reservists and National Guardsmen are called to duty, as many of those agencies have large percentages of their personnel in such units.

What is particularly significant from the Florida experience is the acknowledgement that complete evacuation will not likely be possible given the lead time necessary to do so and that the more highly populated areas will be particularly vulnerable to a "killer" storm.

Many of the lessons learned in Florida held true in South Carolina when Hurricane Hugo came ashore on September 22, 1989. Evacuation of the barrier islands and coastal lowlands was given impetus as the reports of damage in Puerto Rico and the U.S. Virgin Islands were broadcast. The category 4 storm knocked out electrical power and the water system for days (and, in some cases, weeks), destroyed hundreds of homes and businesses and severely damaged others, downed most of the trees in the city and outlying areas, and put an estimated 270,000 residents out of work.

The relief effort was massive as volunteer organizations, National Guard and other military units, church groups, and local, state, and federal emergency management agencies responded. Unlike the response to the California earthquake a month later, the emergency response to Hugo's damage was characterized by a lack of coordination in delivering relief supplies where they were most needed, conflicts between residents attempting to return home and National Guard and police units guarding the disaster area to prevent looting, charges that the federal (FEMA) response was slow, large numbers of looters (in fact, too many to jail according to the Charleston police chief), price gouging by local businesses, and long lines of victims awaiting assistance. Near riot conditions were common as frustrated residents waited hours for food and other assistance.

FEMA was the focus of most of the criticism for its slowness in delivering emergency aid (primarily food, emergency shelter, and emergency power generators), opening disaster assistance centers, and generally assuming a reactive rather than a proactive role. While the federal response was very slow, the organization of emergency preparedness and response in South Carolina may also have been to blame. According to FEMA spokespersons, federal aid was forthcoming when requests were received from South Carolina officials. However, with primary responsibility for emergency management vested in an adjutant general's office, rather than in or very near the Office of the Governor, coordination of the emergency response was difficult at best. That difficulty was exacerbated by the lack of an effective communication network (the

Governor's Office used a state police network to maintain contact with the affected communities) and a general lack of good disaster planning. In short, the formal emergency management program was poorly designed and implemented and grossly inadequate to the task of disaster response. The expectation of a coherent and functioning chain of command, with requests for aid by local officials being funneled through the Governor's Office to FEMA and other agencies, was unrealistic. The loss of communications with the power failure further confused the situation. (See note at end of chapter). When Hurricane Jerry hit the Texas coast a few days later, the FEMA response was much quicker. Moreover, FEMA did assume a proactive role in responding to the devastation in the U.S. Virgin Islands because agency officials perceived that local authorities were unable to maintain order, assess damage, and request aid formally.

CONCLUSION

The hazard presented by tropical cyclones is one that has to be addressed. Storms can be 500 miles in diameter and strike coastlines with devastating impact. Indeed, as seen on radar maps, Hurricane Gilbert in 1988 seemed to fill the Caribbean. While nature has provided barrier islands, tidal marshes, and other environmental means of blunting the force of storms, such hurricanes can change the contours of coastlines. Beaches are moved, inlets are created, marshes are covered, and so on. In large measure, there is little communities can do to change those processes. Primitive communities simply avoided the hazardous areas or perished when severe storms struck.

There are actions that can be taken, however, to preserve some of the development along the coast when severe storms strike. Structural mitigation approaches are generally the least effective. Approaches that attempt to blunt or redirect the force of tidal surges, particularly with natural buffers, are generally more effective, although people may not be willing to move their residences and businesses to safer ground. Land-use and zoning, i.e., nonstructural approaches, may be the most realistic means of hazard reduction given the reluctance of most communities to forego development near the shore. The regulation of development can minimize wind and flood damage and it is the responsibility of local officials to identify and implement effective measures. Whether they are willing to do so is another question. It will be instructive to watch whether or to what extent South Carolina enforces its Beachfront Management Act to limit new construction and the rebuilding of structures that sustained major damage from Hugo.

The Gulf Shores case suggests that the National Flood Insurance Program has provided important guidance concerning building codes and land use in coastal communities and necessary sanctions to assure compliance. State governments, too, appear reluctant to regulate development. Indeed, if the Texas case is any indication, there are strong political and economic pressures to promote development inspite of the hazard. The experience with the NOAA simulations and other technical assistance also suggests that they may be the most effective means of preparing communities for hurricanes. There fundamental questions that have to be answered about the capacities of communities and states to develop and maintain effective mitigation and preparedness programs without federal funding and technical assistance.

Evacuation, even vertical evacuation, may be the most effective response to hurricanes. However, while science may be able to increase the lead time for evacuations somewhat, many coastal areas will never have enough warning to move all endangered residents to safety. Recent hurricane experience is providing valuable information on how to evacuate more quickly and how to deal with special populations that cannot evacuate themselves. But, the highly populated, densely developed coastal areas will continue to be at risk and a strong, force 4 or 5, hurricane may result in the loss of hundreds lives if it makes landfall near one of the larger metropolitan areas.

A choice that should not be overlooked is to rely more heavily on the natural means of reducing the hazard of hurricanes. A step in that direction has been taken with the recent changes in the National Flood Insurance Program to withhold eligibility from areas being developed along the barrier islands. Without utilities, highways, and bridges, development will be discouraged. Reducing exposure to disaster is the most effective approach.

REFERENCES

Note: The information on Hurricane Hugo was gleaned from numerous press reports during and immediately following the disaster. The basic information on the South Carolina response was gathered in telephone conversations with Mr. John Eichels, a reporter for the _Charlotte_ (North Carolina) _Observer_.

Chang, Semoon (1983) "Disasters and Fiscal Policy: Hurricane Impact on Municipal Revenue," Urban Affairs Quarterly (June): 511-523.

Clary, Bruce B. (1985) "The Evolution and Structure of Natural Hazards Policies," Public Administration Review 45 (January): 20-28.

Congressional Research Service, Library of Congress (1984) Information Technology for Emergency Management, Report prepared for the Subcommittee on Investigations and Oversight, Committee on Science and Technology, U.S. House of Representatives, 98th Congress, 2nd Session, October 9.

Eagleman, Joe R. (1983) Severe and Unusual Weather (New York: Van Nostrand Reinhold Company).

Funk, Ben, "Hurricane!," National Geographic 158 (September 1980), pp.346-365, 372-379.

Godschalk, David R. (1988) "Rebuilding After Hurricane Frederic," pp. 199-212 in Crisis Management, edited by Michael Charles and John Choon Kim (Springfield, Ill.: Charles C. Thomas Publishers).

Leavenworth, Geoffrey (1986) "The Barrier Island Gamble: Is Galveston a Catastrophe Waiting to Happen," Insurance Review (September): 40-40.

McDonald, Franklin, and Philippe Boulle (1988) "Hurricane Gilbert," UNDRO News (September/October), pp. 15-16.

May, Peter J. (1988) "Disaster Recovery and Reconstruction," pp. 236-251 in Managing Disaster, edited by Louise K. Comfort (Durham, NC: Duke University Press).

Miller, Christopher, and Geraldine Bachman (1984) "Planning for Hurricanes and Other Coastal Disturbances," Urban Land (January): 18-23.

Mittler, Elliot (1988) "Agenda-Setting in Nonstructural Hazard Mitigation Policy," pp. 86-107 in Managing Disasters, edited by Louise K. Comfort (Durham, NC: Duke University Press).

National Research Council, U.S. National Academy of Sciences, and U.S. National Academy of Engineering (1987) Confronting Natural Disasters: An International Decade for Natural Hazard Reduction (Washington, DC: National Academy Press).

Simpson, Robert H., and Herbert Riehl (1981) The Hurricane and Its Impact (Baton Rouge: Louisiana State University Press).

Stokes, Herman O., Jr. (1986) "Back to Back Hurricanes in Florida," Paper presented at the National

Conference of the American Society for Public Administration, Anaheim, California, April 13-16.

U.S. General Accounting Office (1983a) <u>Management of the Federal Emergency Management Agency--A System Being Developed</u> (Washington, DC: USGAO, GAO/GGD-83-9, January 6).

____ (1983b) <u>Review of the Federal Emergency Management Agency's Role in Assisting State and Local Governments to Develop Hurricane Preparedness Planning</u> (Washington, DC: USGAO, GAO/RCED-83-182, July 7).

____ (1980) <u>States Can Be Better Prepared to Respond to Disasters</u> (Washington, DC: USGAO, CED-80-60, March 31).

Walker, Barry (1984) "Technology Takes on the Hurricane," <u>Insurance Review</u> (September/ October): 28-34.

Waugh, William L., Jr. (1988) "Current Policy and Implementation Issues in Disaster Preparedness," pp. 111-125 in <u>Managing Disaster</u>, edited by Louise K. Comfort (Durham, NC: Duke University Press).

Waugh, William L., Jr. (1990) "Emergency Management and the Capacities of State and Local Governments," in <u>Cities and Disaster: North American Studies in Emergency Management</u>, edited by Richard Sylves and William L. Waugh, Jr. (Springfield, Ill.: Charles C. Thomas Publishers).

6

Floods

Beverly A. Cigler and Raymond J. Burby

Flooding, any abnormally high water flow that overtops a waterway's natural or artificial confining boundaries, is the most destructive and costly natural disaster faced by the United States. Floods, and the resulting mud and debris flows, are caused not only by rain, but also by human-induced changes to the earth's surface, making the term "natural disaster" somewhat of a misnomer. Farming, deforestation, and urbanization, for example, increase runoff that inundates areas that would not otherwise experience flooding. Careless building in hazard-prone areas, poor watershed management, failure to control flooding, and other human actions increase the impact of the flood disaster (National Research Council, 1987).

Flash floods result from torrential rain or cloudbursts on relatively small and widely dispersed streams, dam failures, and/or breakups of ice jams. This type of flood is especially common to mountainous areas and desert regions. The threat to life from local flash floods, which are characterized by great volume and short duration, is increasing (Kusler, 1982). Riverine floods are caused by precipitation over large areas, the spring snow melt, or both. These floods can last from a few hours to many days and affect river systems with tributaries draining large geographic areas and encompassing many independent river basins.

Seven percent (about 160 million acres) of U.S. land is estimated to be in floodplains and flooding is found in every region of the nation. The urban expansion into those floodplains, which is increasing at a rate of 1.5 to 2.5 percent annually accounts for a rising proportion of flood losses (National Science Foundation, 1980). Floods affect over half of U.S. communities, with risks ranging from chronic flooding in some one to two hundred communities to potential flooding of fringe areas of floodplains in most of the flood-prone communities (White, 1979).

The toll of flood losses is rising most along modest tributary creeks and streams in developing metropolitan areas. Small watersheds respond more dramatically than larger ones to changes in land use through urbanization in terms of rapidity and volume of flood runoff. When natural land surfaces are paved over, built upon, or sewered, small streams that drain only a few square miles become more dangerous relative to larger streams with a watershed of several hundred or thousand square miles (Anderson, 1970; Platt, 1987). It is the smaller U.S. metropolitan areas, moreover, that are experiencing the highest levels of population increase and, therefore, rise in flood loss potential. Many of these areas are in the Sunbelt and the West and other metropolitan areas with little or no previous experience in coping with metropolitan growth, including the flood problem (Platt, 1987).

The dominant strategies for dealing with the flood problem, historically, have been flood control projects (e.g., dams, levees) and federal disaster relief. Each year, however, floods take an increasing number of lives and property and disaster relief costs rise. From 1965-1985, floods in the United States caused 1,767 deaths and accounted for more than 63 percent (337 out of 531) of the federally declared disasters (National Research Council, 1987). The Federal Emergency Management Agency (FEMA) depicts the customary sequence of events as: flooding, flood losses, disaster relief, flood control projects attempting to modify the flood potential through provisions for storage, accelerating, blocking, or diverting flood waters, renewed encroachment and development onto the floodplain and upstream watershed, flooding, flood losses, disaster relief, more projects, more encroachment and development, ad infinitum (FEMA, 1986a). Increased attention has been devoted in the last two decades to nonstructural alternatives for dealing with the flood problem through regulatory land-use measures and subsidized flood insurance.

A comprehensive estimate of future flood control needs cannot be developed because the service provided is one the of costs avoided. However, available data indicate the continued necessity for flood reduction measures. The traditional measure of flood control need is the amount of damage occurring. The National Weather Service (NWS) collects data on losses for presidentially declared disasters from FEMA, major events reported by the U.S. Army Corps of Engineers and the Soil Conservation Service (SCS), and from the news media, but no attempt is made to total annual floods for a single year in comprehensive fashion. The U.S. Army Corps of Engineers and SCS forecast flood damages only for individual projects.

Some recent federal aggregated projections suggest that average annual losses from floods are rising. Average annual cost estimates climbed from $1 billion in 1966 (Task Force on Flood Control Policy, 1966) to $2.2 billion in the mid-1970s (U.S. Water Resources Council 1977), using 1967 dollars. In the 1980s the costs are estimated to be $5 billion annually (Council on Environmental Quality, 1981). Flood losses in 1985 met the $5-billion prediction due to several major hurricanes.

THE HISTORY OF U.S. FLOOD MANAGEMENT POLICY

The major impetus for the federal government's role in reducing flood damages was the enactment of the Flood Control Act of 1936 (PL 74-738), with emphasis on structural solutions valued at more than $20 billion in historical investment-while preventing damages of nearly $150 billion (Schilling et al., 1987). The U.S. Army Corps of Engineers attempts to reduce property damage from flooding by constructing protective works. The Tennessee Valley Authority (TVA) was authorized in 1933, in part, to construct dams and reservoirs in the Tennessee River and its tributaries. Today, nine TVA dams span the river itself and an additional thirty dams provide flood control on tributaries. The Bureau of Reclamation and the Department of Agriculture's SCS construct flood control projects and upstream water projects. NWS is responsible for flood warnings.

Structural Projects

The most visible structural projects are dams and reservoirs. However, these are very costly and pose environmental and social drawbacks. Channel modifications are a much used flood damage reduction measure to deal with localized flooding problems, although continued local maintenance is necessary and, over a period of years, land-use changes in the watershed upstream of the project can make its design capacity inadequate, posing serious problems.

Stream renovation and erosion control programs offer yet another relatively cost effective and environmentally benign alternatives to projects involving significant stream channel straightening and enlargement, typical of agricultural flood damage prevention projects. The Soil Conservation Service often takes the lead in such activities as selective removal of silt, sand and gravel, log jams, snags, downed trees, and other channel debris.

Many areas of the country use levees and floodwalls extensively, such as along the lower Mississippi River. The overtopping or failure of a levee could be disastrous so such structures must be able to withstand flood events with an extremely low probability of occurrence. Consequently, a favorable cost/benefit ratio is difficult to achieve for construction, operating, and maintenance costs.

The Flood Control Act of 1936 included the principle of cost sharing with local interests, although requirements were sharply reduced in flood control acts passed in 1937 and 1938. Rutherford H. Platt (1979) argues that the federal government investment of more than $10 billion in structural measures by the end of the 1960s gave many local communities a false sense of security and also led to a local ideology that placed little interest in managing the land within their floodplains. In recent years, an important trend has been to increase the state and local cost-sharing requirements.

Flood control facilities too often proved to be impracticable and economically unfeasible for the great majority of flood-prone communities. Development occurred rapidly in flood hazard areas. The federal government was unable to provide protection through flood control works, especially when an unwise use of natural floodplains led to increased losses from development. In the absence of local laws and regulations designed to protect floodplains from urban encroachment, federal construction projects made possible the continued, and even more intensive, use of flood hazard areas (White et al., 1958; Burby and French, 1981: 289; 1981; Burby et al., 1985). A dangerous drawback, moreover, is the tendency for residents of "protected areas" to ignore warnings of the possibility of floodwaters overtopping flood control structures and remaining in hazardous areas until disaster strikes.

If gains are to be made in lessening the increases in flood losses and in maintaining environmental quality, investment in some new flood control projects is essential. Most of the nation's largest structures have now been completed, however. New structures will likely be small and more localized, with greater sharing of responsibility by nonfederal interests and project beneficiaries.

The TVA reservoir system is a good example of the difficulties of sole reliance on a structural project approach. In the early 1950s, TVA engineers realized that for every community with a flood problem for which relief through flood control structures was feasible, there were some twenty communities where such works were not feasible (Tennessee Valley Authority, 1983). Nearly 150 communities prone to significant flood damages were identified, even with the major TVA reservoirs in place. Annual potential flood loss is estimated at $35 million in the Tennessee Valley and is growing at the rate of about 4 percent per year (Tennessee Valley Authority, 1986).

Development of Nonstructural (Land-Use and Insurance) Options

The structural options (dams and levees) for flood hazard mitigation are designed to shield people and development from harm. Another, less feasible, option is to act upon the hazard itself (e.g., cloud seeding). Recognizing the problems with exclusive reliance upon structural approaches to reducing flood hazards, federal attention in the mid-1960s turned to nonstructural alternatives to avert disaster losses through such means as flood warning systems, land-use regulations, construction regulations, land acquisition, and property relocation. Most nonstructural alternatives either prevent or limit the location of vulnerable development and of populations in hazardous areas (land-use controls, financial incentives or disincentives) or alter the design or construction of development or redevelopment (via building code provisions) to make it less vulnerable to flooding.

Discussion of the use of such approaches dates as far back as the 1930s. In 1952, President Truman advocated a flood insurance program and noted the need for limits to be placed on the use of floodplains via state and local zoning laws. Congress, however, did not respond with any funded legislation until the Flood Insurance Act of 1968 (PL 90-448), which explicitly included the mandating of floodplain regulations.

Several events prior to the landmark flood insurance legislation are noteworthy in the development of the nonstructural approach. The concept of floodproofing of structures received national exposure in the 1960s with the publication of John Sheaffer's works. Gilbert White's (1945) paper, entitled "Human Adjustment to Floods," made a case for averting local flood damage by careful land-use planning relying on a combination of engineering, architectural, and hydrologic measures and finally received the attention of federal agencies, especially TVA. That agency first used the term "floodplain management" and pioneered a floodplain management assistance program for local communities in 1953 that helped them define their flood problems and land-use options, but left it to the local communities themselves to enact ordinances.

By 1959, six years after the initial experience with floodplain management in the Tennessee Valley, TVA recommended adoption of such a program on a national scale. In 1966 the Task Force on Federal Flood Control Policy, formed by the Bureau of the Budget and chaired by Gilbert White, recommended a "Unified National Program for Managing Flood Losses" (Task Force on Federal Flood Control Policy, 1966). President Johnson endorsed the task force's report and referred it to the House Committee on Public Works which printed it as House Document 465, providing the first major policy level recommendations for alternative techniques (beyond structural works) such as flood insurance, floodproofing, relocation, forecasting and warning, and floodplain regulations. It signaled the need for a coordinated federal-state-local program for managing floodplains and advocated improved floodplain mapping, coordinated intergovernmental planning, improved technical services, changes in flood control project surveys, and cost sharing to provide for greater state and local involvement.

Simultaneously, President Johnson issued Executive Order 11296, which directed all federal agencies to evaluate the flood hazard in administering grants, loans, mortgages insurance, property disposal, and construction programs. The U.S. Army Corps of Engineers established a Floodplain Management Services program, closely patterned after the TVA program, as a result of the task force report.

At the same time that House Document 406 was written in 1966, a report on flood insurance by the Department of Housing and Urban Development (U.S. Senate Committee on Banking and Currency, 1966) recommended a federal flood insurance program. The program was designed to meet the insurance needs of flood-prone areas, shift the costs of floodplain occupancy from the national government (via disaster relief and structural measures) to the beneficiaries of flood-prone locations (floodplain owners and occupants), and encourage local land-use and building regulations to reduce the susceptibility of new construction to flood losses. Insurance for existing structures would be subsidized in order to facilitate participation in the programs since prohibitively high insurance costs would otherwise be borne by participants. Actuarially sound rates would be applied to new construction to reflect fully the potential for property damage from flooding. Local governments would be required to adopt and enforce floodplain regulations as a condition for participation by their residents in the program, preventing insurance availability from inducing an increase in floodplain development.

In 1968, Congress responded to the two 1966 recommendations by the Bureau of the Budget and the Department of Housing and Urban Development (HUD) with passage of the National Flood Insurance Act (PL 90-448), which called for the president to develop a unified national program for floodplain management, a responsibility he delegated to the U.S. Water Resources Council. A conceptual framework and recommendations for federal and state actions, especially for reducing losses through floodplain management, were developed by the council and published in 1976.

National Flood Insurance Program

The National Flood Insurance Program (NFIP), originally administered by HUD was the main focus of the National Flood Insurance Act. Eligibility for the insurance was conditioned on community adoption of building regulations to reduce the susceptibility of new construction to flood damage. Since House Document 465 and NFIP, state and local governments have an increased awareness of floodplain problems and have exercised additional responsibility over flood-prone lands. States have taken enabling action, allowing their local communities to establish floodplain management regulations. (Of 20,000 flood-prone communities, some 17,500 now participate in NFIP.)

In the first year of the program, however, only four communities joined and only twenty flood insurance policies were sold (Platt, 1976), reflecting the lack of initial local government commitment and capacity to undertake the required floodplain regulations. An "emergency" phase of NFIP participation was created by Congress in 1969 (PL 91-152), reflecting congressional recognition that sufficient flood data were necessary before local governments could institute regulations. The emergency phase authorized provisional eligibility of flood-prone communities and allowed property owners to purchase flood insurance even before studies were conducted to establish actuarially sound premium charges. As detailed flood maps became available and local regulations were adopted, communities became eligible for the "regular" program which offered larger amounts of insurance coverage.

Even with inducement to participate, interest in the voluntary NFIP program was weak. Fewer than one-fifth of the flood-prone communities in the nation were participating in NFIP, even when the United States was experiencing some of its worst flooding in history-Hurricane Agnes and the Rapid City, South Dakota flash flood. (Agnes alone caused over $2 billion in losses and damaged more than 300,000 structures in 1982.)

The Flood Disaster Protection Act of 1973 (PL 93-234) virtually made local government participation in the program compulsory since it required state and local governments, as a condition for future federal financial assistance for property acquisition or construction in flood hazard areas (including sewerage system financing), to participate in NFIP. In addition, severe sanctions for owners of floodplain property resulted if their local governments did not participate. Not only could flood insurance not be purchased, but floodplain property owners would not be eligible for federal disaster assistance for any flood-related damages, and they would not be eligible for loans-such as home mortgages-from any federally supervised, regulated, or insured agencies or institutions. Finally, direct federal grants and loans, such as those from the Small Business Administration, would be barred.

The lending sanctions of the strengthened NFIP program led to strong opposition by the banking industry. The prohibition against federally insured institutions making loans to residents of flood-prone communities that had no floodplain regulations was relaxed in 1977 when the flood insurance act was amended (PL 95-128). The lending sanction was replaced by a requirement that financial institutions making loans had to notify recipients that federal disaster relief assistance would not be made available unless flood insurance was purchased.

Today, the federal role in flood protection clearly includes both structural and nonstructural options. While federal participation in structural programs includes direct building of public works structures through increasing cost arrangements with other sectors, the federal role in promoting nonstructural alternatives ranges from administering the subsidized flood insurance program to facilitating of state and local regulatory land-use actions via the sanctions of NFIP.

A BROADENED NATIONAL FLOODPLAIN MANAGEMENT PHILOSOPHY

In 1977 the president issued a comprehensive environmental message calling for better management of floodplains, wetlands, coastal barrier islands, and marine sanctuaries. Executive Order 11988 (Floodplain Management Executive Order) accompanied the message. The order reinforced the need to strengthen federal policies to reduce the risk of flood loss to minimize the impact of floods on human safety, health, and welfare and to restore and preserve natural floodplain values. In linking together the earlier stated objectives of protecting lives and property with the environmental objective of protecting natural and beneficial floodplain values, this executive order offered a more comprehensive and stronger policy directive. In addition, Executive Order 11988 requires federal agencies to provide leadership and take action to ensure the practice of sound floodplain management by avoiding public investment in the floodplain-including grants-in-aid to local governments-if practicable alternatives exist.

Similarly, Executive Order 11990 (Protection of Wetlands), also issued in 1977, was designed to reduce the adverse impacts associated with the destruction or modification of wetlands. Section 73 of the Water Resources Development Act of 1974 (PL 93-251) had already required the U.S. Army Corps of Engineers and other federal construction agencies to give full consideration to building and land-use alternatives to flood control structures when evaluating ways to reduce flood losses. It also provided for cost sharing for nonstructural as well as structural flood damage reduction measures.

To reflect the increased concern for natural floodplain values enunciated in Executive Orders 11988 and 11990, the Water Resources Council (1979) revised its unified program by modifying the conceptual framework and the recommendations. To address the growing costs of coastal flooding, the Coastal Barriers Resource Act (PL 97-348) was enacted in 1982. It prohibits the selling of federal flood insurance in designated barrier islands along the Atlantic and Gulf coasts, but applies only to improvements or new construction in designated areas.

Other environmental quality legislation affecting water resources helped set the stage for the far-reaching implications of the Floodplain Management Executive Order (11988). This includes the Coastal Zone Management Act of 1974 (PL 92-583) and its amendments. That federal initiative helps the states minimize life and property losses and environmental degradation caused by improper development along coastal areas.

The United States has 3,000 federal and 80,000 nonfederal dams; 2,900 of the total are believed to be unsafe. Ninety-nine percent of these are nonfederal dams and 75 percent are privately owned. The Federal Dam Safety Act (PL 92-367) promotes dam inspections, a model state dam safety program, and seed funding for states to develop dam safety programs for dealing with nonfederal dams. Funding for the key part of the program, the seed money for state dam safety programs, has dwindled in recent years, however.

The early Clean Water Acts of 1972 and 1977 (PL 92-500 and 95-217) assigned the U.S. Army Corps of Engineers the responsibility of issuing permits for the discharge of dredged or fill material into water of the United States (Section 404 permits), after consultation with the Environmental Protection Agency (EPA) and other appropriate units. The laws also gave EPA power to restrict discharges with unacceptable environmental impacts. Other sections of these laws and other legislation require planning coordination within and among levels of government on matters concerning floodplain management, such as planning for waste treatment facilities and the preparation of basin plans (Water Resources Planning Act, PL 89-80).

Federal Emergency Management

Federal floodplain management responsibilities, originally housed in HUD where the flood insurance program originated, were assigned to the Federal Emergency Management Agency (FEMA) by Executive Order 12148 (which established FEMA IN 1979). FEMA recently updated the U.S. Water Resources Council (1986b) document, "A Unified National Program for Floodplain Management," since the council no longer exists. This document is the best official source for summaries of national flood policy and information on FEMA's policy recommendations.

To implement Executive Orders 11988 and 11990, FEMA developed an eight-step floodplain management and wetlands protection decision-making process that must be followed by federal agencies. In addition to, and supportive of NFIP, FEMA offers state and local governments a variety of information resources (guides, handbooks, manuals, maps, and training), financial assistance (planning grants and repair and reconstruction of flood-damaged structures), and technical assistance (design standards, model ordinances, demonstration projects, and expert consultation networks).

FEMA is also, of course, the lead federal agency for developing, coordinating, and implementing federal policy for recovery from flood disasters. It works closely with state governments in shared arrangements for promoting local mitigation efforts and disaster relief and recovery.

In addition to the Flood Disaster Protection Act of 1973, which virtually required participation in NFIP, several other pieces of disaster relief legislation dovetail with the NFIP inducements for land-use approaches to the flood problem and strengthen the existing federal floodplain management framework. Realizing that many federal expenditures, especially those for disaster relief, were used only to restore facilities to their predisaster condition, Congress expanded its pre- and postdisaster mitigation goals and requirements in Section 406 of the Disaster Relief Act Amendments of 1974 (PL 93-288). A condition for receiving federal disaster loans or grant assistance for any type of disaster is the requirement that all levels of government identify and take steps to mitigate hazards (through land-use and construction regulations). A hazard mitigation clause is incorporated in the FEMA-state agreement for disaster assistance, thereby establishing the evaluation of mitigation opportunities as a condition for receiving federal assistance in disasters declared by the president. States experiencing a disaster must prepare, within 180 days, a hazard mitigation plan for the disaster area.

While the preparation of the 406 mitigation plan is primarily a state responsibility, the federal government takes the lead in another set of activities related to a flood disaster. An Interagency Hazard Mitigation Team (IHMT)-a coordinated interagency and intergovernmental group mobilized by the FEMA regional director-is activated after a presidential declaration of a flood-related disaster. The IHMT process draws immediate attention to mitigation measures since the first in a series of reports containing recommendations for mitigation actions is due fifteen days after a disaster declaration. The FEMA reports often help improve federal-state-local relations since all levels of government are represented on the team.

FEMA administers grants for federal disaster assistance to the states from the president's disaster relief fund and coordinates the disaster assistance functions of all federal agencies. The state government is a partner in the FEMA-state agreement signed after the president's disaster declaration and, in addition to the 406 responsibilities already discussed, plays an important role in the disbursement of federal assistance. Many state laws also extend authority to state agencies for provision of technical or financial assistance or for identification of local funding sources for recovery and mitigation.

In 1983, FEMA began using an Integrated Emergency Management System (IEMS) to encourage state and local progress in dealing with all hazards, both natural and technological. This systematic approach to planning includes identification and analysis of hazards, assessment of capabilities to prepare for and respond to hazard events, and the planning of multiyear programs for all phases (preparedness, response, recovery, and mitigation) of emergency management.

Flood hazard mitigation is also related to the implementation of Section 402 of the Disaster Relief Act which authorizes the president to make contributions to state or local governments to help repair, reconstruct, or replace public facilities damaged or destroyed by a disaster.

Several other federal agencies are important to federal flood mitigation efforts (FEMA, 1986a). Most of these are associated with early U.S. efforts in building structural control projects, but all are important today in nonstructural options as well. The U.S. Army Corps of Engineers conducts and/or funds beach erosion control projects (limited to 70 percent of the funding of a project or $1 million), flood control works (fifty to two hundred rehabilitations per year, ranging from $2,000 to more than $1 million each), small flood control projects not specifically authorized by Congress, obtaining and clearing projects for flood control protection for essential highways and bridges, floodplain management services, planning assistance to the states, and assistance in emergency flood fighting and rescues. State and local cost-sharing principles apply to these activities.

The U.S. Soil Conservation Service in the Department of Agriculture provides technical assistance, including watershed protection and river basin surveys, flood protection projects, other floodplain management studies, resources conservation and development, emergency watershed protection, and soil and snow surveys. Cost-sharing requirements vary depending on the service.

The Federal Highway Administration in the Department of Transportation provides formula and project grants to state highway agencies to aid in the cost of rebuilding flood-damaged highway facilities on the federal aid system, assists in surveying roadway damage in flood areas, and is involved with debris removal and erosion control as well as channel cleaning.

Other federal agencies provide a gamut of services. The Department of Agriculture's Farmers Home Administration offers loans from recovery losses from disasters and for watershed protection. The Small Business Administration has made loans to individuals and businesses for property repair and replacement in disaster areas. HUD's Community Development Block Grant Program (CDBG) allows use of funds for mitigation-related projects, including acquisition, rehabilitation of certain public work facilities, housing rehabilitation, code enforcement, relocation assistance, and urban renewal.

The U.S. Geological Survey conducts mapping programs and assists communities and state agencies in collecting, developing, and computing basic data for floodplain engineering studies and investigations. The National Weather Service forecasts the water levels of the nation's rivers and issues flood warnings to the public and mass media. Both the National Weather Service and the National Oceanic and Atmospheric Administration provide a variety of technical assistance to state and localities, such as establishing local flood warning systems.

The Evolving Federal Role

The diverse federal role in dealing with the flood problem is discussed in great depth elsewhere (National Science Foundation, 1980; Changnon et al., 1983; White, 1975; Platt, 1976). The major federal policies are the structural flood control projects undertaken directly or indirectly by federal agencies, flood disaster assistance programs, and the fiscal subsidies and guarantees that influence private sector investment and locational decisions through subsidized flood insurance. Other federal policies affect the flood problem, however: general regulatory measures that protect public health, safety, and welfare (e.g., water quality regulations); taxation and personal and corporate income (depreciation policies and casualty write-offs); and improvement and management of navigable waterways (e.g., permit regulations for construction or fill along rivers and shorelines)(FEMA, 1986b).

Legislation relating to nonstructural options demonstrates both the clear mandate for a federal regulatory role in floodplain management and the complexity of such a policy. Under the U.S. constitutional system, the management of private land-use is the responsibility of state and especially local governments. With approximately 17,500 of the 20,000 U.S. flood-prone communities currently participating in NFIP, the federal government's role is to build the commitment of local governments to floodplain management and to develop local governments' capacities to design, enact, and enforce the required floodplain regulations.

The NFIP program implemented by FEMA includes activities which relate to insurance (enrolling individual participants, establishing rates, and paying claims) and activities which relate to floodplain management (establishing flood zones, enrolling communities in regular and emergency phases, and establishing standards). Although the two sets of activities are housed separately within FEMA, the regulatory "stick" is driven by the "carrot" provided by flood insurance availability (May and Williams, 1986).

FEMA's regulatory role in NFIP includes the development of guidelines concerning minimal standards for floodplain management, standards which serve as the criteria for evaluating whether a community's regulations justify certification so that residents can be eligible for subsidized flood insurance. Communities not meeting FEMA-developed standards can be suspended, a power used not infrequently by FEMA-140 communities were suspended in 1983 (May and Williams, 1986). Communities and individuals may appeal FEMA actions.

FEMA also devotes resources to regional offices which work with states and local communities to promote the program and respond to inquiries about it. The Comprehensive Cooperative Agreement (CCA) between FEMA and a state or eligible territory allows all emergency management programs and activities for each state and its local governments to be funded through a single instrument. All of FEMA's mitigation programs, with the exception of NFIP, are funded through the state's CCA with FEMA.

FEMA considers the states as the key providers of NFIP technical assistance. Each governor has designated a specific state agency to coordinate its flood insurance program. Seed money provided by FEMA enables state programs to implement technical assistance activities, in conjunction with regional FEMA offices. The state role in NFIP is still evolving but research found that state officials viewed the states as appropriate vehicles for providing local technical assistance and planning and coordination activities--despite the fact that only 52 percent of the local officials were aware of their state's NFIP assistance program (Burby and Cigler, 1984).

Most states do not devote a great deal of their own resources to NFIP. In addition, state flood-related programs are usually fragmented among several agencies, with land-use floodplain management and structural control programs handled by water resource agencies and flood relief handled by emergency services agencies. After the flood disaster strikes, the relief agencies do not have the necessary commitment to undertake mitigation efforts or to work with other agencies which have more expertise in mitigation programs, such as land-use measures.

FEMA funding for NFIP is primarily for the preparation of the detailed flood maps that are necessary before flood-prone communities can begin to develop their regulations. Other activities include special flood studies (mobile home anchoring and mudflows) and since 1981 a small property acquisition program for acquiring flood-prone properties (authorized under Section 1362 of the 1968 Flood Insurance Act).

EVALUATION OF FEDERAL FLOOD CONTROL PROGRAMS

Increasing flood damage, despite enormous past flood control investments at all levels of government, leads many observers to judge past programs--particularly structural projects--as ineffective. The perception persists because benefit estimation techniques concentrate on property damage avoided and net income change, despite the view that the authors of the 1936 Flood Control Act envisioned social welfare flood control benefits in addition to reducing physical property damage and income losses. In this section, a broad set of federal goals is used to assess the overall federal effort in dealing with the flood problem.

Reducing Flood Losses

In contrast to popular perception and traditional measures of past program effectiveness, Douglas Woolley (1986) offers an alternative view which examines flood damages in relation to Gross National Product (GNP). He argues that an assessment of flood damage trends should consider three factors: inflation, population, and wealth. The consumer price index, a measure of inflation, has increased sixfold since 1930. Population and wealth increases affect the demand for floodplain land, suggesting that investments on such land will increase as the land takes on increased social value. Thus, the current measure of GNP will reflect price, population, and wealth trends. By dividing annual estimates of flood damages by GNP for a given year, a measure of flood damages that is adjusted for the economic conditions of the period is obtained. Since damages vary substantially from year to year, the trend over time is most interesting.

Woolley found no increase or decrease in the ratio of flood damages to GNP over the time period of 1929 to 1983. This finding suggests the possibility that substantial economic benefits have been realized from structural projects. If flood damages have been stable while significant increases in the developmental intensity of floodplains have occurred, it can be inferred that the nation has realized the benefits of intensified land uses without paying a penalty in increased damages. Still, whether the land-use benefits--net of damages--have exceeded the cost of project construction cannot be determined (Woolley, 1986; Schilling et al., 1987). Woolley's study dovetails with conclusions from other work that estimates losses prevented by the federal flood control program (White, 1975).

Most of the literature on the evaluation of nonstructural projects (land-use measures) is advocacy in nature, although some studies have attempted to assess costs and benefits of various measures (Carson, 1975; U.S. Department of Housing and Urban Development, 1981). Several national studies by researchers associated with the Center for Urban and Regional Studies at the University of North Carolina at Chapel Hill, however, shed some light on the effectiveness of floodplain regulations. Raymond J.

Burby and his associates (1985, 1987) and Beverly A. Cigler and her colleagues (1988) use perceptual data gathered from mail surveys of local officials to gauge the effectiveness of various regulatory land-use measures. Others compared changes in floodplain conditions between 1976 and 1985 in ten communities to assess the effectiveness of NFIP-induced regulations (Burby et al., 1988).

The University of North Carolina studies, plus a series of case studies by Peter J. May and Walter Williams (1986), and estimates of cost savings by John R. Sheaffer and Roland Scheaffer (1979) all find that the federal government's promotion of nonstructural options has achieved congressional objectives for reduction of flood losses through NFIP-induced regulatory measures. The recent ten-city comparative study by University of North Carolina researchers, for example, estimated that local nonstructural programs resulted in a 35 percent reduction in potential average annual flood damages.

Most flood loss progress has been made in reducing losses to new development occurring in flood hazard areas, while improvement in protecting existing developments from flooding and in preserving the natural values of the floodplain (water quality, wildlife habitat, flood storage, aquifer recharge) has been less successful. Forty-eight percent of the local officials surveyed in the 1979 and 1982 University of North Carolina studies rated flood hazard management as very effective in preventing flood losses to new construction. For most new construction, developers and builders avoided flood hazard areas (94 percent). Just 21 percent of the local officials rated flood hazard management as very effective in reducing the exposure of existing development to flooding.

Preserving Natural Values

Only 33 percent of the local officials in the 1979 and 1982 University of North Carolina studies rated their programs as very effective in preserving the natural values of flood hazard areas. In fact, only 18 percent of the local officials cited this as a goal of their community's flood management program. Just as federal flood control structures have been found to induce floodplain development, and thus damage the natural environment, NFIP has had a somewhat similar effect. Flood insurance reduces property owners' and lenders' fears of experiencing the adverse consequences of flooding and may encourage development. NFIP's other benefits, however, appear to have a stimulating effect on development.

The goal most stressed by NFIP--protection of new construction--achieves higher compliance than goals developed in the broader philosophy embodied in Executive Order 11988 for protecting natural floodplain degradation as well as overall life and property in flood hazard areas.

Increased State and Local Responsibility for Flood Hazard Management

The federal government has also experienced much success in achieving its objective of developing local government participation in NFIP, with subsequent adoption of the required minimal building regulations and prohibition of new development in floodways. As stated earlier, more than 17,500 (over 90 percent of flood-prone U.S. communities) participate in NFIP and most of these units enforce the required building elevation and floodway protection requirements. The North Carolina research effort reported that 74 percent of state governments offer technical assistance to local governments on NFIP-related concerns, and 68 percent are involved in planning and coordination activities.

Cost Shifting among Governments

The federal objective of having the beneficiaries of successful flood control and management programs absorb more of the costs can be assessed by several measures: cost-sharing arrangements for structural and nonstructural programs, the number of flood property owners holding purchased flood insurance, the amount of subsidy for flood insurance premiums paid by the national government, and trends in federal payments for disaster relief. Using these measures to determine the federal role in flood control yields mixed findings.

Cost sharing for both flood control works and nonstructural management approaches has clearly shifted to the beneficiaries of these policies. The steady growth in federal disaster relief spending spurred actions to limit federal expenditures, to increase disaster loan interest rates, to eliminate loan-forgiveness clauses to eliminate federal funding for long-term reconstruction, and to shift toward private risk sharing for flood insurance (May, 1985).

As federal arrangements for structural and nonstructural options require more cost burdens to be assumed by state and local governments, these governments have developed their own expertise through investment of their own funds, paired with federal seed monies. In addition, states and communities bear costs when participating in the Interagency Hazard Mitigation Teams developed after a disaster strikes and through Section 406 of the Disaster Relief Act of 1974 (PL 93-288), which requires identification of hazards and a mitigation plan as a condition of receiving federal disaster assistance in the future.

It must be remembered also that federal disaster assistance as defined in the Disaster Relief Act of 1974 (PL 93-288) is supplemental to state and local capabilities to respond to a disaster. Each year, many floods strike states and their communities for which no federal disaster assistance is requested or provided. Even with a presidentially declared disaster, substantial recovery costs are borne by the state and local governments and the private sector. The amount of federal disaster assistance for eligible public facilities, moreover, has gone from 100 percent to 75 percent (25 percent from state and local) in recent years. It is proposed that regulations be developed stipulating a 50-50 cost share.

Recent changes in the National Flood Insurance Fund of NFIP also require more cost sharing. The cumulative loss for the program is projected to be $1.4 billion at the end of 1988. The deficit, historically, has been partially financed through appropriations of $1.2 billion. The national government's goal has been to reduce that subsidy, as indicated in the president's 1986 budget submission (U.S. Congress, 1985). A substantial increase in premiums for 1988 along with coverage changes and optional deductibles, and rating system changes are expected to make the program self-supporting--at least for the "normal" year (the average year experienced to date as compared to the average resulting from a time period including a truly catastrophic event). Beginning in 1986, administrative and other associated costs of flood insurance were folded into the flood insurance fund and are expected to be recovered eventually through flood insurance premiums.

Since NFIP achieved large-scale penetration of the market in 1980 (approximately 2 of 7 million flood-prone structures are covered), there has not been a truly catastrophic flood event (one with more than a billion dollars in flood insurance claims). There is no evidence that the administrative costs of NFIP, moreover, are too high in comparison with those of the private insurance industry, despite the statutory requirements of extensive flood risk studies, loss reduction studies, and other requirements. The latest two-year average expense ratio of .34 is the same as the latest two-year average expense ratio of the private insurance industry for property insurance (Federal Register, 1987).

CONTINUING PROBLEMS FOR FEDERAL FLOOD POLICIES

Despite much progress and significant success, the federal effort to help avert flood disasters is fraught with many problems relating to intergovernmental coordination, equity considerations, and private property rights.

Intergovernmental Coordination

Fragmented and uncoordinated responsibility for floodplain management at all levels of government is a key characteristic of flood policy. Programs are marked by a lack of consistency, overlapping, and duplication. State programs, for example, are usually fragmented among water agencies and emergency management agencies that focus on preparedness and response but not mitigation. Federal water programs are housed across several key agencies while FEMA houses NFIP.

An intergovernmental paradox exists in that the governments most responsible for dealing with flood problems are least equipped to do so. These subnational governments, in addition, hold flood problems to be less salient than do decision makers at the national level--who must be concerned about the aggregate of all losses in the United States, not just those of a single community or state (Cigler, 1988b).

A number of other facts associated with how governments have organized to deal with hazards in general militate against cooperation among and between governments (Cigler, 1988a):

1. Existing government programs are based on legislation addressing specific concerns (e.g., floods, water issues) which vary among states and local governments.

2. Hazards officials are a diverse group; physical planners, financial planners, and risk managers rarely work with other emergency management officials.

3. Most hazards officials devote only part-time efforts to hazards policies, complicating opportunities for coordination.

4. The engineering, scientific, and economic expertise involving hazards is limited and fragmented by academic disciplines.

5. Interaction among and between technical staff and public decision makers is not well established.

Equity Considerations

Much is still unknown about the distribution of impacts--both of flood disasters and of disaster assistance--across income classes and geographic areas. This raises many questions for federal policy decisions relating to cost sharing and cost shifting. Many argue that we have relied too heavily on public investment strategies in dealing with our national flood problem. Our knowledge regarding the redistributive effects of existing grant, loan, insurance and tax provisions is sparse. Peter J. May's (1985) analysis of research findings on the current redistributive influence of current disaster relief programs (which primarily entail low interest loans without forgiveness features) on individuals suggests that higher-income, higher-loss disaster victims are favored. The existence of more accurate data to help evaluate policy options still might not, however, settle all of the normative questions about the role of the national government relative to state and local roles.

Private Property Rights
and Nonstructural Mitigation

Many useful land-use regulations are not enacted or enforced due to unresolved conflicts between private property rights and local, state, and national interests in the flood problem. Attempts to resolve conflicts lead to costly litigation for all parties, including suits by the national government against localities for not complying with NFIP.

CONCLUSION

Federal policy debate will likely continue to focus on questions of economic efficiency, especially those relating to cost shifting to state and local governments and the private sector for flood insurance, flood control works, mitigation measures, and disaster relief. The debate will be difficult because of the equity issues which must be brought to bear. Normative questions about the respective roles of the national, state, and local governments in the federal system will dominate the debate.

The complexity of data and perception problems when dealing with natural hazards suggests a continued focus on single hazards by most governments, despite FEMA's attempts at an integrated emergency management system. Thus, existing arrangements and programs for dealing with flood problems will not change dramatically.

REFERENCES

Anderson, D. G. (1970). Effects of Urban Development on Floods in Northern Virginia, Geological Survey Water Supply Paper #2001-C. (Washington, D.C.: U.S. Government Printing Office).

Burby, Raymond J., and Beverly A. Cigler (1984). "Effectiveness of State Assistance Programs for Flood Hazard Mitigation," in Regional and State Water Resources Planning and Management, ed. Randall Charbeneau, pp.179-88 (Bethesda, Md.: American Water Resources Association).

Burby, Raymond J., and Steven P. French (1981). "Coping with Floods: Land Use Management Paradox," Journal of the American Planning Association 47: 289-300.

Burby, Raymond J., et al. (1985). Flood Plain Land-Use Management: A National Assessment (Boulder Colo.: Westview Press)

Burby, Raymond J., and Edward J. Kaiser (1987). An Assessment of Urban Floodplain Land-Use Management in the United States: The Case for Land Acquisition in Comprehensive Floodplain (Madison, Wis.: Association of State Floodplain Managers, Technical Report No. 1, June).

Burby, Raymond J., et al. (1988). Cities under Water: A Comparative Evaluation of Ten Cities' Efforts to Manage Floodplain Land Use (Boulder, Colo.: University of Colorado, Institute of Behavioral Science, Monograph #47).

Carson, William D. (1975). Estimated Costs and Benefits for Nonstructural Flood Control

Measures (Davis, Calif.: Hydraulic Engineering Center, U.S. Army Corps of Engineers, October).

Changnon, Stanley A., et al., eds. (1983). Floods and Their Mitigation in the United States (Champaign, Ill.: Illinois State Water Survey).

Cigler, Beverly A. (1987). "Political and Organizational Considerations in Infrastructure Investment Decisionmaking," in Local Infrastructure Decisionmaking, ed. Thomas G. Johnson, pp. 201-13 (Boulder, Colo.: Westview Press).

_____ (1988a). "Current Issues in Mitigation," in Managing Disaster: Strategies and Policy Perspectives, ed. Louise K. Comfort, pp. 39-52 (Durham, N.C.: Duke University Press).

_____ (1988b). "Emergency Management and Public Administration," in Crisis Management: A Casebook, ed. Michael T. Charles and John Choon Kim, pp. 5-19 (Springfield, Ill.: Charles C. Thomas).

Council on Environmental Quality (1981). Environmental Quality--1980 (Washington, D.C.: U.S. Government Printing Office).

Federal Emergency Management Agency (FEMA)(1986a). Disaster Assistance Programs: Making Mitigation Work--A Handbook for State Officials (Washington, D.C.: Federal Emergency Management Agency, June).

_____ (1986b). A Unified National Program for Floodplain Management (Washington, D.C.: Federal Emergency Management Agency, March).

_____ (1987). Integrated Emergency Management System: Mitigation Program Development Guidance (Washington, D.C.: Federal Emergency Management Agency, March).

Federal Register (1987). 52/39 (February 27): 59-79.

Kusler, Jon A. (1982). Regulation of Flood Hazard Areas to Reduce Flood Losses, vol. 3 (Washington, D.C.: U.S. Water Resources Council).

May, Peter J. (1985). Recovering from Catastrophes: Federal Disaster Relief Policy and Politics (Westport, Conn.: Greenwood).

_____ and Walter Williams (1986). Disaster Policy Implementation: Managing Programs Under Shared Governance (New York: Plenum).

National Research Council (1987). Confronting Natural Disasters: An International Decade for

Natural Hazard Reduction (Washington, D.C.: National Academy).

National Science Foundation (1980). A Report of Flood Hazard Mitigation (Washington, D.C.: National Science Foundation).

Platt, Rutherford H. (1976). "The National Flood Insurance Program: Some Mainstream Perspectives," Journal of the American Institute of Planners 42 (July): 303-13.

_____ (1987). Regional Management of Metropolitan Floodplains: Experience in the United States and Abroad (Boulder, Colo.: University of Colorado, Institute of Behavioral Science, Monograph #45).

Schilling, Kyle, et al. (1987). The Nation's Public Works: Report on Water Resources (Washington, D.C.: National Council on Public Works Improvement, May).

Sheaffer, John R. (1960). Flood Proofing: An Element in a Flood Damage Reduction Program (Chicago, Ill.: University of Chicago, Department of Geography, Research Paper No. 165).

_____ (1967). Introduction to Flood Proofing (Chicago, Ill.: University of Chicago, Center for Urban Studies).

Sheaffer, John R. and Roland (1979). Evaluation of the Economic, Social and Environmental Effects of Floodplain Regulations (Washington, D.C.: Federal Emergency Management Agency).

Task Force on Flood Control Policy (1966). A Unified National Program for Managing Flood Losses, House Document 465, 89th Congress, 2d Session (Washington, D.C.: U.S. Government Printing Office).

Tennessee Valley Authority (TVA)(1983). Floodplain Management: The TVA Experience (Knoxville, Tenn.: Tennessee Valley Authority, Division of Economic and Community Development).

_____ (1986). Pathways for Floods (Knoxville, Tenn.: Tennessee Valley Authority, Division of Economic and Community Development).

U.S. Congress (1985). House of Representatives Doc. No. 99-17, 99th Congress, 1st Session (February 4, 1985). Part 5, p. 85-- President's FY86 budget submission.

U.S. Department of Housing and Urban Development (1981). Evaluation of the Economic, Social and Environmental Effects of Floodplain Regulations (Washington, D.C.: Federal Emergency Management Agency, FIA-8, March).

U.S. Senate Committee on Banking and Currency (1966). _Insurance and Other Programs for Financial Assistance to Flood Victims_ (Washington, D.C.: U.S. Government Printing Office).

U.S. Water Resources Council (1976). _A Unified National Program for Floodplain Management_ (Washington, D.C.: U.S. Government Printing Office).

_____ (1977). _Estimated Flood Damages, 1875-2000_, Appendix B, Nationwide Report (Washington, D.C.: U.S. Government Printing Office).

_____ (1979). _A Unified National Program for Floodplain Management_ (Washington, D.C.: U.S. Government Printing Office).

White, Gilbert F. (1945). _Human Adjustment to Flood_ (Chicago, Ill.: University of Chicago, Department of Geography).

_____ (1975). _Flood Hazard in the United States: A Research Assessment_ (Boulder, Colo.: University of Colorado, Institute of Behavioral Science, Monograph #6).

_____ (1979). _Nonstructural Floodplain Management Study: Overview_ (Washington, D.C.: Water Resources Council, Consultant Report).

White, Gilbert F., et al. (1958). _Changes in the Urban Occupance of Flood Plains in the United States_ (Chicago, Ill: University of Chicago, Department of Geography, Research Paper No. 87).

Woolley, Douglas (1986). "An Economic and Historical Perspective of Flood Damage: The Viability of Structural Solutions," in _Strengthening Local Flood Protection Programs_, proceedings of the tenth annual conference of the Association of State Floodplain Managers, Pittsburgh, Pa., June 17-19, 1986 (Boulder, Colo.: Natural Hazard Research and Applications Information Center, Institute of Behavioral Science, Special Publication #15).

7

Tornadoes

Loran B. Smith and David T. Jervis

A tornado is the most violent storm nature produces. As a natural phenomenon, it is unpredictable as to when, where, and how long it will last. There is nothing an individual can do that will guarantee protection for life or property under the onslaught of a tornado. While an individual hurricane may cause more death and destruction than a single tornado, a hurricane is a slow-moving storm that can be easily tracked, and advance warning can be given about where it will strike. Neither of these conditions applies to tornadoes, as they often strike quickly with little advance warning. These surprise attacks are one reason why tornadoes have caused more deaths during the past forty years than any other natural catastrophe. Even today, with all the technical and scientific breakthroughs, tornadoes claim the lives of about one hundred people each year. The violence, the unpredictability, and the potential for death and vast destruction of property have made tornado-caused disasters a major challenge to emergency management systems (Flora, 1954: 3; Fuller, 1987: 50-52; Reichelderfer, 1957: 29).

This chapter will focus on the nature of tornadoes, their vast potential for causing death and destruction, and the steps taken by the government to meet the challenges they present. The chapter will also address each of the four phases of emergency management discussed in detail elsewhere in this book: mitigation, preparedness, response, and recovery. Finally, several emergency management issues will be discussed. Although at least two of these issues are concerned with overall federal disaster policy rather than "tornado policy" per se, they are discussed here because tornadoes are the most frequently occurring of all natural hazards (with the exception of floods) and because they constitute a significant portion of all major disaster declarations issued by the president.

CHARACTERISTICS OF TORNADOES

A tornado is a violently rotating column of air in contact with the ground. It is formed as a result of the clash of two massive air masses in the presence of a strong jet stream. Tornadoes in the United States are usually formed when cool, dry air from the west or northwest moves over warm, moist surface air from the Gulf of Mexico. When the warm air mass is able to pick up additional heat and humidity generated by the solar heating of the ground, huge cumulonimbus clouds (thunderstorms) are formed. If conditions are right, the warm air is prevented from escaping because of the massive blanket of heavy cold air that covers it. As the warm air rises, it begins to cause the cooler air it meets to spin around the upward draft. This spinning begins to form a column which has to extend downward because the blanket of cold air will not let it go upward. This is the beginning of the funnel cloud that is a tornado (Reichelderfer, 1957: 31; Laffoon, 1975: 22-23; Eagleman et al., 1975: 1).

Unlike a hurricane, a tornado cannot be tracked with any degree of precision. Meteorologists at the National Severe Storms Forecast Center (NSSFC) in Kansas City, Missouri, can forecast the possibility of severe thunderstorms and/or tornadoes up to six hours in advance. But the typical severe thunderstorm watch issued by NSSFC includes an area containing 20,000 to 25,000 square miles (Reichelderfer, 1957: 32; Fuller, 1987: 33). Within that area, it is impossible to state with any certainty where, when, or even whether a tornado will actually hit. A tornado can usually be identified by radar by its distinctive "hook echo" signature, but even then there is no certainty that a tornado is actually on the ground. For confirmation, an actual sighting of a tornado by a trained observer, or spotter, is needed. In those few locations where high-resolution Doppler radar is operative, it is possible that advance warning of up to thirty minutes might be given. Because this radar can measure how fast precipitation is moving toward an area and the velocity of the wind in which the raindrops are embedded, it can alert meteorologists to the presence of a tornado still in the cumulonimbus cloud. If there is no precipitation inside the rotating cell, however, the Doppler radar provides only a weak signal which might be missed. Thus, while the forecast and detection of tornadoes has improved considerably in the past forty years, there is still much to be learned (Fuller, 1987: 140, 189-90).

The United States has experienced more tornadoes than any other country. Within the United States, no state is completely immune from the threat of tornadoes. During the past sixty years, tornadoes have struck in all fifty states and the District of Columbia. Even so, the area of greatest threat is the Great Plains region east of the Rocky Mountains and the Midwestern states of Wisconsin, Michigan, Illinois, Indiana, and Ohio. In of fact, the Great Plains area from Texas to Canada is dubbed "Tornado Alley" for the frequency of the tornadoes that strike that area. Figure 7.1 shows the mean annual number of tornadoes by state and clearly reveals a north/northeastward trend from Texas to the Great Lakes states. One should be careful to note that the reported incidence of tornadoes is overrated or exaggerated, as the case may be, by the size of the state. Thus, Texas, which is usually ranked first or second in the number of annual tornadoes, has a relatively low incidence rate compared to Massachusetts, but this is a function of its geographical size, not the number of tornadoes (Eagleman et al., 1975: 18; Reichelderfer, 1957: 31; Fuller, 1987: 21)

Tornadoes have been known to strike at all hours of the day and all months of the year. The weather conditions necessary for the formation of tornadoes, however, generally prevail only during certain months of the year and times of day. In addition to the cool, dry air and the warm, moist air, the existence of a strong jet stream appears to be critical to the formation of tornadoes. During the winter months, the jet stream usually flows across the southern portion of the United States. During the spring, it migrates northward through the central Great Plains to Ohio, Pennsylvania, and southern New England. In the summer, the jet stream flows across the U.S.-Canadian border and northern New England before it starts migrating southward again in the fall. This migration of the jet stream helps to explain why the months of peak tornado activity will vary from state to state (see figure 7.2). In southern Texas and the states of the deep South, the tornado season is usually in early spring or late fall. As one travels northward, the tornado season comes later: June in South Dakota, Minnesota, and Wisconsin; and July in North Dakota and northern New England (U.S. Department of Commerce, 1984: C7; Eagleman et al., 1975: 17).

Figure 7.1

Mean Number of Tornadoes per 10,000 Square Miles per Year

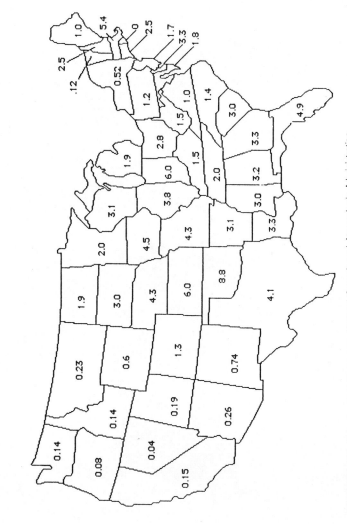

SOURCE: U.S. Department of Commerce, National Oceanic and Atmospheric Administration, Tornado Safety: Sruviving Nature's Most Violent Storms, p. C6.

Figure 7.2

Months of Peak Tornado Activity

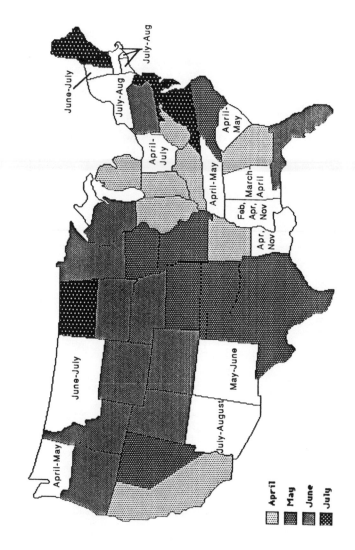

Source: U.S. Department of Commerce, National Oceanic and Atmospheric Administration, Tornado Safety: Surviving Nature's Most Violent Storms, p. CZ.

Tornadoes have been known to form at all hours of the day and night. Since the solar heating of the ground appears to be an important ingredient in the formation of tornadoes, however, one should expect most tornadoes to strike in the late afternoon and early evening. Statistics indicate that 82 percent of all tornadoes occur between noon and midnight and about 43 percent occur between 3:00 p.m. and 7:00 p.m. (Reichelderfer, 1957: 31; Flora, 1954: 58-59; U.S. Department of Commerce, 1984: C9). Divided into six-hour time spans, the most dangerous period for a tornado is between 3:00 p.m. and 9:00 p.m., when approximately 57 percent of all tornadoes strike. The least dangerous six hour time span is between 3:00 a.m. and 9:00 a.m., when only 8 percent of tornadoes occur. The remaining 35 percent of tornadoes is divided almost evenly between the two remaining six-hour time spans. Because of their warm, humid climate, Southern states are more likely to experience morning tornadoes than states of the Great Plains or Midwest (Flora, 1954: 58-59).

Tornadoes are probably the most devastating of naturalhazards. While an individual hurricane may cause more deaths or property damage than an individual tornado, the overall total number of deaths and amount of property damage caused by tornadoes exceeds that caused by hurricanes. Because of the disparity between verified tornado sightings and unconfirmed reports of tornado touchdowns, determining the exact number of tornadoes during any given period is difficult. One source indicates that over 23,000 tornadoes struck the United States between 1930 and 1980, while the U.S. Weather Bureau reports approximately 7,100 confirmed tornado touchdowns between 1916 and 1980. The death toll for those tornadoes is reported at approximately 8,780 or about 1.2 per tornado. Thus, just the frequency of tornadoes makes their potential for death and destruction more serious than that of any other natural hazard (Insurance Information Institute, 1980: 2; Flora, 1954: 32-37; U.S. Department of Commerce, 1984: C7).

Tornadoes can generate wind speeds in excess of three hundred miles per hour. It is these violent winds that cause most property damage, and the flying debris picked up by these winds cause most deaths and injuries. While reinforced concrete structures are generally able to withstand the tremendous winds (although windows facing the tornado are likely to be blown inward), most other structures are subject to severe damage or total destruction if struck by a tornado. Thus, a key to assessing the property damage caused by tornadoes is where the tornado occurs. If the tornado strikes a city or a residential community, the amount of property damage will be much higher than if a tornado hits a rural area. As a result, the amount of property damage sustained by states hit by tornadoes is only roughly correlated with the average number of tornadoes to hit that state. For example, in one compilation of tornado-caused property damage sustained by states from 1916 to 1953, Georgia, Massachusetts, Ohio, and Michigan ranked among the top eight states in property damage, yet none of these states ranked among the top ten in the number of tornadoes--as a matter of fact, Massachusetts ranked thirty-fifth in the latter category. Conversely, the essentially rural states of Kansas, Arkansas, Alabama, and Louisiana all rank in the top ten in the number of tornadoes, but none are ranked higher than eleventh in the amount of property damage sustained (U.S. Department of Commerce, 1984: C10; Flora, 1954: 35, 58-59).

Geographical location also helps to explain the death toll from tornadoes. Since much of Tornado Alley is sparsely populated, the large number of tornadoes that strike that area, especially the in southern portion, generally cause few deaths. But when tornadoes move over densely populated areas such as the Great Lakes states, the death toll rises dramatically.

This fact is particularly relevant when one realizes that very severe thunderstorms can generate more than one tornado. Thus, it is possible for a "family" of tornadoes to march across the countryside on a front as wide as three hundred miles. If that front passes over densely populated areas, the death toll can be in the hundreds. It was such a storm that generated the largest known outbreak of tornadoes on April 3-4, 1974. On that day, 148 separate tornadoes struck an area from southeastern Mississippi to western Ohio (including Xenia, Ohio) leaving a death toll of 315 and property damage in excess of $600 billion. Another storm on March 18, 1925, generated only seven tornadoes in the Tri-State area of Illinois-Missouri-Kentucky but killed 740 people--the greatest tornado death toll recorded in the United States (U.S. Department of Commerce, 1984: C9-C10).

GOVERNMENT POLICY

In dealing with natural hazards such as tornadoes, the federal government's emergency management policies are fragmented. In the disaster phases of mitigation and preparedness, emergency management is often shared between the Federal Emergency Management Agency (FEMA) and the Department of Commerce's National Oceanic and Atmospheric Administration (NOAA) and, more specifically, the National Weather Service within NOAA.

There is little that the government can do to reduce the tornado risk to people and property. There is no such thing as a windproof building (Wright and Rossi, 1981: 151). While it is true that some construction techniques and building materials resist tornadoes better than others, the cost of such buildings would be prohibitive, especially when balanced against the small probability that a tornado will occur in any specific area.

Given the number of tornado-related deaths that occur within them, one structural mitigation policy would be to abolish the use of mobile homes in areas of high tornado risk. In recent years, 40 percent of all tornado-related deaths occurred in mobile homes. Even more significant, the risk to mobile home dwellers appears to be six to eight times higher than for a conventional home dweller. Despite these facts, the 5 to 6 percent of the population which lives in mobile homes and the manufactured housing industry would aggressively fight any attempt to limit the sale or location of mobile homes (National Weather Service, 1987b: 2).

As a result, much of the federal government's tornado mitigation policy is based on a program of public education. In conjunction with the National Oceanic and Atmospheric Administration's National Weather Service, FEMA publishes a large number of materials warning of tornado dangers and warning citizens about how to reduce their risk. The National Weather Service encourages its field offices to enlist state and local officials in promoting Tornado Awareness Weeks or Severe Weather Awareness Weeks in their areas. These are often accompanied by drills which enable emergency management personnel to assess their degree of preparedness and responsiveness to the potential hazard. In 1986, emergency management drills or severe weather/flood awareness campaigns were conducted in every state (National Weather Service, 1987a: 3-6; National Weather Service, 1987c: 8-10).

In addition, the National Weather Service has an active speakers bureau, maintains regular contacts with the local media, and works closely with local government officials (National Weather Service, 1987c: 10). The emphasis in all of these programs, of course, is to impress upon people the nature and potential severity of natural hazards and to teach them basic self-defense measures.

Professionals in the field of emergency management focus on preparedness as a means of minimizing the damage from any disaster. Given the unpredictability of tornadoes, the major thrust of FEMA's tornado preparedness policies is to provide citizens with an adequate warning that a tornado will occur. The task of providing adequate warning is shared with the National Weather Service and state and local governments. The first portion of this warning system originates with the National Severe Storms Forecast Center in Kansas City, Missouri, which alerts National Weather Service field offices to the possibility of severe weather in their regions. If a tornado watch is posted for an area, meteorologists using radar look for the tell-tale hook echo on their radar screens, while trained ground spotters look for signs of a tornado. Generally, the presence of a tornado can only be confirmed by a visual sighting by one of these ground spotters. When a tornado is sighted, emergency management personnel and the broadcast media stations in the area are notified immediately in order to alert the general public through broadcasts and, in those cities that have them, the sounding of civil defense or fire sirens. The civil defense Emergency Broadcast System is also activated whenever a tornado or other emergency is imminent. In 1983, the Emergency Broadcast System was activated 1,186 times for civil emergency situations, many of these related to tornadoes or severe thunderstorms (Fuller, 1987: 33; Eagleman, et al., 1975: 19-20; FEMA, 1984: 5).

FEMA's preparedness activities also include considerable emphasis on planning and training. At its National Emergency Training Center in Emmitsburg, Maryland, FEMA conducts seminars and training sessions to prepare state and local emergency managers to deal with a wide range of emergencies. Through the use of computers to simulate particular hazardous situations, trainees can evaluate the response capabilities of their own communities. In recent years, FEMA has expanded its training programs to include video teleconferencing via satellite. This permits a large number of local officials to participate in training activities at a relatively low cost. In 1984, these training sessions reached an average audience of 4,200 per event in more than two hundred cities (FEMA, 1985: 3, 6; Giuffrida, 1984: 32-33).

In trying to prepare for a major disaster, two primary problems are the loss of communications and inadequate medical assistance. FEMA has planned to deal with these problems in several ways. First, it has a Mobile and Transportable Telecommunications

System (MATTS) van which can be sent to the site of a major disaster to establish communications. Second, under the National Emergency Management System, emergency managers can use FEMA's computer data base to identify all hospitals, port facilities, power facilities, population concentrations, and other critical emergency data that can facilitate planning before and response after a disaster. Third, a National Disaster Medical System would, in a catastrophic situation, augment regional, state, and local medical resources when the number of patients overwhelms the medical care capabilities of the local health care system. While the scope of a typical tornado-caused disaster is unlikely to require the implementation of these plans, their existence indicates the degree to which FEMA is prepared for disasters (FEMA, 1984: 10; FEMA, 1985: 5-6).

The weak link of tornado preparedness is the warning system. Evidence suggests that even a few minutes of warning can save lives. Yet, despite the existence of federal grants to state and local governments for this purpose, many communities do not have a siren warning system at all and many others have a system that is inadequate. In the Tornado Alley of the Great Plains, just about every city has a network of warning sirens. In other areas of the country, however, the warning system is incomplete or nonexistent. For example, in 1980, the civil defense director of Kalamazoo, Michigan, estimated that only 17 percent of the entire city's residents were within hearing range of the sirens. Despite that fact, and despite the fact that Kalamazoo had earlier that year suffered a tornado that killed five people, the city council refused to appropriate money for additional sirens (Hodler, 1982: 48).

To be sure, sirens are good only so long as the electricity continues to flow. Once the power is cut, sirens are worthless (Fuller, 1987: 88). Still, they can provide some warning which can enable alert citizens to take cover. The real problem is that watches, warnings, and even sirens are ignored by some segment of the population, especially in those areas with little experience with tornadoes. Only one percent of the public learned of the May 1985 tornadoes in western Pennsylvania through early warning systems; 27 percent of the population first learned of the tornadoes when they saw them (Comfort and Cahill, 1988: 193). It is for this reason that the deadliest tornadoes, causing the most concentrated fatalities, hit the heavily populated East and southeast where they are least expected, where warning systems are least deployed, and where warnings are more often ignored. Even in Tornado Alley, there are always some people who deny that they could be under risk. In the Kalamazoo tornado of 1980, 18 percent of the people who heard the warning sirens ignored them (Fuller, 1987: 13, 52; Hodler, 1982: 48).

Because many mitigation measures are often controversial and unpopular (e.g., flood insurance), and because the public and local officials are often apathetic about preparedness issues, most of the publicity surrounding the federal government's efforts in emergency management centers around the response and recovery phases. In one sense, the emphasis is somewhat surprising because the federal government's role in these areas is less than forty years old. Historically, state and local governments were expected to utilize their own resources to deal with emergencies. In a severe catastrophe, Congress might appropriate funds and allocate resources to aid the victims and communities in that particular case, but there was no general federal disaster aid policy other than the federal chartering of the American National Red Cross. It was anticipated that the Red Cross would provide disaster victims with food, clothes, medical care, shelter, and eventually, rehabilitation, while state and local governments would perform all the other tasks associated with response and recovery (Wright and Rossi, 1981: 49; Peterson, 1957: 52).

Experience with several major catastrophes indicated that the traditional assistance policies were insufficient. For one thing, the work of the Red Cross was often hampered by the disruption of public facilities: bridges were washed out, roads were clogged with debris, power lines were down, and many public buildings were either destroyed or severely damaged. Many communities did not have the equipment necessary to clean up the debris from a disaster. For this reason, the first general federal policy of disaster assistance, the Surplus Property Disaster Act of 1947, authorized state and local governments in disaster areas to draw upon the federal government's war surplus equipment to assist in disaster clean-up operations (Peterson, 1957: 53).

When the war surplus property was depleted, Congress expanded its disaster assistance program in the Disaster Act of 1950. The intent of the law was that the Red Cross was to continue in its traditional role of relieving human suffering, while the federal government was to assist state and local governments in clearing debris and repairing local government facilities. In the aftermath of Hurricane Betsy (1965), Congress passed emergency legislation that permitted "forgiveness" of $1,800 on loans a family

obtained from the Small Business Administration (SBA).
By this action, Congress recognized that it was not
only state and local governments that needed
assistance to recover from disaster; families and
small businesses also needed short-term help if
recovery was to be achieved. In subsequent years, as
other disasters occurred, Congress renewed this
legislation and the forgiveness sum began to rise
(Peterson, 1957: 53; Laffoon, 1975: 113).

In the aftermath of Hurricane Camille, Congress
passed the Disaster Relief Act of 1970. It set the
forgiveness amount at $2,500 and, for the first time,
pledged the federal government to pay totally for the
rebuilding of damaged public works in the disaster
area. After Hurricane Agnes in 1972, Congress
increased the forgiveness amount to $5,000 and dropped
the SBA interest rate to one percent. Underlying all
of these acts was the basic premise that state and
local governments and individuals must primarily rely
upon their own resources to achieve recovery. The
federal government would provide immediate and short-
term disaster assistance, but it would not be
responsible for long-term recovery. Even under these
conditions, federal disaster assistance was expensive.
In 1965, with Hurricane Betsy, federal inputs
compensated for about 12 percent of disaster losses;
in 1972, they had risen to 88 percent. Clearly, this
level of generosity could not continue (Laffoon, 1975:
114).

In April 1973, Congress retreated from its
commitment to private individuals. It dropped the
forgiveness feature entirely and raised interest rates
on SBA loans to 5 percent. One year later, in April
1974, the worst tornado outbreak in American history
created a path of death and devastation from
Mississippi to Michigan and from Illinois to West
Virginia. The 148 tornadoes left 315 dead and over
$600 billion in damages. These tornadoes hastened
congressional effort to revise federal disaster
assistance policies and in May 1974, the Disaster
Relief Act of 1974 was adopted (88 Stat. 143). This
law still serves as the basic guiding principle of
federal disaster relief efforts and, as such, deserves
closer scrutiny.

The 1974 law made it clear that, once again,
federal aid was to supplement, not supplant, the
relief efforts of the affected state and local
governments (Section 301[a]). Federal aid came in two
forms: (1) less extensive and more specialized
assistance to meet a smaller emergency (i.e.,
temporary housing, mass care, debris removal, etc.)
when the president declared that an "emergency"

existed; and (2) a presidential declaration of a major disaster which mobilizes the entire federal relief apparatus. The law requires that both the emergency and major disaster declarations must be requested by the governor(s) of the affected state(s) and that such requests must be accompanied by an accounting of state and local resources that will be used to alleviate the conditions and a certification of a reasonable expenditure of state and local funds for disaster relief. If a governor is requesting a major disaster declaration, the law requires that the state's emergency plan be activated prior to making such a request. A governor's request for assistance is usually made to the nearest FEMA regional director who passes it along to FEMA headquarters for review. In turn, FEMA forwards the request to the president along with its recommendations (FEMA, 1987: 3-4).

Once the president issues a major disaster declaration for an area, a FEMA official is designated as the federal coordinating officer (FCO). This officer makes an initial appraisal of the type of relief needed, coordinates the federal assistance efforts with state and local emergency management officials, and coordinates the relief efforts of the government with those of the American National Red Cross, the Salvation Army, and the Mennonite Disaster Service. To assist the FCO, Emergency Support Teams composed of emergency specialists from various federal agencies are sent to each disaster area. The underlying goal of all the federal activity is to clear debris, protect public health and safety, meet the immediate needs of the victims, and restore essential public services as quickly as possible, with a minimum of red tape (FEMA, 1987: 5; Laffoon, 1975: 116).

The Disaster Relief Act of 1974 permits the federal government to engage in emergency work to save lives and protect and preserve property, public health, and safety. In practice, this means that federal personnel are authorized to engage in search and rescue activities; provide for medical care, mass care (food, etc.) and shelter; remove debris; clear roads; construct temporary bridges; demolish unsafe structures and hazards, and so forth. The law also authorizes federal officials to perform these activities on both public and private property (see Section 306[a][4]).

For individuals whose homes or property have been struck by a tornado, the result is often chaos. Not only are homes and businesses often destroyed or severely damaged; important papers and documents are often destroyed or disappear as well. To alleviate some of this chaos, the FCO and the Emergency Support Team establish Disaster Application Centers, a sort of one-stop shopping center for individuals needing assistance. This assistance extends from unemployment insurance and job placement help to applications for Small Business Administration loans, tax information and assistance, and agricultural assistance. The Federal Emergency Management Agency is also required by law to contract with area mental health professionals to provide crisis counseling to disaster victims (FEMA, 1987: 7-8; Section 413).

Perhaps the most immediate problem facing relief forces arriving on the scene of a disaster is providing mass care for displaced individuals. In conjunction with private relief agencies, FEMA makes provision for the food, clothing, and shelter needs of the displaced. Individuals and families with no other resources may receive federal grants of up to $5,000 to meet disaster-related expenses. Moreover, FEMA is able to finance the cost of restoring a home to habitable condition if no major restoration or rehabiliation is needed. For those whose homes are habitable but who are unable to make rental or mortgage payments because of disaster-related unemployment, FEMA will make such payments for a period not to exceed one year. Finally, for those whose homes are destroyed, the federal government will underwrite 100 percent of the temporary housing costs for up to one year after the disaster (Section 404 et seq.; Section 408[b]).

The federal government will assist state and local governments in clearing debris; providing emergency protective measures for the preservation of life and property; repair or replace roads, bridges, streets, water control facilities, public buildings, public utilities, public facilities, recreational facilities and parks, and eligible private nonprofit education, utility, emergency medical, and custodial care facilities. By law, the federal contribution to state and local governments cannot exceed 100 percent of the net cost of repairing or restoring facilities as they existed immediately prior to the disaster. In addition, FEMA is authorized to grant loans to local governments in the disaster area which suffered a substantial loss of tax revenue. These loans may be issued for an amount up to 25 percent of the annual operating budget of the affected government. Finally, the Disaster Relief Act of 1974 permits federal officials to establish temporary public transportation service in the disaster area (FEMA, 1987: 9-10; Section 402 et seq.; Section 414[a]; Section 416).

Although the major federal role in managing disasters is to assist state and local governments in responding to the immediate needs of the victims, the Disaster Relief Act of 1974 also makes some provision for assisting state and local governments in providing for the long-term recovery of the disaster area. Under the provisions for economic recovery, an economic development plan for the disaster area will be prepared. This plan will aim at restoring the economic and employment base of the community. In formulating and implementing this plan, technical assistance will be provided by federal personnel. Once the plan is approved, federal grants and loan guarantees will be made available to both the public and the private sector to facilitate the process of economic recovery (Section 801 et seq.).

TORNADO-RELATED ISSUES

Given the unpredictability and physical characteristics of tornadoes, there are few mitigation issues related to tornado-caused emergencies. As previously noted, a limitation on the location of mobile homes might be a wise mitigatory measure, but it has never been given serious consideration. Thus, the major issues, or controversies, dealing with tornadoes involve preparedness, response, and recovery. Three of these issues appear to be most important, but only one of the three is specifically directed at tornadoes. These issues are: (1) the degree of preparedness, (2) the definition of disaster, and (3) the amount of federal aid that should go to individuals and state and local governments after a disaster.

It seems clear that most state and local governments are not as prepared to meet the threat of tornadoes as they could be. The fact that Doppler radar, an innovative device that can increase the warning time for those in the path of a tornado, has not been widely deployed can be traced to the deficit reduction policies of the federal government. But the lion's share of blame for inadequate preparedness must rest with the state and local governments. In both the 1969 and 1970 Disaster Relief Acts, 50 percent matching grants up to $250,000 were available to each state to assist them in developing plans and programs to combat major disasters. Only fourteen states took advantage of the 1969 law and used a total of only $217,000, while only eleven states used $712,000 under the 1970 law. California was the only state to use its entire $250,000 allotment. These disappointing results prompted Congress, in the 1974 law, to authorize one-time, outright, nonmatching grants of $250,000 per state to encourage more disaster planning and preparedness (U.S. Code, 1974).

Even with outright grants, emergency preparedness has not improved as much as it could. For one thing, unless a community is located in an area that has been repeatedly visited by tornadoes, floods, or other fast-moving natural emergencies, it is difficult to persuade citizens to invest in something that they may never need. Moreover, emergency preparedness has, in the minds of many, been linked with the controversial subject of civil defense and nuclear war.

When the Federal Emergency Management Agency was established in 1979, five separate agencies were combined under its umbrella. Civil defense, heretofore a separate agency, was one of the five. The only thread linking these agencies together was their involvement in one or more aspects of emergency management. This tenuous connection was made even more difficult because emergency management professionals resented the inclusion of civil defense.

Things went from bad to worse when Congress, in the 1981 amendments to the Federal Civil Defense Act, permitted civil defense funds to be used in preparing and responding to natural disasters with the proviso that such expenditures be consistent with, contribute to, or not detract from attack-related civil defense preparedness (FEMA, 1986: 1, 4). This "all-hazards" approach mandated by Congress was formalized by FEMA into the Integrated Emergency Management System which might be described as a generic approach to emergency management. Instead of emphasizing civilian defense from a nuclear attack, IEMS emphasized "population protection planning" that would integrate the functional elements common to any emergency regardless of whether it was a peacetime natural disaster or a nuclear war.

IEMS sparked criticism and dissent from both emergency management professionals and state and local governments. Emergency management personnel felt that their calling was receiving second billing in both funding and attention. They had no intention of becoming the supporting cast for the antics of the military. State and local governments found that in order to use federal money to plan and prepare for disasters, they would also have to consider the needs of civil defense such as evacuation plans, shelter surveys, and so forth. Many state and local governments vigorously resisted IEMS, believing it was a front for civil defense planning, which they believed to be futile. Between 1980 and 1984 about 120 government units refused to participate in drawing up evacuation plans for their areas. While the controversy has become more subdued in recent years, it still exists. One result, of course, is that the level of state and local preparedness to meet the threat of tornadoes did not significantly improve. Oregon and Washington refused to conduct preparedness exercises in March 1987 because they involved preparing for a nuclear attack (Oreskes, 1984: B1; Moore, 1987: 933-34; Witt, 1988: 20).

Another issue involves the question of what constitutes a disaster. In the three years that the Disaster Relief Act of 1970 was in effect, the president used its provisions to declare 111 major disasters--forty-six of them in 1973 alone. From 1982 to 1986 President Reagan issued 115 major disaster declarations (U.S. Code, 1974; Moore, 1987: 933). The large number of disaster declarations suggests that, in the past twenty years or so, there has been a veritable plague of disasters causing widespread death and destruction. Yet, data compiled from records of the American National Red Cross reveal that, between 1960 and 1970, the average disaster-impacted county experienced losses that amounted to less than one person killed and about twelve injuries with four dwellings destroyed and another twenty-two dwellings severely damaged. When tornado events are considered separately, the same average losses are revealed (Davis and Seitz, 1982: 552; Rossi, et al., 1981: 19-20).

This suggests that many disaster declarations include events that are not all that disastrous. To some extent, this has been caused by the tendency of Congress to establish federal disaster policy in response to statistically rare major natural catastrophes rather than to base policy on the average "normal" disaster. In 1960, 1965, 1969, 1970, and 1974, Congress revised and expanded federal disaster policy specifically in response to major natural catastrophes in the form of hurricanes or, in the case of the 1974 act, the blitz of tornadoes that swept through the Midwest. In so doing, Congress made it possible for any community affected by a flood, hurricane, or tornado to believe that it had been struck by a "major" disaster. Thus, the definition of what constitutes a disaster has been expanded (Rossi et al., 1981: 21; U.S. Code, 1974).

This trivialization of what constitutes a disaster has several important policy consequences. First, because a presidential declaration of a major disaster will bring about a major transfer of money, goods, and services that might otherwise have to be supplied by state and local governments, communities and state governments are encouraged to exaggerate their losses and underestimate their resources in order to get a disaster declaration and its accompanying federal largesse. Second, the large number of disaster declarations has placed tremendous pressure on the disaster relief funds available, prompting FEMA to reduce its contributions to repair the infrastructure of state and local governments. This, in turn, has angered many state and local governments which complain that they are not receiving their "fair share" of federal aid funds. Finally, the expanded definition of what constitutes a disaster undermines federal efforts to encourage state and local governments to adopt mitigation and preparedness plans, because it is assumed that federal relief aid can be used to rebuild or even improve communities struck by a tornado, hurricane, or flood (Davis and Seitz, 1982: 552; Voisin, 1987: 49).

Several provisions of the Disaster Relief Act of 1974 seem to anticipate the gamesmanship that would eventually develop around disaster assistance. For example, the law requires governors requesting a presidential declaration to pledge a reasonable amount of state and local resources to alleviate the conditions of the disaster. The act implies that FEMA may ask a governor to increase the amount of state and local commitment before it forwards the request to the president if the agency believes the original amount is inadequate. In addition, the 1974 law requires that any property replaced, repaired, or restored through federal funds must secure adequate insurance to protect against future loss. If insurance is not secured, or if the state acts as self-insurer of its own facilities, then no federal assistance will be available on those facilities in the event of another disaster. Finally, the law allows federal assistance up to 100 percent of the net costs of repairing, restoring, or replacing public facilities as they were immediately prior to the disaster. This provision allows FEMA to determine which costs are eligible and which are not. It also clearly attempts to limit the efforts of local governments to build new, bigger, and better public facilities at the expense of the federal government (Sections 301, 314, 402).

Needless to say, state and local governments are not happy with these provisions or with the way that FEMA has interpreted them. This irritation with FEMA's management of disaster assistance represents the third major issue involving emergency management. It is an issue that disaster victims as well as state and local governments have all cited in recent years, namely, the stinginess of FEMA in providing disaster aid.

For disaster victims, this issue is usually symbolized by the controversy over mobile homes. Because FEMA is charged with securing temporary housing for people displaced by disaster, the victims often come to believe that such housing should consist of government-owned mobile homes; in their minds, nothing else will do. For its part, FEMA resists this belief, preferring instead to house people in undamaged homes and apartments in the area. While the cost of transporting and maintaining mobile homes is a factor underlying FEMA's reluctance to use them, it is not the only factor. FEMA sees its role as a provider of emergency relief; it comes in, gets the job done, and gets out as fast as possible. In its experience, the agency has found that mobile homes are counterproductive to its goals. Once on the scene, they create a bureaucracy of their own. Moreover, for many of the victims who use them, a mobile home is the best housing they have ever known. Thus, there is little incentive for these people to find and pay for their own housing. This, of course, increases federal expenditures, but it also makes it much more difficult for the community to return to near-normal conditions which is itself a goal of emergency management. As a result, FEMA, although allowed to provide temporary housing for up to one year, tries to resolve housing problems long before that time and strongly resists placing mobile homes in a disaster area (Fuller, 1987: 153; Laffoon, 1975: 116; Quarantelli, 1982: 278-279).

For state and local governments, FEMA's stinginess is reflected in its unwillingness to pay the full cost of repairing, reconstructing, or replacing public facilities. According to the Disaster Relief Act of 1974, the federal government is authorized to pay up to 100 percent of these costs. Since 1980, however, FEMA has reduced the federal share of these costs to 75 percent of the "eligible" costs. Because FEMA decides what is an eligible cost, the actual reimbursement to state and local governments can be a significantly smaller percentage. For example, in one California county hit by floods in three separate years, the local government received 71 percent of its costs in the first year, 50 percent in the second year, and 38 percent in the third year (Moore, 1987: 933-34; Voisin, 1987: 3).

For its part, FEMA was faced with administering a program in which costs spiraled out of control. In the last year of full 100 percent reimbursement, disaster relief accounted for approximately 60 percent of FEMA's $631- million budget. Clearly, that situation could not continue. Since FEMA reduced the reimburseable percentage to 75 percent of eligible costs, disaster aid has accounted for approximately 30 percent of the agency's budget. Even so, the agency has been under considerable pressure from the Office of Management and Budget to reduce its outlays to state and local governments. As a result, FEMA has begun to tighten its standards as to what constitutes an eligible cost (FEMA, 1980: 61; FEMA, 1984: 29; FEMA, 1985: 34; Moore, 1987: 932).

One of the key elements of this controversy has been an apparent change of guiding principle for federal disaster assistance. As previously noted, that principle has always maintained that federal aid supplements, not supplants, state and local resources. In practice, this means that state and local governments must still expect to bear the lion's share of the burden of repairing, restoring, and replacing public facilities. Judging from the criticism of FEMA's disaster assistance policies by state and local governments, however, one would think that the federal government is primarily responsible for disaster relief and recovery. Even in the 1950s, when the effective law provided federal reimbursement only for emergency or temporary repairs, state and local governments complained bitterly when they discovered that they, not the federal government, had to pay all the costs for restoration and replacement. Now that the federal government has pledged to pay a larger share of the costs, state and local governments are still complaining that it is too little (Peterson, 1957: 62; Moore, 1987: 935).

The present disaster relief act creates much of this confusion, especially for those communities without much experience, because it makes reference to assisting the primary efforts of state and local governments while apparently guaranteeing 100 percent reimbursement for the cost of repairing, restoring, or replacing public facilities. In other words, some sections of the law imply that the federal government is the primary funder of response and recovery costs. If true, this would clearly be a major change in federal disaster policy. Unfortunately for state and local governments, it is not true. FEMA, by requiring richer states to pay a larger share of disaster assistance and recovery costs and by tightening reimbursement eligibility requirements, appears to be doing nothing more than affirming an almost thirty-year federal policy; that is, primary and major responsibility for disaster relief and recovery is borne by the state and local governments (Moore, 1987: 934-35; Voisin, 1987: 49).

This controversy is likely to continue into the future, at times abating while at other times, especially after disasters, becoming more strident. Already, at least one U.S. Congressman has introduced legislation which would require the federal government to reimburse 100 percent of the repair, reconstruction, and replacement costs of public facilities and would limit FEMA's role in determining eligibility formulas (Moore, 1987: 935). Such attempts will be observed closely by emergency management professionals, because they involve reopening discussions about what constitutes a disaster and to what extent the federal government and the state and local governments should be responsible for mitigation, preparedness, response, and recovery from disaster. Whether intended or not, if these attempts to modify the Disaster Relief Act of 1974 succeed, they would make the federal government primarily responsible for disaster response and recovery. What the state and local governments may not realize, however, is that these same modifications make it easier for the federal government to assume responsibility for mitigation and preparedness-- something that, in light of the civil defense controversy, they would vigorously oppose.

CONCLUSION

The first chapter of this text cited three major problems inhibiting the development of effective emergency management policy--salience, fragmented government responsibility, and technical expertise questions. Tornado policy is affected by each of these impediments. The salience of tornadoes is limited to Tornado Alley. Consequently, many local governments do not install warning systems. Doppler radar systems have not been widely utilized. Residents often ignore warnings when they hear them. Furthermore, disputes about the extent of federal assistance to tornado-impacted communities illustrate the problems of fragmented government responsibility common to emergency management. Additional intergovernment concerns include the use of emergency planning funds for civil defense activities rather than for more likely emergencies, and the state and local attitude that the federal government should pay for all aspects of emergency management, not simply relief and recovery. Finally, the limited ability to predict tornadoes is a manifestation of the impediment of unanswered technical questions upon effective emergency management. In these ways, government's response to tornadoes--the most common natural disaster--reflects many of the problems common to emergency management.

REFERENCES

Comfort, Louise K., and Anthony G. Cahill (1988). "Increasing Problem-solving Capacity between Organizations: The Role of Information in Managing the May 31, 1985, Tornado Disaster in Western Pennsylvania," pp. 180-198 in Managing Disaster: Strategies and Policy Perspectives, ed. Louise K. Comfort (Durham, N.C.: Duke University).

Davis, Morris, and Steven Seitz (1982). "Disasters and Governments," Journal of Conflict Resolution 26 (September).

Eagleman, Joe R., et al. (1975). Thunderstorms, Tornadoes, and Building Damage (Lexington, Mass.: Lexington).

Federal Emergency Management Agency (FEMA)(1980). A Report to the President on Comprehensive Emergency Management, 1979 (Washington, D.C.: U.S. Government Printing Office).

____ (1984). Annual Report, 1983 (Washington, D.C.: U.S. Government Printing Office).

____ (1985). Annual Report, 1984 (Washington, D.C.: U.S. Government Printing Office).

____ (1987a). Report to the Senate and House Committees on Armed Services on National Civil Defense Program (Washington, D.C.: Federal Emergency Management Agency).

____ (1987b). Disaster Assistance Programs: A Guide to Federal Aid in Disasters (Washington, D.C.: Federal Emergency Management Agency).

Flora, Snowden (1954). Tornadoes of the United States (Norman, Okla.: University of Oklahoma Press).

Fuller, John G. (1987). Tornado Watch #211 (New York: William Morrow).

Giuffrida, Louis O. (1984). "An All-Hazards Approach to Emergency Management," Police Chief 51 (May).

Hodler, Thomas W. (1982). "Residents, Preparedness and Response to the Kalamazoo Tornado," Disasters.

Insurance Information Institute (1980). Tornado Safety---Before-During-After (New York: Insurance Information Institute).

Laffoon, Polk, IV (1975). Tornado (New York: Harper and Row).

Moore, W. John (1987). "After the Deluge," National Journal 19 (April 18).

National Weather Service (1987a). Disaster Preparedness Report (April).

____ (1987b). Disaster Preparedness Report (July).

____ (1987c). Disaster Preparedness Report (December).

Oreskes, Michael (1984). "Civil Defense Futile, Cuomo Says," New York Times (May 15).

Peterson, Val (1957). "Co-ordinating and Extending Federal Assistance," Annals of the American Academy of Political and Social Science 309 (January).

Quarantelli, E. L. (1982). "General and Particular Observations on Sheltering and Housing in American Disasters," Disasters.

Reichelderfer, F. W. (1957). "Hurricanes, Tornadoes, and Other Storms," Annals of the American Academy of Political and Social Science 309 (January).

Rossi, Peter H., et al. (1981). "Are There Long-Term Effects of American Natural Disasters?" in Social Science and Natural Hazards, eds. James D. Wright and Peter H. Rossi (Cambridge, Mass.: Abt).

U.S. Code (1974). Congressional & Administrative News Vol. 2, 93rd Congress, 2d Session (St. Paul, Minn.: West).

U.S. Department of Commerce, National Oceanic and Atmospheric Administration (1984). Tornado Safety: Surviving Nature's Most Violent Storms (Washington, D.C.: U.S. Department of Commerce, NOAA).

Voisin, Elizabeth (1987). "Bill Would Avoid Cuts in Federal Disaster Aid," City & State 4 (July).

Witt, Elder (1988). "The Civil (Defense) War Between the States and the Federal Government," Governing (June).

Wright, James D., and Peter H. Rossi (1981). "The Politics of Natural Disaster: State and Local Elites," in Social Science and Natural Hazards, eds. James D. Wright and Peter H. Rossi (Cambridge, Mass.: Abt).

8

Wildfire Hazards

Diane Moskow-McKenzie
and John C. Freemuth

During the summer of 1988, the Yellowstone area was
ravaged by severe fires. The fires, which raged
through America's first national park, captured the
attention of the national and international media.
Reaction to the fires was intense, with both
condemnation and support of the U.S. government's fire
policy. The public thus was exposed to the subtleties
of wildland fire management.

This chapter examines wildland fire policy from
the perspective of emergency response and management.
It thus hopes to set the groundwork for the reader's
understanding of wildland fire management. It will not
attempt an intricate analysis of wildland fire policy,
but rather provide the tools to understand the outline
of current policy and policy debate. It therefore
serves as an introduction to this complex and
controversial area of public policy and emergency
management.

EARLY POLICY

According to Ted Williams, "for virtually all of the
20th century, scientists have been aware that forests
evolved with fire and that, therefore, fire has a
place in forests" (1989: 44). During the summer of
1910, 5 million acres of western forest land burned.
Because of the severity of these fires, the United
States Forest Service (USFS) began a campaign to rid
the forests of fire. In 1927 the American Forestry
Association organized a group called the Dixie
Crusaders who began spreading the word about the evils
of wildfire. In 1935, USFS instituted its "10 A.M.

Fire Control" policy which stated that every wildfire should be extinguished by 10:00 a.m. the next morning.

Walt Disney's 1942 animated motion picture "Bambi" was an important influence on both fire management policy and public attitudes toward wildfire. Smokey the Bear was also a very important character in spreading the word with the slogan "Remember, only you can prevent forest fires." Williams concludes: "As the general public went off in one direction, science proceeded in another. To those who knew how to look (scientists), it became patently obvious that fire not only had a place in the natural landscape but that many plant communities absolutely required it" (1989: 51).

According to Stephen J. Pyne, a noted fire historian,

> The problem of fire oppressed and preoccupied the Forest Service from its beginnings. In 1898, when the Service was still a bureau with only advisory powers, there was a fear that the question of forest fires would be shelved. After 1910 there was little danger that the problem would be shelved. Chief Forester Henry Graves declared in 1913 that "the necessity of preventing losses from forest fires requires no discussion. It is the fundamental obligation of the Forest Service and takes precedence over all other duties and activities" (Pyne, 1982).

The history of fire policy and that of the Forest Service thus go hand in hand.

A wildland fire control program was started in New York in the Adirondacks Reserve in 1885. Wildfire suppressions began in Yellowstone National Park in 1886. The park superintendent protected the forests from both fire and axe during that time.

From 1886 to 1916, the U.S. Army administered the national parks. The development of the fire suppression policy may be attributed, at least in part, to the fact that the army was also responsible for the invention of the public campground.

In 1916, the National Park Service (NPS) was created as part of the U.S. Department of the Interior. Fire control responsibility in the parks was transferred to NPS from the U.S. Army. The Park Service relied heavily on the Forest Service for fire protection. During this initial period, the Park Service lacked the professional cadre and sense of shared values already well developed in the U.S. Department of Agriculture's Forest Service.

NPS fire fighting did not come until the 1930s when the Park Service began its own fire program. New policy books were released by the Park Service in 1968. Following its experience with extensive fires in the Everglades in the 1950s, the Park Service began to change its fire suppression and prescribed burning policies. By 1968, the Park Service accepted a more natural role for fire in park ecosystems. The changes were given further impetus by the lightning-caused fires in the Sequoia-Kings Canyon National Parks and several other major fires that occurred in parks between 1968 and 1972. Recognizing the natural ecological role of fire, lightning fires were permitted to burn in certain zones within the areas managed by NPS. Currently, approximately 58 million acres of national park lands are classified as natural fire zones (Federal Register, 1988).

In the 1970s experimentation with fire programs by other researchers and administrators began. As wildland fire protection programs became larger and more sophisticated, federal and state agencies found it necessary to coordinate their programs, procedures, and standards. The National Wildfire Coordinating Group (NWCG) was chartered in 1976 for this purpose. The National Interagency Fire Qualification System (NIFQS) was developed under the sponsorship of NWCG for the purpose of assuring a nationwide source of professional wildland fire fighting personnel. On the national level, the National Park Service joined the NWCG and the Boise Interagency Fire Center which consolidated logistical support for on-going wildfires. This period also welcomed the beginning of a strong Bureau of Land Management fire organization which supported the collective action of the Interior agencies (Pyne, 1982).

In 1972 the U. S. Department of Agriculture's Forest Service began allowing lightning-caused fires to play a more natural role in the wilderness. The Forest and Rangeland Resources Planning Act of 1974 and the National Forest Management Act of 1976 required that both the use of prescribed fire and the control of wildfire play an important role in Forest Service land management. By 1976, policy prescriptions allowed lightning-caused fires to burn under carefully prescribed conditions and were put into effect in parts of the western wilderness area. In 1978 Forest Service fire policy was revised with authority to approve wilderness fire management plans being given to Regional Foresters, as part of a revised policy that called for "fire management programs." This revision, which is part of the current policy, called for well-planned and -executed fire protection and fire-use programs. The objective of suppressing wildfire changed to minimizing costs and damage consistent with land and resource management goals.

Forest Service wilderness fire management policy was revised in 1985, clarifying the objectives of wilderness fire management. The use of prescribed fires was authorized when necessary and lightning fires were to be allowed to play their natural role. The risk of wildfire to life, property, and resources both within and outside wilderness areas was reduced.

FEDERAL FIRE POLICIES TODAY

Traditionally, the fire policies of federal land management agencies were to control all wildland fires as promptly as possible. When initial attack failed in controlling a fire the first day, personnel and equipment were organized to control the fire by 10:00 a.m. the next day.

Generally speaking, today's fire management programs and activities are executed in support of land and resource management plans and objectives. That is, burning may be permitted to achieve broader objectives, such as reducing the accumulation of fuels that may cause a larger or less controllable fire. Two kinds of wildland fires are acknowledged: prescribed fires and wildfires. Prescribed fire is the application of fire to wildland fuels in a predetermined area to produce fire behavior characteristics required to accomplish specified management objectives. Fire is used scientifically to realize maximum net benefits at minimum impact and with acceptable costs. A prescribed natural fire is a lightning-caused fire that is allowed to burn in a prescribed area. "Prescription" is a written statement for a designated geographic area defining weather and fuel limits and conditions necessary to attain fire and resource management objectives. Elements at a minimum consist of temperature, humidity, wind direction and speed, and fuel moisture under which the fire will be allowed to burn. These conditions and limits are generally expressed in an acceptable range of fire-related indices. Prescribed fires may thus be ignited, or allowed to burn, under specified conditions to achieve established management objectives.

Wildfire is a free-burning fire requiring suppression response, in other words, all fire other than prescribed fire that occurs on wildlands. Suppression strategies considered in determining the appropriate action range from prompt control, minimizing acreage burned, to more indirect suppression action to contain or confine wildfires when these alternatives are less costly than control in terms of suppression costs, damage from fire, and other adverse impacts. Unsuppressed wildfires may result in loss of life, serious damage to natural resources, and damage to or destruction of man-made developments. However, the use of prescribed fire under carefully controlled conditions can lessen that threat and, thus, be a useful tool in wildland resource management.

According to the Federal Register (1988), these policies as applied to parks and wilderness areas allow for the prescribed use of fire, either by natural causes or man-made, in support of land management objectives. The suppression of all wildfires is required, using economically efficient and environmentally compatible methods. All prescribed fires require preplanning and decision criteria addressing expected fire behavior and effects.

Overall management objectives for the woodland area, the historical occurrence of fire and its natural role, the degree of suppression being proposed, the specific fire's expected behavior, acceptable suppression techniques, the existence of buffer zones, smoke management concerns, and anticipated effects on landowners must all be taken into consideration when determining agency land or resource management objectives.

Prescribed fires are conducted by qualified personnel under prescribed fire plans or written prescriptions. The fires must be monitored to ensure that they remain within prescription. Once a prescribed fire exceeds the limits of an approved fire plan, it will be reclassified as a wildfire and suppressed. Such fires are not returned to prescribed fire status, according to policy.

WILDLAND FIRE MANAGEMENT: BOISE INTERAGENCY FIRE CENTER

The Boise Interagency Fire Center (BIFC) was established in 1965. The center coordinates fire support activities among federal and state fire fighting agencies. BIFC is staffed by fire management personnel from the Bureau of Land Management, the Bureau of Indian Affairs, the National Park Service, and the Fish and Wildlife Service (all federal land resource agencies under the U.S. Department of the Interior) and the Forest Service (under the U.S. Department of Agriculture). The National Weather

Service (under the U.S. Department of Commerce, National Oceanic and Atmospheric Administration) is another agency making up the Interagency Fire Center. All BIFC agencies, except the National Weather Service, have Washington-level fire management staff.

Since each agency has its own mission and funding, the coordination of fire management activities, blending of expertise, and sorting out of budgetary matters are the central concerns of BIFC. According to BIFC's public affairs officer, Arnold Hartigan, "when the presuppression budget of BIFC has been depleted, the center then borrows from other accounts. Congress is then asked to approve supplemental funding." All agencies cooperate in programs to improve the efficiency and economics of support to wildfire suppression efforts nationwide. The Boise Interagency Fire Center also assists during floods, earthquakes, and other natural disasters, as well as fighting wildfire, when local, state, and regional resources have been exhausted.

Bob Webber, supervisory range technician of the Bureau of Land Management, notes that "the Boise Interagency Fire Center is a pioneer in the development of fire suppression equipment and fire training. Fire training courses are used nationally and internationally. BIFC's fire suppression equipment and fire training are considered to be state-of-the-art, but are continually being evaluated and improved upon."

The Bureau of Land Management

The Bureau of Land Management (BLM) is the host agency of the fire center. BLM owns and operates the center site with other agencies involved paying their appropriate operating expenses and sharing in the responsibility of overseeing the center's interagency programs. BLM has four divisions: management services, fire management, information systems, and training.

The Division of Management Services operates the BIFC fire warehouse and all buildings and grounds at the center. Within the division, the Supply Branch is responsible for the warehouse and aircraft ramp activity. It is responsible for the procurement, warehousing, maintenance, and speedy movement of fireline and personnel support items to fire sites and fire agencies whenever and wherever needed. The branch must be prepared to support about eight thousand fire fighters at any given time. The Base Services Branch does payroll for emergency fire fighters, provides ground transportation at BIFC, and furnishes administrative support at fire camps, as well as maintaining the buildings and grounds of the sites.

The Division of Fire Management supports BLM field units in fire program planning and implementation. The Field Operations Branch provides fire suppression specialists to all agencies and oversees equipment standardization within BLM. The Logistic Support Branch is a combined Forest Service/Interior logistic support office which receives and processes fire orders from across the United States and Canada. It is also responsible for the gathering of fire intelligence, analysis, and dissemination. The logistic support office has aircraft, manpower, and equipment coordinators who assist in getting equipment and fire fighters from where they are to where they are needed.

The Information Systems Division provides fire communications networks and a great deal more. The division maintains and operates the Interior Department's National Radio Support Cache which has been combined with the Forest Service National Fire Radio Cache, according to Arnold Hartigan of BIFC. Communications officers and technicians are available to design, install, and operate complete communications systems for fires and other emergencies. The division also installs and maintains automatic lightning detection (ALDS) units as part of the western U.S. fire detection system. ALDS units can detect an air-to-ground lightning strike from up to 225 miles away and pinpoint it within a mile at that distance. These units are used in conjunction with Remote Automatic Weather Stations (RAWS), solar-powered devices that gather weather information and feed it to a satellite passing overhead. A satellite dish at the fire center acquires this data from all RAWS devices, as relayed by the satellite, and disseminates it through the Administrative Forest Fire Information Retrieval and Management System (AFFIRMS) computer program to resource management agencies by land line. AFFIRMS has computer programs in the system that provide a national fire danger safety rating system. The subsystems of AFFIRMS provide weather data with outputs giving the probability of fire starts and the rate of spread. ALDS and RAWS information is combined with observed data from several other sources, utilizing computer-based data manipulation and display techniques, into the initial Attack Management System. This system provides fire suppression managers with a totally integrated information package that allows faster response time when making initial attack decision.

The Training Division develops and carries out fire courses for BLM and cooperating agencies. Courses include basic through advanced training in fire suppression, prevention, prescribed fire, and related subjects. Courses and materials support performance and qualification requirements for over seventy fire positions ranging from basic fire fighter to incident commander. Training is developed centrally by participating agencies and taught at the lowest practical organizational level. Assistance and materials are also provided to state and local agencies, universities, and foreign governments.

The division's Technical Development Branch develops courses and materials, conducts national courses, and assists field offices with regional and local training programs. The Training Support Branch provides audiovisual production, facilities, and related services. The training standards office provides instructional systems technology and assists in program evaluation. A member of the division is also assigned as assistant director of the National Advanced Resource Technology Center at Marana, Arizona. In an average year, the division develops eight new training products and twelve audiovisual productions. It conducts or directly supports over sixty courses throughout the United States and trains approximately two thousand personnel.

The U.S. Forest Service

The Forest Service jointly operates the Logistic Support Office with BLM to support incidents, whether wildfires or other emergencies. In addition, the needs and capabilities of the fifty state forestry organizations are also integrated. Staff personnel also oversee the FIREBASE and AFFIRMS computer systems for fire data.

The National Aviation Contracting Offices at BIFC contract for air tankers, medium helicopters, and transport aircraft. That staff also contracts catering and shower services for fire camp use.

The National Aviation Operations Officer and staff provide aviation expertise for the Forest Service. They conduct inspections of air tankers, transport aircraft, and helicopters. They set inspection standards and inspector qualifications and conduct national instrument refresher training for all Forest Service pilots. In cooperation with the Interior Department's Office of Aircraft Service, they conduct helicopter pilot training. They also maintain two aircraft for use in national infrared mapping services.

The Infrared Operations and Maintenance staff at BIFC uses infrared remote sensing equipment and techniques on wildfires in the United States. They also assist Canada when requested to do so.

The Forest Service National Fire Radio Cache (NFRC) is located at BIFC. The NFRC staff is responsible for maintenance, packaging, and shipping of all Forest Service communications systems and service nets used on large fires throughout the United States. NFRC also maintains three systems for use on insect and disease control programs.

The U.S. Fish and Wildlife Service

The Fish and Wildlife Service (FWS) maintains its headquarters office fire management staff at BIFC. The staff provides interagency coordination with the other agencies located at BIFC and provides technical guidance, program review, coordination, and leadership for the fire management program within the National Wildlife Refuge Systems. The FWS staff stationed at BIFC coordinates, on a national level, an interagency cooperative concept that had previously been handled by the individual field stations. Such coordination includes: training course identification, development, and presentations; fire equipment specifications, purchase, and inventory; and fire suppression team support and fire reporting services to the seven regions of FWS.

The National Park Service

The National Park Service, Washington Office, Branch of Fire Management is located at BIFC, except for its head. It exercises both a policy formulation role as well as a direct technical support role for all the regions and the parks on the full range of wildland fire activities, from prevention to and including prescribed fire. Two Interagency Hot-Shot Crews are also managed by this office with duty stations in parks. The location at both BIFC and the other land management agencies facilitates coordination and promotes efficiency in operations. In the forests where roads are scarce, hand crews are needed rather than engine companies. The hot-shot units fulfill this need.

The National Weather Service

The National Weather Service (NWS) Forecast Office in Idaho is part of the fire center. It is responsible for ten programs: public weather, aviation weather, fire weather, agriculture forecasts, hydrologic forecasts, surface and upper air observations, weather wire, weather radio, and pilot weather briefings.

The fire weather forecast staff gives daily in-depth briefings to BIFC, interagency training course development, and meteorological expertise on both national and international levels.

Regionally, the staff provides daily fire weather forecasts for an area that extends from southeastern Oregon across central and southern Idaho and into western Wyoming. Site-specific forecasts are prepared for wildfires, prescribed burns, tree planting, and herbicide spraying. Two mobile weather units and a modularized unit are available for dispatch with an accompanying meteorologist for on-site weather forecasts and warnings. The staff also coordinates the dispatch of additional NWS mobile units throughout the Western states. ALDS data is collected at the Office and computer processed for distribution to NWS offices throughout the western and central United States (BIFC).

Wildland Fire Management:
The National Interagency Incident Management System

In 1981, the National Wildfire Coordinating Group adopted the National Interagency Incident Management System (NIIMS). NIIMS has been developed to provide a common system which fire protection agencies can utilize at local, state, and federal levels. The system consists of two major components: the National Interagency Fire Qualifications System and the Incident Command System.

The National Interagency Fire Qualifications System (NIFQS) consists of the standards for qualification and certification and the standard training courses applicable to Incident Command System positions. At present, NIFQS standards for qualification and certification and training courses stress the application to the wildland/urban interface fire protection problem. Today, many man-made developments, such as residential areas, are on the borders of the wildlands and create new fire protection problems.

The Incident Command System (ICS) was developed through a cooperative interagency (local, state, and federal) effort. The basic organizational structure of ICS is based upon a large fire organization which has been developed over time by federal fire protection agencies. ICS is designed to be used for all kinds of emergencies (see, e.g., the discussion of adapting fire fighting programs to respond to the Mount St.

Helens eruption in 1980 in the chapter on volcanoes) and is applicable to both small day-to-day situations as well as very large and complex incidents.

The following are basic system design operating requirements for the Incident Command System. The system must:

1. provide for the following kinds of operation: single jurisdiction/single agency, single jurisdiction with multiagency involvement, and multijurisdiction/ multiagency involvement

2. have an organizational structure adaptable to any emergency or incident to which fire protection agencies would be expected to respond

3. be applicable and acceptable to users throughout the country

4. be readily adaptable to new technology

5. be able to expand in a logical manner from an initial attack situation into a major incident

6. have basic common elements in organization, terminology, and procedures which allow for the maximum application and use of already developed qualifications and standards and ensure continuation of a total mobility concept

7. present the least possible disruption to existing systems when implemented

8. be effective effective in fulfilling all of the above requirements and yet be simple enough to ensure low operational maintenance costs

In the summer of 1988 more than 15,000 people organized under the Forest Service, Bureau of Land Management, National Park Service, Bureau of Indian Affairs, the U.S. Army, and a conglomeration of state and local agencies worked within a single command to battle the blazes in the wildlands of the West. Fire fighters and equipment from all fifty states and the Virgin Islands assisted in the effort. The total cost of the operation approached half a billion dollars.

Using the Incident Command System, the fire fighters were able to respond to the diverse demands of the physical and social environment. The structure of the system is solid enough to bring a variety of agencies and skills together effectively.

The mobility of fire crews is essential to the Forest Service's system of fire management. This alleviates the need to station fire fighting crews and equipment in each area, which would be a very costly venture.

The Incident Command System is uniform nationwide. The Forest Service has set up training courses at each of ten regional offices in the United States. Federal, state, and local government employees are trained at these centers. The system has been so successful that it has been used in other emergency situations, such as hazardous waste spills, manhunts, floods, and earthquakes, and crowd control.

THE 1988 YELLOWSTONE FIRES

The summer of 1988 came early to Yellowstone National Park and surrounding areas, along with dry conditions. Thunderstorms moved through the park, bringing lightning that started several fires in areas covered by Yellowstone fire management plans. Fire managers set out to determine whether to suppress the fires. Their decisions were based on predicted weather and fire behavior, the fires' current locations, and available suppression resources.

The last few summers had been wet and it is possible the fire management personnel relied too extensively on the past weather. The most uncertain element in the decision process was the long-term weather forecast. In the end, officials decided that certain fires were within prescription policy and could be allowed to burn without suppression efforts. However, normal rains did not occur. In midsummer, drought conditions combined with strong winds forced park officials to begin control efforts on several of the fires. Along with visitor evacuation during midsummer came visits from members of Congress and allegations of mismanagement on the part of the park officials. Since the fires of 1988, public hearings on federal fire policy have been held and federal agencies have publicly questioned each other's policies. The final report is not yet out.

On December 15, 1988, a Fire Management Policy Review Team coordinated by the Department of Agriculture and the Department of the Interior presented their findings on the current prescribed natural fire policy. Members of the policy review team included representatives from the Department of Agriculture; Department of the Interior; Rocky Mountain Region of the U.S. Forest Service; Stanislaus National Forest of the U.S. Forest Service; Alaska Region of the National Park Service; Division of Wildlife Refuges of the U.S. Fish and Wildlife Service; Lands and Renewable Resources of the Bureau of Land Management; Boise Interagency Fire Center; Bureau of Indian Affairs; Western Region of the National Park Service; and National Association of State Foresters.

The Fire Management Policy Review Team found that:

1. Prescribed natural fire policy has had many notable successes but has been interpreted to allow prescribed natural fires with essentially no prescriptions

2. Some agency employees support a policy of allowing naturally caused fires to burn free of prescription so long as they do not cross park or wilderness boundaries

3. Some managers apparently support "naturalness" above all else, allowing fires to burn outside of prescription without appropriate suppression action

4. Planned ignitions can help achieve management objectives; however, there are factors constraining their use

5. Many fire management prescriptions do not place adequate limits on fire management decisions

6. The 1988 fire season revealed the risks inherent in managing wildland fires

7. Many fire management plans do not meet current policy

8. Fire management programs could be strengthened by incorporating improved decision criteria, additional fire management expertise, and more direct line officer involvement

9. Reduction of hazard fuels in selected areas reduces risks and costs

10. Agency training programs are insufficient to maintain the number of knowledgeable personnel to ensure proper and consistent application of policy

11. Environmental effects of prescribed natural fires generally support land management objectives, but social and economic impacts on- and off-site may be unacceptable

12. Dissemination of information and public participation in the fire management planning process needs to be improved

13. Budget structure and funding create dissimilarities in the way agencies plan and implement prescribed natural fire programs

14. Inadequate definition of "light hand on the land" suppression tactics raised serious questions over management of 1988 fires

15. Further research and analysis are needed to provide improved tools for management of fire management programs (Departments of Agriculture and of the Interior, 1988)

The Fire Management Policy Review Team recommended that:

1. Agencies strengthen existing fire management policies

2. Agencies reaffirm their policy that fires are either prescribed fires or wildfires

3. No prescribed natural fires be allowed until fire management plans meet current policy and additional new requirements

4. Current fire management plans be strengthened by joint planning along common boundaries; by improving prescription; by clearly describing the decision process; by including criteria for declaring a prescribed fire a wildfire; by clearly identifying areas that need protection from fire; by clearly stating management objectives; and by identifying community outreach projects

5. Agencies implement a daily certification process verifying that adequate resources are available to assure prescribed natural fires will remain within prescription given certain conditions and, if not, to declare these fires to be wildfires and to initiate suppression action

6. Agencies develop regional and national contingency plans to curtail or constrain prescribed fire programs under extreme conditions

7. Prescribed fire program management be improved by establishing appropriate regional- as well as unit-level prescribed fire program management organizations

8. Additional interagency emphasis be given to addressing opportunities for improving fire management programs

9. Agencies consider opportunities to use planned ignitions to complement prescribed natural fire programs and to reduce hazard fuels

10. Agencies assure that the NEPA process is followed for fire management plans to increase opportunities for public involvement and coordination with state and local governments

11. Agencies improve interpretation and public information before and during fires

12. Agencies review funding methods for prescribed fire and fire protection programs to improve interagency effectiveness

13. Additional research related to fire management programs be undertaken

14. Allegations of misuse of policy be reviewed immediately and acted on as appropriate (Departments of Agriculture and of the Interior, 1988)

The Bush administration scrapped the controversial "let it burn" policy (i.e., prescribed natural fire policy) in Yellowstone and other national parks for the 1989 fire season. In Yellowstone, every fire would be fought, including those caused by nature. In the Interior and Agriculture Departments' detailed study of federal fire policy in December 1988, Interior officials said they would impose a "temporary moratorium" on the "let it burn" policy while the report was being completed. Later, they decided to extend the moratorium through the summer and fall of 1989, despite scientists' endorsement of the traditional policy.

CONCLUSION

Wildland fire management has evolved into a well-structured and well-organized example of emergency management policy. One testimony to this organization is the use of management techniques to cope with other emergencies such as earthquakes. At the same time, however, wildland fire management is bound up with the matrix of the many values associated with public lands.

Fire has come to be perceived as beneficial by members of the scientific and public land management communities, largely through the research of fire ecologists. Yet public perception of the beneficial nature of some wildfires has yet to catch up with the views and policies of scientists and land managers. The on-going review of the 1988 fires in the Yellowstone area suggests that science and public opinion are as yet not completely in agreement. Perhaps the efforts of park interpretation at Yellowstone will begin to affect the way the public views fire management in the future.

At the same time, however, the growing urbanization and development of the West may serve as a counterbalance to prescribed fire policies. According to Richard McCluskey, a biologist and consultant to the U.S. Forest Service, the increased growth in population has created a demand for the use and occupancy of the wildlands and rural areas. As a result, there has been an increase in the number of human-caused wildland fires. Other factors contributing to the wildland fire problem are: homes being built that are extremely vulnerable to destruction by wildfire; new residents causing the start of more fires; subdivisions and individual structures being built without adequate safety measures; and the accumulation of highly flammable vegetable fuel. Oftentimes lands formerly reserved for livestock grazing, forest products, recreation, wildlife, and minerals are converted to residential use. McCluskey states: "Wildfire in these areas destroy many natural resource values and real property such as fences, communication systems, water systems, powerlines, corrals, vehicles, and structures. Each wildland area has a unique degree of fire hazard severity which makes it difficult for federal and local authorities to identify and implement realistic management protection levels" (1989: 11). Increasing real estate values justify an increase in fire protection and management. Local governments are held responsible for the management of land use. These responsibilities include the protection of public health, safety, and welfare.

Many times questions arise concerning who is responsible for the protection of a structure on private land next to federal land and, most importantly, whether natural resources should be sacrificed to protect a structure. Fire fighters are instructed to protect structures before resources because of the political and ethical implications involved. When a fire threatens a structure, the fire is then diverted and allowed to grow and damage forest resources. In addition to the problems of fighting structural fires, wildland fire agencies generally do not have the proper clothing, equipment, or specialized training to fight these types of fires. It is difficult to conduct a cost/benefit analysis and convince the owner of a structure that the natural resources are of greater value in the longterm than his house or corral.

McCluskey suggests that steps be taken to educate the public in order to reduce the risk of fire dangers. These recommendations include: publishing fire hazard maps and distributing them to local government officials and the general public; evaluating the potential of fire hazard before any subdivision or parcel is approved for development; informing the potential property owners of the fire hazard and possible limitations on loss indeminification; preparing a fire hazard assessment which includes structures as part of the fuel component; requiring the use of fire-resistant materials in the construction of structural roofs; and, providing guidelines for reducing fire hazards to property owners and government officials.

The growing urbanization of the intermountain West may create a policy paradox. On the one hand, the fires of Yellowstone and resultant interpretive programs explaining the benefits of fire have the potential to move the general public toward an acceptance of fire. Yet as people continue to seek out the amenities associated with living near parks and wilderness areas, they may press for more fire suppression. Our appreciation of these areas can lead to activities and policies which could cause new harm as well, echoing the fears of the 1960s that these areas were being "loved to death."

REFERENCES

General

Chambers, John (1987). "The Evolution of Wildland Fire Management and Policy," Fire Management Notes 48/2.

Departments of Agriculture and the Interior (1988). "Recommendations of the Fire Management Policy Review Team," Federal Register 53 (December 20).

Fire Management and Policy Review Team (1988). "Memorandum of December 14, 1988," Fire Management Policy Review Team Report (U.S. Departments of Agriculture and the Interior, December).

Graber, David M. (1987). "The Evolution of National Park Service Fire Policy," Fire Management Notes 46/4.

McCluskey, Richard J. (1989). "United States Forest Service Conceptual Framework for Fire in the Forest - Influences on the Landscape and Management Decisions in the West," U.S. Forest Service, Intermountain Region (February).

"National Interagency Incident Management System, National Interagency Fire Qualifications System, Incident Command System and the ICS Operating Requirements" (1981). Operational System Description ICS 120-1, Incident Command System Publication, December 12.

Pyne, Stephen J. (1982). Fire in America (Princeton, N.J.: Princeton University Press).

Williams, Ted (1989). "Incineration of Yellowstone," Audubon 91 (January).

Interviews

Bill Baden, Former director, Boise Interagency Fire Center, U.S. Forest Service, U.S. Department of Agriculture. Interview in February 1989 at BIFC.

Arnold Hartigan, public affairs officer, Boise Interagency Fire Center, Bureau of Land Management, U.S. Department of the Interior. Series of interviews in February, March, April, and June 1989 at BIFC.

Tom   Rios,   intelligence   section   chief,   Boise
        Interagency Fire Center, Bureau of Land
        Management, U.S. Department of the Interior.
        Telephone interview in June 1989.

Bob Webber, supervisory range technician, Bureau of
        Land Management, Boise Interagency Fire
        Center, U.S. Department of the Interior.
        Interview in February 1989.

9

Drought

Donald A. Wilhite

Drought is a normal feature of climate. Although scientists disagree on what constitutes a drought (Wilhite and Glantz, 1985: 111), it represents a common experience that, in a sense, binds certain regions together (e.g., the Great Plains). During the past century, the United States has been plagued by numerous major drought episodes (e.g., 1890s, 1930s) and innumerable dry spells. In fact, it is unusual for drought not to occur somewhere in the United States each year. Recent short-term droughts that have resulted in substantial damage include the drought and heat wave of 1980 in the southwestern, southern, and central plains, and southern Corn Belt states; the 1983 drought in the Corn Belt; the 1985 drought in the northern and central Great Plains and the Northeast; the 1986 drought in the Southeast; and the 1988 drought in the Corn Belt and northern Great Plains states.

Although severe drought generally occurs more frequently in some parts of the United States than others, no part of the nation is immune (Karl and Knight, 1985). Severe drought is generally associated with cumulative moisture deficiencies of sufficient magnitude that, when extended over a substantial length of time, result in far-reaching impacts over a rather large geographical area. For example, the drought of July and August 1983 was so severe that the federal government designated 1,123 counties in twenty-two states as drought disaster areas. In addition to the designations that were made in the Great Plains states of Nebraska, Kansas, New Mexico, and Texas, the federal government also declared parts of Alabama, Georgia, Virginia, West Virginia, Tennessee, Kentucky, South Carolina, Pennsylvania, and parts of most Midwest states eligible for low-interest disaster loans because of drought.

The actions of the federal government in responding to the 1983 drought are not unique. In fact, these actions seem almost inconsequential when compared to the massive drought relief programs formulated in response to the major episodes of severe drought that have occurred in the United States during the twentieth century. For example, during the droughts of the mid-1970s the federal government was responsible for the largest drought relief program in U.S. history. The General Accounting Office (1979: 29) calculated the cost of the drought program to four federal agencies alone at more than $5 billion during 1976-77. D.A. Wilhite and his colleagues (1984) estimated expenditures by all federal agencies involved in the response effort, plus administrative costs at both the federal and state level, to be $8 billion from 1974 to 1977.

Since each drought relief effort in the United States has relied, to some extent, on the precedents set in previous episodes, it is not surprising that mistakes and failures have been repeated. This chapter documents and evaluates efforts to respond to drought in 1976/77, the last major drought episode for which large-scale federal relief efforts are documented. Although ten years have elapsed since this episode, little has been done by the federal government to prepare for, and thus respond more effectively to, the inevitable recurrence of severe drought in the United States. Considerably more progress has been made by state governments. Recommendations are given on ways to improve the effectiveness of federal and state governments' response to future droughts. The concept and advantages of drought planning and a ten-step planning process will be discussed.

FEDERAL RESPONSE TO DROUGHT (1976/77)

That the federal government would attempt to mitigate some of the most severe impacts of widespread drought during the mid-1970s was not unexpected. Droughts of greater intensity and duration during the 1930s and 1950s had produced similar responses. Although the organizational structure for administering drought relief and the forms of assistance available changed significantly during the fifty years before the mid-1970's drought, the fundamental approach did not.

During the mid-1970s, the Federal Disaster Assistance Administration (FDAA) was responsible for administering grants to presidentially declared disaster areas from the president's disaster relief fund. Moreover, FDAA was responsible for directing and coordinating the assistance efforts of all federal agencies (FDAA, 1975). The number of federal disaster assistance programs available in 1975 was extensive. Few, if any, of these programs had been designed specifically to respond to problems caused by drought.

The actions of state and federal agencies that resulted in response to the drought of 1976-1977 are described in detail below. Table 9.1 provides a chronology for these actions.

The 1976 Federal Drought Response

The first federal actions were initiated during the last year of the Ford administration in response to requests from Governor Richard F. Kneip and Representative James Abdnor of South Dakota in July 1976. The governor requested federal agencies to provide maximum assistance to the severely stricken drought areas in his state (Kneip, 1976). This request prompted the president to direct the Domestic Council to review the socioeconomic impacts of drought in the Dakotas, Minnesota, and Wisconsin and to determine if additional assistance could be provided under existing federal laws and programs (May, 1976). The governor's letter was followed by a request from Representative Abdnor to the secretary of agriculture for the creation of a special task force to review and improve current drought assistance programs (Abdnor, 1976). In response to Abdnor's request, a special cabinet-level drought committee was formed by the president in late October. The committee's objectives included the development of a drought monitoring scheme and a comprehensive plan and program for delivering short-term assistance to drought-affected areas.

The special cabinet-level drought committee reported to President Ford on December 28, 1976. By this time, 325 counties had been declared emergency disaster areas. Basically, the report provided a summary of federal response to date, a status report of the current situation, and an indication of problem areas. The committee's findings suggested that current programs "may not be able to cope effectively if the situation deteriorates much further" (Bell, 1976). The report concluded that, "when drought occurs it is difficult to determine the nature and extent of federal assistance required, and some emergency programs are not designed to cope with agricultural drought."

Table 9.1
State and Federal Response to the 1976/1977 Drought

Action/Date	Response/Date
1976	
Request for action from South Dakota governor and others--July	Domestic Council directed by President Ford to review socioeconomic impact--September
Request by Rep. Abdnor (South Dakota) for the creation of a drought task force--July	President Ford appoints special cabinet-level task force--October Task force issues report--December
1977	
States form regional alliances, Western Governors' Task Force on Regional Policy Management meets to discuss drought conditions--January	Western States Water Council begins to monitor drought--January
Western governors meet with Secretary Andrus--January	Commitments by federal and state governments for action; President Carter and governors appoint drought coordinators--January to early March
Federal drought coordinator requests drought-related information from 13 federal agencies--February	Drought appraisal report prepared under leadership of the U.S. Army Corps of Engineers for submission to President Carter--mid-March
Presidential drought package for $844 million submitted to Congress --March 23	Drought package passed almost intact by Congress, except for two items--April to early May
Formation of an Interagency Drought Coordinating Committee to designate Emergency Drought Impact Areas under the president's drought program--April	2,145 counties declared Emergency Drough Impact Areas by this committee between April 25 and September 12
Drought conditions improve between April and August in the Great Plains and Upper Midwest states, and by December in the Far West states	Federal drought assistance estimated between $7 and 8 billion for 1976/77

The drought committee's report reached President Ford on January 3, 1977, seventeen days before the end of his term in office. The committee's report provided only a cursory examination of the drought problem and did not deal with the questions of long-term policy cited among the committee's original objectives. As table 9.2 shows, the report included a tabulation indicating federal assistance in presidentially declared emergency areas up to December 1, 1976.

Federal drought response during the Ford administration is best summarized as reaction-oriented. Little if any planning was done to develop alternative actions for possible future conditions. No new programs were developed and no coordinated effort was made to respond to deteriorating conditions.

The 1977 Federal Drought Response

In January 1977, regional alliances put added political pressure on Washington for action. On January 23, 1977, the Western Governors' Task Force on Regional Policy Management met to discuss the scope and magnitude of the western drought (WESTPO, 1978). Following this meeting, the lead agency for water policy and development, the Western States Water Council (WSWC), began to monitor the drought situation at regular intervals. The governors met with the secretary of the interior, Cecil Andrus, to discuss state needs and federal actions to mitigate the societal impact of drought. Although many areas of the nation were entering their second, and a few locations their third, consecutive year of drought, this was the first such joint discussion of mitigation alternatives by state and federal officials.

The meeting with Secretary Andrus concluded with several commitments by the secretary and the governors. The secretary agreed to seek the appointment of a federal drought coordinator and to encourage the president to discuss the drought issue at the National Governors Conference. The governors also agreed to consider the need for alternative approaches to cooperative, multilateral drought response actions and to designate state drought coordinators.

In response to these initiatives, President Carter appointed Jack Watson to be federal drought coordinator. One of Watson's first actions was to request each of thirteen federal agencies to prepare a report by March 3 (a lead time of less than one week) that would include: (1) a brief evaluation of the impacts and drought-related problems in each agency's area of responsibility; (2) a list and description of drought assistance programs; (3) a statement of administration or funding problems; (4) an evaluation of complaints from state and local governments and drought victims; and (5) suggestions of legislative changes or initiatives that might help to better organize and deliver federal assistance in support of state and local government efforts (Watson, 1977).

The agency reports submitted to Watson totaled several thousand pages and were, not surprisingly, lacking in uniformity and consistency. Watson recognized the inability of his staff to restructure the raw information provided by the agencies into a format that would be useful in the decision-making process (Kallaur, 1977). The U.S. Army Corps of Engineers was asked to coordinate this assimilation process. The Corps accepted this task and completed it within one week, as directed. The thirteen reporting agencies became known as the White House Drought Study Group. The Drought Appraisal Report, as it was called, was completed on March 18 and served as the basis for President Carter's drought program.

The Drought Appraisal Report described drought conditions in the United States and addressed questions of water conservation, water supply augmentation, and management measures; it also suggested possible immediate mitigating actions. The report concentrated heavily on drought impacts in the Far West, sometimes to the point of downplaying, if not neglecting, those areas plagued by extreme drought in the Midwest and northern plains states.

Federal response activities continued to expand during March as drought conditions intensified and encompassed larger geographic areas. Emergency loans from FmHA were made available to 706 counties in twenty-seven states. Livestock feed assistance was provided in 436 counties in twelve states by ASCS. By the end of March FDAA was providing aid to sixteen states, by presidential declaration, through three assistance programs (FDAA, 1977). The three programs provided assistance for hay transportation, cattle transportation, and emergency feed. USDA was responsible for coordinating most of the assistance activities in the agricultural sector.

President Carter sent a request to Congress on March 23 for $844 million in loans and grants for farmers, ranchers, communities, and businesses stricken by drought. The president's request for this program was passed intact by Congress, except for the Small Business Administration legislation and a reduction in funds, from $225 to $175 million, for the Economic Development Agency (EDA) loan and grant program (Crawford, 1978: 143). The water bank bill was signed by the president on April 7. Other portions of the "package" were delayed until early May. Program funds were to be expended or committed by September 30, 1977.

Table 9.2

Federal Grant and Loan Programs Providing Assistance in Disaster Areas Through December 1, 1976

Agency/Program	Applications Received	Estimated Amount	Applications Payments	Amount Paid
Federal Disaster Assistance Administration, DHUD Hay and Cattle Transportation Assistance	18,456	$83,312,926	9,701	$7,154,121*
Small Business Administration Economic Injury Disaster Loans	31	$1,101,500	19	$701,500
Agricultural Stabilization and Conservation Service, USDA Disaster Payment Program	151,869	$172,050,000	70,712	$65,497,000
Emergency Livestock Feed Program (now being phased out due to lack of CCC-owned feed grain stocks)	N/A	$4,300,000	N/A	$4,300,000
Farmers Home Administration, USDA Emergency Loans	7,300	$207,263,000	2,956	$133,263,000
Economic Development Administration, DOC Economic Development-Special Economic Development and Adjustment Assistance Program	22	Undetermined**	8	$1,556,000*

Source: Bell, 1976.

*Partial payments on some applications
**Amount to be determined after further evaluation

Note:
This summmary reflects applications for grants and loans received and funds requested therein following the presidential emergency declarations and through November 1976 in the States of Minnesota, Missouri, North Dakota, South Dakota, Virginia, and Wisconsin. Eleven counties in Arkansas were declared eligible for assistance on December 3, 1976. The data contained herein was limited to assistance provided in the areas covered by the presidential emergency declarations due to drought. The assistance included in this report was provided through emergency and regular program authorities.

In April the Interagency Drought Coordinating Committee (IDCC) was created. The major function of IDCC was to designate areas eligible for federal assistance. This federal assistance, however, referred only to programs authorized in President Carter's "drought package." Members of IDCC included representatives of the U.S. Department of Agriculture (chairman), the Small Business Administration and the Departments of Interior and Commerce. Geographic areas designated by IDCC were referred to as Emergency Drought Impact Areas (EDIAs).

During the first formal meeting of IDCC, held on April 25, 1977, the committee designated 1183 counties as EDIAs. Of these, 842 had already received presidential or secretarial declarations (Stockton, 1977). The EDIAs were located in 24 western and midwestern states. The list of declarations grew during the summer months. By September 12, 1977, the date of the last declaration, 2,145 counties (70 percent of all counties in the United States) were included as EDIAs. These designations were to expire on September 30.

In the early stages of IDCC there were no distinct criteria for the designation of EDIAs. At least half of the counties designated during this time period were so designated with no supporting documentation. The need for such criteria was discussed during the third meeting of IDCC on May 3. It was agreed that ASCS would draft a list of criteria, which was presented to and approved by the committee on May 20. The list included the Palmer Drought Severity Index (PDSI). This index was apparently the principal criterion used by IDCC to determine eligibility for drought assistance (General Accounting Office, 1979: 29).

Considerable confusion appears to have developed over IDCC designations. Many federal and state officials assumed that counties were automatically eligible for all federal programs after they had been designated by IDCC. Although it is not so specified in the original memorandum of agreement, IDCC designations were intended to apply only to programs included in the presidential drought package. Following IDCC designation, counties automatically became eligible for only one of the many drought package programs, FmHA's Emergency Loan Program. To qualify for other programs in the package, counties had to meet the special eligibility requirements of each program. Eligibility for programs not included in the presidential drought package was determined on a program-by-program basis and was not linked to IDCC designations.

The only distinction between IDCC-designated and non-IDCC counties was that the former had access to the special drought funds associated with the president's drought package. IDCC designations were sweeping, usually focusing on states rather than individual counties. The detailed, county-level evaluation process was left to the several involved federal agencies.

Although the presidential drought package was substantial ($844 million)--one of the largest single appropriations for drought relief in the nation's history--it represented only a small portion of the total federal drought assistance program. Forty programs were available to provide assistance to the private sector during 1976/77. However, six programs accounted for the vast majority of funds disbursed: (1) the Farmers' Home Administration's Emergency Loan Program; (2) the Small Business Administration's Disaster Loan Program; (3) the Department of Commerce's Community Emergency Drought Relief Program; (4) the Bureau of Reclamation's Emergency Fund Program; (5) the Bureau of Reclamation's Emergency Drought Program; and (6) the Farmers' Home Administration's Community Program Loans and Grants. The authorizations and activities associated with each of these programs during the 1976/77 drought have been summarized in a General Accounting Office report (1979: 29) entitled "Federal Response to the 1976-77 Drought: What Should Be Done Next?" GAO reported that the Departments of Agriculture, Commerce, and Interior and SBA alone administered more than $5 billion in drought relief programs to water users during 1976/77. However, if the cost of programs administered by other federal agencies is included, as well as the cost of the relief programs of 1974 and drought-related administration costs to states during 1974-77, the total cost of the drought to the government can be conservatively estimated at $7 to 8 billion (Wilhite et al., 1984).

IMPROVING FEDERAL RESPONSE TO DROUGHT

In view of the experiences of the mid-1970s and previous drought relief efforts, certain lessons emerge about ways to improve governmental response to periods of widespread and severe drought. Based on the foregoing information, four basic requirements for more effective response by federal government are suggested: (1) reliable and timely information and dissemination plans; (2) objective and reliable impact assessment procedures; (3) objective and timely designation procedures; and (4) appropriate disaster programs and efficient program administration and delivery systems.

Information Products and Dissemination Plans

The drought response efforts of the mid-1970s were not based on adequate and systematic provision of timely information on drought conditions and impacts to persons and agencies involved in administering programs. Although the availability of reliable, current, and properly formated information does not ensure correct and timely decisions on the part of government officials, it is at least reasonable to believe that good decisions are less likely to be made on the basis of inadequate or incorrect information.

Many types of information are needed during periods of drought if the wide-ranging impacts associated with water shortages are to be adequately addressed. For example, meteorological data is necessary to describe the degree of water shortage and to identify those geographical areas most affected. Such data, in conjunction with information on soil moisture conditions, can be used for early projections of yield. Commodity prices, in conjunction with projected yield figures, can be used to estimate monetary losses for principal grain, vegetable, and hay crops. Data on stream flow and ground water depletion rates provide important information on the outlook for water supply to the agricultural, municipal, and industrial sectors.

A common requirement for all types of drought-related information is that it be reliable, effectively organized, and timely. In almost all cases during the mid-1970s' drought, government agencies did not make assessments of the drought situation until drought conditions had reached critical proportions.

To improve the ability of government to respond effectively in times of drought, the drought situation and its consequent impacts must be continually monitored. Since weather data form the basis for virtually all other assessments, special attention should be given to providing relevant observations of precipitation and calculations of evapotranspiration and soil moisture status. Networks of automated weather stations (such as the one developed in Nebraska, South Dakota, Colorado, Kansas, Wyoming, and Iowa under partial support of the National Climate Program Office) can provide the data needed for the aforementioned calculations. This network currently provides near-real time data for seven meteorological parameters--solar radiation, wind direction and speed, precipitation, humidity, temperature, and soil temperature (Hubbard et al., 1983: 213; Hubbard, 1987: 97).

Regional automated weather networks in drought-prone areas and terrestrial sensors in space can provide the data base for drought early warning and surveillance systems. Atmospheric scientists have a significant contribution to make in the improved collection and interpretation of weather data for drought management.

Impact Assessment Procedures

A long-standing problem in responding to drought has been the lack of reliable procedures for assessing probable impact. Because drought normally has its most immediate and substantial impact on the agricultural sector, improved techniques for assessing, in near-real time, the impact of weather conditions on crops and rangeland should greatly improve our ability to identify (and therefore speed assistance to) areas affected by drought.

Historically, the most common government criterion to identify areas stricken by drought has been amount of normal precipitation. This information and local reports of crop, pasture and livestock conditions, and human distress were used extensively during the 1930s and 1950s.

During 1976/77 PDSI was used by federal agencies and IDCC to establish eligibility of areas for drought relief (General Accounting Office, 1979: 29). A map showing the distribution of PDSI values was (and is) published regularly in the Weekly Weather and Crop Bulletin. PDSI is intended to describe long-term moisture conditions. More recently, the Crop Moisture Index (CMI), a modification of PDSI and more agriculturally appropriate, has been used by federal agencies to assess short-term moisture conditions (Palmer, 1968: 157; National Weather Service, 1977). CMI was not widely used during 1976/77.

PDSI has been increasingly criticized in recent years by scientists (Changnon, 1980: 5; Wilhite, 1983: 22; Alley, 1984: 22). Inconsistencies have been noted between PDSI and actual severity of the drought impacts observed. There are several reasons for the lack of agreement between calculated PDSI values and actual drought severity, particularly with respect to agricultural drought. Specific crop responses to drought were not considered in the derivation of the index, nor do they figure in the calculation of index values. Yet, PDSI is used, qualitatively, to assess drought impacts on crops. Additionally, the Thornthwaite method (Thornthwaite, 1948: 38) of estimating evapotranspiration (ET) is used in the calculation of PDSI values. The Thornthwaite method is unable to account for sensible heat advection, a major source of the energy that drives the ET process in the Great Plains region. Thus, there is concern that the Thornthwaite method severely underestimates ET in subhumid and semiarid regions (Rosenberg et al., 1983) and, accordingly, that the PDSI tends to overestimate the amount of water remaining in the soil (Smith, 1983).

Regional differences in land use and cropping systems should be considered in the impact assessment issue. For example, a PDSI of -3.0 in July may signal substantial reduction in yield of nonirrigated corn because of destruction of reproductive tissue. Were moisture conditions to improve, corn yield would still be low but soybeans, whose reproductive activity continues through much of the growing season, may produce near-normal yields.

Clearly, new techniques must be developed to enhance our drought impact assessment capability. Impacts are most precisely estimated on a crop-specific basis. Agricultural meteorologists and agronomists, working together, have the skills needed to develop crop-specific drought indices. Automated weather data networks are now providing the data to support the development and operation of these indices in some drought-prone regions. These data can also support numerous other assessment-related activities of state government. Therefore, states should play an important role in supporting the development and maintenance of these networks.

Drought Designation Procedures

The development of objective and timely procedures to determine eligibility for federal disaster assistance is a necessary condition for the improvement of government response to drought. Although standby legislation and response plans may reduce delays in program formulation and implementation, the lack of appropriate designation procedures and reliable, objective criteria on which to base those designations hampers the delivery of programs to the affected area and leads to ineffective response.

Procedures for designating counties eligible for assistance have changed with each drought episode. During a particular episode, procedures may have been altered in response to deteriorating weather conditions. Changes in political administration in the middle of a drought can also be expected to result in changing designation procedures. During the mid-1970s' drought the procedure for designating counties eligible for disaster assistance was more complicated and confusing than it had been in previous droughts, partly because more agencies and committees were involved in administering the programs (Wilhite et al., 1984).

The General Accounting Office (1978: 95) has summarized the substantial differences in the disaster declaration procedures used by major agencies--FmHA and SBA--during 1977. The effect of these differences in disaster declaration procedures was such that, during the period July 1977 through January 1978, FmHA and SBA operated their programs in forty-five and fourteen states, respectively. Within states where both agencies operated, certain counties were covered by only one of the two agency programs.

One examination and evaluation of the function, procedures, and actions of IDCC has identified several specific problem areas (Wilhite et al., 1984). First, the existence and precise function of IDCC were poorly understood by government officials, especially at the state level. In many cases, designations by the committee were interpreted by government officials as an automatic qualification of their state or county for all federal disaster assistance programs. FmHA's Emergency Loan Program was the only government program actually enabled by IDCC action.

Second, IDCC designations were broad and sweeping, and impacts identified by states were not verified by the committee on the basis of a common set of objective data. No IDCC evaluation criteria were actually available until early June, and then they were not widely understood. Of the 2145 counties designated by IDCC between April 25 and September 12, 1977, approximately 1575, or 73 percent, were approved before the criteria had been properly defined. Although entire states were often designated by IDCC, actual impact areas were of limited geographical extent. For example, the primary impact area in Nebraska in 1977, in terms of production losses of the principal grain crops, was confined to a nine-county area in the extreme southeastern corner of the state. IDCC designated the entire state (ninety-three counties) on April 25. These sweeping designations provided many counties throughout the nation not affected by the severe drought with access to FmHA emergency loans. This action also led to the illusion of a severe nationwide drought. Such an illusion can, in the long run, be detrimental to the establishment of drought relief programs.

Third, the criteria established by IDCC were not fully reliable for the purpose of identifying affected areas, although they were probably the best available at the time. Assessments by federal agencies were improvised from the data at hand. However, these needed data were not available to the committee that was charged with evaluating all requests for assistance. Also, the data available to the committee was, in some cases, out of date. Therefore, decisions were, at times, based on information that may not have represented the situation accurately.

Disaster Programs, Administration, and Delivery Systems

As many as forty separate programs were available to provide assistance to drought victims in the form of loans, grants, and insurance during the mid-1970s (see table 9.3). These programs can be clustered into two broad categories. The first included short-term actions to avoid or lessen the impact of drought by augmenting water supplies. This was the primary objective of President Carter's drought program. The second group involved programs designed to make loans to farmers to compensate them for production losses and to provide them with working capital. The wide range of assistance programs available reflects the variety of groups and economic sectors affected by drought and the lack of a coordinated federal disaster response plan.

Two characteristics of these disaster programs can be noted. First, only a few of the programs available in the mid-1970s were designed to address the specific problems associated with drought. Rather, they were orginally formulated by Congress to respond to problems of soil and water conservation and to other natural disasters such as flooding. Second, other than the on-going programs implemented in response to previous twentieth-century drought episodes (e.g., Great Plains Conservation Program), the programs of the mid-1970s were intended to be short-term or tactical. No new long-term program initiatives were instituted during this period.

The General Accounting Office (1979: 29) indicated four major problem areas in its study of the programs and the administration of programs that were part of the 1976/77 federal drought response effort. First, several drought programs were enacted too late to lessen the effects of drought. For example, President Carter's drought program did not receive congressional approval until April and, in some cases, May. In the Far West it had been apparent since January 1977 that a water shortage would occur during the irrigation season. As another example, delays in congressional approval also sharply reduced the effectiveness of certain programs. For example, $75 million was authorized to the Bureau of Reclamation for the Water Bank Program. However, only $4.8 million was spent in this manner because most growers of lower-value annual crops had already planted by the time the program was implemented. It was too late to reallocate water to the higher-value perennial crops.

Second, many projects that were approved violated congressional intent to augment water supplies on a short-term basis. Several projects were initiated so late that water could not be supplied during the drought for which the aid had been given. Construction of other projects did not even begin until after the drought had ended. Also, drought loans and grants appear to have been used to provide a low-cost source of federal financing for nondrought-related projects.

Third, eligibility and repayment criteria for emergency drought programs were inconsistent, inequitable, and confusing. Although substantial differences in criteria existed between many disaster programs, the differences between the FmHA's Emergency Loan Program and SBA's Disaster Loan Program are, perhaps, the most interesting because they were directed to the same target groups. (For specific differences between these two programs, see the 1978 GAO report). Loans obligated through the two programs totaled $4.63 billion during 1976/77.

Fourth, inadequate coordination among agencies led to program overlap and nonuniform standards for determining eligible drought relief projects. GAO cites several specific examples of loan applicants applying to two agencies. In some cases, applications were approved by both agencies, and applicants could choose the loan with the most favorable terms.

The General Accounting Office (1979:29) concluded its examination of the 1976/77 federal drought response effort with the recommendation that Congress direct the four primary agencies administering assistance programs (USDA, SBA, Departments of Interior and Commerce) to assess the problems encountered in providing emergency relief. Based on the findings of this assessment, GAO recommended that a national drought plan be developed to provide assistance in a more timely, consistent, and equitable manner. According to GAO, this plan should identify the respective roles of agencies to avoid the overlap and duplication that has been associated with previous drought response efforts. GAO recommended that Congress consider legislation that would more clearly define those roles. GAO also recommended standby legislation (i.e., authorizing assistance programs) to permit more timely response to drought-related problems.

In light of past experiences, the recommendations of GAO appear eminently sensible. The number of agencies participating in drought assistance activities during 1976/77, as well as the number of programs available, indicates the obvious need for an assessment and response plan organized under the leadership of a single agency. In the process of developing such a plan, all disaster assistance programs should be reviewed in terms of their consistency, efficiency, and equity, as well as their relevance in dealing with the problems and impacts associated with drought. Most assistance programs were originally developed to address problems resulting from the occurrence of natural hazards other than drought or in response to specific water supply problems. During droughts these programs have simply been redirected. Also, more attention needs to be given to alleviating drought impact and facilitating recovery in the agricultural sector.

Multidisciplinary studies should be initiated to define the impacts of past droughts. In addition, scenarios should be used to help evaluate probable impacts of future drought. The results of such studies could aid in identifying real needs for drought assistance programs, reduce the number of such programs, and lead to improved efficiency in their administration.

DROUGHT POLICY AND THE DEVELOPMENT OF PLANS

The Goals and Objectives of Drought Policy

The underlying question in this discussion is: Should government be involved in providing assistance to those economic sectors or persons that experience hardship in times of drought? Because of the frequency, severity, and spatial extent of drought, governments in the United States and elsewhere have elected to provide assistance through a wide range of measures. These drought assistance measures are the instruments of a de facto policy that has evolved over the past fifty years. The decision on whether to provide aid has been based more often on political than economic reasoning. Thus, government involvement in drought relief seems to be a political reality, and one that should be dealt with in a more effective and efficient manner.

Previous discussion has concentrated on government response to a recent episode of widespread, severe drought in the United States. This drought relief effort has been shown to be largely ineffective, poorly coordinated, and untimely. Governments have reacted to, rather than prepared for, recurrent and inevitable episodes of drought.

For purposes of contingency planning, the goals of government drought policy must be stated explicitly. Without clearly stated drought policy goals, contingency planning will lack direction and purpose. Also, the effectiveness of drought assessment and response actions will be difficult to evaluate.

Three goals for drought policy are proposed here. First, assistance measures should not discourage agricultural producers, municipalities, and other groups from adopting appropriate and efficient management practices to help alleviate the effects of drought. Second, assistance should be provided in an equitable, consistent, and predictable manner to all without regard to economic circumstances, industry, or geographic region. Third, the importance of protecting the natural and agricultural resource base must be recognized. Although these goals may not be achievable in all cases, they do represent a model against which recent drought policies and measures--the instruments of that policy--can be evaluated. Drought policy goals are also the foundation of any planning effort by federal and state governments.

The specific objectives of drought policy will, of course, vary between levels of government and from country to country. In the United States, for example, the objectives of a national drought policy might be:

1. To prepare an organizational structure for assessing and responding to drought-related problems and water shortages

2. To develop standby legislation that adequately addresses the impacts of drought through relevant assistance measures

3. To encourage and support basic and applied research leading to the development of appropriate management strategies for all drought-prone regions

4. To foster and support water planning and management activities at both the state and regional level

To be successful, whether in the United States or elsewhere, drought planning must be integrated within the national and state--or provincial--levels of government, involving existing regional (multistate)

organizations as well as the private sector where applicable. At the national level in the United States, however, the diversity of impacts associated with drought and the multitude of federal agencies with responsibility for drought assessment and response make it difficult for a single federal agency to assume leadership in the development of a national drought assessment and response plan. The development of a national policy requires an interagency approach in these instances, under the leadership of a single agency. For this as well as other reasons, such as unique local water management problems, Wilhite and his colleagues (1986: 22) have suggested that where a complex federal bureaucratic structure exists, as it does in the United States, drought planning efforts may be most effective if first initiated at the state level. In other settings, such as in less-developed countries, the drought planning process may be coordinated more easily at the national level since the bureaucratic structure may be less formidable.

The objectives of drought policy at the state level will differ from those at the national level, reflecting the unique physical, environmental, socioeconomic, and political characteristics of a particular area. For example, drought policy objectives might be:

1. To develop a monitoring system that provides early warning of impending drought conditions and impacts

2. To develop an organizational structure that enhances drought preparedness and response by linking levels of government

The development of the organizational structure referred to in the second objective will provide the necessary integration with drought policies at the national level and should ensure adequate coordination between the two levels.

Regional actions should be directed toward fulfilling at least three objectives:

1. To improve data collection and dissemination efforts between states

2. To identify or establish a regional organization to facilitate much of the drought planning effort and to improve coordination and cooperation within and between levels of government

3. To develop a strategy whereby the designated organization can focus federal attention on drought-stricken areas so that they receive appropriate assistance in a timely manner

Successful regional drought planning efforts have three prerequisites. First, the governors of the region in question must be convinced of the advantages of risk versus crisis management. This usually requires an event or series of events (i.e., the occurrence of a severe drought) to first capture their attention. An intensive educational effort must then be directed toward these decision makers. Second, states must have the full cooperation of federal agencies. Water planning and management is a complex problem, one whose solution involves all levels of government. Federal agencies can play a key role in identifying and implementing solutions to these problems. Third, drought planning should begin at the state level and then progress to the regional and national level. States that are cooperating in a regional planning effort must first establish the necessary institutional infrastructure within their state. This action will facilitate the planning effort at higher levels of government.

DROUGHT POLICY FEATURES

The principal features of drought policy are grouped into three categories: organization, response, and evaluation.

Organizational features are planning activities that provide timely and reliable assessments, such as a drought early warning system, and procedures for a coordinated and efficient response, such as drought declaration. These characteristics would be the foundation of a national or state drought plan. Only a few states in the United States have drought plans (Wilhite and Wood, 1985: 21).

Response features refer to assistance measures and associated administrative procedures that are in place to assist individual citizens or businesses experiencing economic and physical hardship because of drought. Numerous assistance measures are available in the United States, but few are intended specifically for drought. An all-risk crop insurance program has been evolving in the United States since 1939 (Federal Crop Insurance Corporation, 1980), although the level of participation by farmers is quite low.

Evaluation of organization procedures and drought assistance measures in the postdrought recovery period is the third category of drought policy features.

Governments in some countries (e.g., Australia) have been more conscientious in their evaluation of recent drought response efforts. In the United States, the government does not routinely evaluate the performance of response-related procedures or drought assistance measures. An evaluation of the 1976/77 drought response activities was made by the General Accounting Office (1979: 29) at the request of the chairman of the Subcommittee on Environment, Energy, and Natural Resources, the late Congressman Leo J. Ryan. Wilhite and his colleagues (1984) evaluated government response to the mid-1970s' drought under the sponsorship of the National Science Foundation. These were the first systematic evaluations of federal drought response efforts in the United States. Earlier efforts were only documentations of federal, and possibly state or private, involvement in drought relief, avoiding judgments of its effectiveness (Murphy, 1935; U.S. Executive Office of the President, 1959).

DROUGHT PLANNING: WHAT IS IT?

Drought planning can be defined as actions taken by government, industry, individual citizens, and others in advance of drought for the purpose of mitigating some of its effects. Drought planning should include, but is not limited to, the following activities:

1. A monitoring/early warning system to provide decision makers at all levels with information about the onset, continuation, and termination of drought conditions and their severity

2. Operational assessment programs to reliably determine the likely impact of the drought event

3. An institutional structure for coordinating government actions, including information flow within and between levels of government and drought declaration and revocation criteria and procedures

4. Appropriate drought assistance programs with predetermined eligibility and implementation criteria

5. Financial resources to maintain operational programs and to initiate research required

to support drought assessment and response activities

6. Educational programs designed to promote the adoption of appropriate drought mitigation strategies among the various economic sectors most affected by drought

As figure 9.1 illustrates, drought planning has been described by D. A. Wilhite and W. Easterling (1987) as a ten-step process. This process is intended to be flexible so that it can be easily adapted to many sociopolitical situations and levels of government. Continuous evaluation and updating of the procedures included within each step of the process are recommended to ensure that the plan remains most responsive to the needs of the region involved. This process should be useful to governments desiring to implement some level of drought contingency planning activity.

FEDERAL AND STATE DROUGHT PLANNING: CURRENT STATUS

Earlier in this chapter, four basic requirements were suggested as necessary to improve the effectiveness of federal drought response efforts: (1) reliable and timely information and dissemination plans; (2) objective and reliable impact assessment procedures; (3) objective and timely designation procedures; and (4) appropriate disaster programs and efficient program administration and delivery systems. A national drought plan has been suggested as the best way to attain significant progress in each of these four areas.

Although debate on the need for a national drought plan continues, no movement toward the development of such a plan has occurred. Some improvement in the delivery of reliable and timely information to decision makers during the 1988 drought can be noted. Much of the credit for this improvement must be given to the leadership provided by the Joint Agricultural Weather Facility of the U.S. Department of Agriculture and the National Oceanic and Atmospheric Administration. However, the actions of government in responding to widespread and severe drought remain uncoordinated because of the lack of an organizational structure within the federal government. Clearly, the Federal Emergency Management Agency (FEMA) must play a major coordinating role in this effort. It should also be recognized that the speed with which the Congress passed the 1988 drought relief legislation can be attributed largely to an election year spirit of cooperation among members of Congress. If drought continues into 1989, impacts will be even more pervasive, requiring more comprehensive assistance programs. Such bipartisan actions should not be expected in future droughts. A national drought policy needs to be established that defines goals and objectives of federal drought assessment and response programs.

Figure 9.1
A Ten-Step Drought Planning Process

Appointment of
Drought Task Force
(STEP 1)

Statement of Purpose
and Objectives
(STEP 2)

Inventory of Natural and Human
Resources, Financial Constraints
(STEP 3)

Development of Drought Plan
(STEP 4)

Identification of Research Needs
and Institutional Gaps
(STEP 5)

Synthesis of Drought Management
Science and Policy
(STEP 6)

Identification of Response Options
(STEP 7)

Implementation of Drought Plan
(STEP 8)

Development of Educational
and Training Programs
(STEP 9)

Development of
System Evaluation Procedures
(STEP 10)

State governments in the United States have typically played a passive role in assessing and responding to drought. This was certainly the case in the mid-1970s and in earlier drought episodes as well. In recent years, state governments across the nation have made impressive strides in preparing for drought-related water shortages. For example, in 1982 only three states had prepared formal drought plans--Colorado, South Dakota, and New York. At present, about twelve states have plans and another ten states are developing plans. Certainly, the widespread occurrence of severe episodes of drought in the United States over the past decade, and especially since 1985 in the Southeast and Far West, has demonstrated the vulnerability of our society to drought impacts and highlighted the importance of government actions as a mitigation tool.

Today, a number of resources are available that can help state governments prepare for the recurrence of drought. First, states can learn from the planning experiences of other states. The Colorado Drought Plan is probably the most duplicated approach. Second, a model drought plan developed by the Western States Water Council in the fall of 1987 helped many Western states hastily assemble some plan of action in 1988. This model is based on the Colorado plan but incorporates ideas and elements from other plans. Finally, the ten-step planning process referred to in the previous section of this chapter provided some focus and direction to a few states during 1988. This ten-step process is now being expanded with funding from the National Science Foundation to incorporate a model drought plan that will be applicable to all regions of the United States (Wilhite and Easterling, 1988). The availability of this model in the spring of 1989 should facilitate the development and revision of plans in drought-prone areas.

CONCLUSION

The U.S. government often responds to drought through crisis management. This was the case in the mid-1970s as well as in previous episodes of widespread and severe drought. In crisis management the time to act is perceived by decision makers to be short. Reaction to crisis often results in the implementation of hastily prepared assessment and response procedures that lead to ineffective, poorly coordinated, and untimely response. If planning were initiated between periods of drought, the opportunity would exist to develop an organized response that might more effectively address issues and specific problem areas.

Also, the limited resources available to government to mitigate the effects of drought might be allocated in a more beneficial manner.

In 1979 the General Accounting Office recommended the formulation of a national drought plan to provide assistance in a more timely, consistent, and equitable way to drought-affected areas (GAO, 1979: 29). GAO proposed that this plan identify the respective roles of agencies involved in drought response to avoid overlap and duplication; the need for legislation to more closely define these roles; and the need for standby legislation to permit more timely response to drought-related problems.

This chapter has identified four requirements for effective response to drought by government. First, reliable and timely information on drought conditions and drought-related impacts must be developed and properly assembled and disseminated. This requires near-real time meteorological data on which informational products can be based. Second, impact assessment techniques must be improved. In the case of agriculture, usually the first economic sector to experience the hardships of drought, new types of analyses must be developed to provide decision makers at all levels with the types of information necessary to understand the severity of drought and its impacts so that appropriate actions can be implemented in a timely manner. Third, designation procedures must be centralized under a single agency or committee with complete authority to determine eligibility for all assistance programs. Criteria must be determined in advance of drought, well-publicized when drought occurs, and applied in a consistent manner. Finally, assistance programs must be developed in advance of drought to avoid the delays in program formulation and congressional approval that occurred in the mid-1970s. These programs should be administered by a single agency through the mechanism of an interagency committee composed of representatives from all federal agencies with responsibility in drought assessment and response. State and/or regional representatives should be included in the membership of this committee. Assistance programs must address the specific problems associated with drought.

GAO's recommendation for a national drought plan has considerable merit. For such a plan to be effective, however, states must take a more active role in planning for drought. In the past, most states have played a passive role, relying almost exclusively on the federal government to rescue residents of the drought area. Although federal government has, for lack of an alternative, accepted this role, improving government response to drought requires a cooperative effort. States must develop their own organizational plans for collecting, analyzing, and disseminating information on drought conditions. This information should form the basis for more objective and timely assessments of impact. Today, more than twenty states have developed or are developing drought plans. Each plan is unique, reflecting the water supply characteristics and problems of the state and potential impact areas. However, state plans should be linked to a national drought plan through the interagency committee(s) with responsibility for drought designation and program administration. Because of the limited resources available to states, they can be expected to provide only a minimal level of financial assistance to drought disaster victims.

One unique aspect of the mid-1970s' drought was the effectiveness of regional organizations of states in focusing the attention of federal government on the problem. The Western Region Drought Action Task Force, the Western Governors' Policy Office, and the Western States Water Council, working in concert, were able to make a more unified representation to federal officials. This lesson should not be forgotten. Regional organizations are sure to play an even more important role in the future.

It is proposed that drought planning efforts be initiated at various levels of government and that these efforts be closely coordinated. A ten-step planning process is proposed that is adaptable to each level of government and should facilitate the development of drought plans. Regional organizations, such as the Tennessee Valley Authority, the Ohio River Basin Commission, and the Western Governors Association, must be included in this planning process. Regional organizations should consider centralizing their monitoring and assessment activities as one means of improving the efficiency and accuracy of information flow to the federal government and, by so doing, increasing their influence on drought policy.

REFERENCES

Abdnor, J. (1976). Letter to Secretary of Agriculture Earl Butz, August 24, Gerald R. Ford Library, Ann Arbor, Michigan.

Alley, W. M. (1984). "The Palmer Drought Severity Index: Limitations and Assumptions," Journal of Climate and Applied Meteorology 23.

Bell, R. E. (1976). Letter to President Ford, December 28, Official Secretary of Agriculture files, Records Section, Washington, D.C.

Changnon, S. A. (1980). "Removing the Confusion over Droughts and floods: The Interface between Scientists and Policy Makers," Water International 5.

Crawford, A. B. (1978). "State and Federal Responses to the 1977 Drought," in North American Droughts, ed. N. J. Rosenberg (Boulder, Colo.: Westview, AAAS Selected Symposium 15).

Federal Crop Insurance Corporation (1980). An Inside Look at All-Risk Crop Insurance (Washington, D.C.: Federal Crop Insurance Corporation).

Federal Disaster Assistance Administration (1975). FDAA Digest (Washington, D.C.: Federal Disaster Assistance Administration).

____ (1977). FDAA Bimonthly Report (March 31).

General Accounting Office (GAO)(1978). Difficulties in Coordinating Farm Assistance Programs Operated by Farmers' Home Administration and the Small Business Administration (Washington, D.C.: U.S. General Accounting Office).

____ (1979). Federal Response to the 1976-77 Drought: What Should Be Done Next? (Washington, D.C.: General Accounting Office).

Hubbard, K. G.; N. J. Rosenberg; and D. C. Nielsen (1983). "Automated Weather Data Network for Agriculture," Journal of Water Resources Planning and Management 109.

Hubbard, K. G. (1987). "Surface Weather Monitoring and the Development of Drought and Other Climate Information Delivery Systems," in Planning for Drought: Toward a Reduction of Societal Vulnerability, eds. D. A. Wilhite and W. E. Easterling (Boulder, Colo.: Westview).

Kallaur, W. (1977). "Memo for Members of the Drought Study Group" (March 11).

Karl, T. R., and R. W. Knight (1985). "Atlas of Monthly Palmer Hydrological Drought Indices for the Contiguous United States," Historical Climatology Series 3-6 (1895-1930) and 3-7 (1931-1938), National Climate Data Center, Ashville, N.C.

Kneip, R. F. (1976). Letter to President Ford, July 11, Gerald R. Ford Library, Ann Arbor, Mich.

May, F. L. (1976). Letter to Governor Kneip, August 11, Gerald R. Ford Library, Ann Arbor, Mich.

Murphy, P. G. (1935). Drought of 1934: The Federal Government's Assistance to Agriculture, report to the President's Drought Committee, July 15, Washington, D.C.: National Agricultural Library, Beltsville, Md.

National Weather Service (1977). Memo to Recipients of Technical Procedures Bulletin No. 204: Crop Moisture Index, National Weather Service, Silver Springs, Md.

Palmer, W. C. (1968). "Keeping Track of Crop Moisture Conditions Nationwide: The New Crop Moisture Index," Weatherwise 157.

Rosenberg, N. J.; B. L. Blad; and S. B. Verma (1983). Microclimate: The Biological Environment, 2d ed. (New York: Wiley).

Smith, D. T. (1983). "A Comparison of Techniques for Estimating Potential Evapotranspiration in Nebraska," CAMaC Progress Report 83-6, Center for Agricultural Meteorology and Climatology, University of Nebraska-Lincoln.

Stockton, B. (1977). Memo to Cliff Ouse Concerning Emergency Drought Impact Designation, July 6, Washington, D.C., Official Secretary of Agriculture files, Records Section, Washington, D.C.

Thornthwaite, C. W. (1948). "An Approach Toward a Rational Classifiacation of Climate," Geographical Review 38.

U.S. Executive Office of the President (1959). "Drought, a Report," Washington, D.C.

Watson, J. (1977). Memo to John F. O'Leary, Federal Energy Administration, reply to drought information request, February 25, Official Secretary of Agriculture files, Records Section, Washington, D.C.

WESTPO (1978). Managing Resource Scarcity: Lessons from the Mid-Seventies Drought (Denver, Colo.: Western Governors' Policy Office).

Wilhite, D. A. (1983). "Government Response to Drought in the U.S. with Particular Reference to the Great Plains," Journal of Climate and Applied Meteorology 22.

____ (1986). "Drought Policy in the U.S. and Australia: A Comparative Analysis," Water Resources Bulletin 22: 425-438.

Wilhite, D. A., and W. Easterling (1987). Planning for Drought: Toward a Reduction of Societal Vulnerability (Boulder, Colo.: Westview).

Wilhite, D. A., and M. H. Glantz (1985). "Understanding the Phenomenon of Drought: The Role of Definitions," Water International 9.

Wilhite, D. A., and D. A. Wood (1985). "Planning for Drought: The Role of State Government," <u>Water Resources Bulletin</u> 22.

Wilhite, D. A.; N. J. Rosenberg; and M. H. Glantz (1984). "Government Response to Drought in the United States: Lessons from the Mid-1970's," <u>Center for Agricultural Meteorology and Climatology Progress Reports</u>, 84-1 TO 84-4, University of Nebraska-Lincoln.

Wilhite, D. A.; N. J. Rosenberg; and M. H. Glantz (1986). "Improving Federal Response to Drought," <u>Journal of Climatology and Applied Meteorology</u> 25.

10

Hazardous Materials Transport Emergencies

Jeanette M. Trauth and Thomas J. Pavlak

It is estimated that each day 500,000 shipments of hazardous materials are made throughout the United States (Office of Technology Assessment, 1986). The term "hazardous materials" applies to a wide range of substances, from everyday household products such as hairspray in aerosol containers to highly toxic or poisonous substances such as PCBs. The U.S. Department of Transportation (DOT) is the lead agency responsible for the establishment and enforcement of regulations governing the movement of hazardous materials. DOT considers a substance hazardous if it is explosive, flammable, corrosive, poisonous, radioactive, a compressed gas, a human disease-causing microorganism, or if the substance is on one of the various lists of hazardous materials designated by other federal agencies such as the Environmental Protection Agency and subject to DOT regulations (National Conference of State Legislatures, 1984). Hazardous materials are transported via air, water, highways, and railroads.[1] Depending on the type and quantity of material to be shipped and the points of origin and destination, different modes of transport are utilized. For instance, materials moved in bulk shipments are usually shipped via water or rail, whereas relatively small packages of hazardous materials can be shipped via air transport. The nation's highways, by contrast, can be used to transport almost any type or quantity of hazardous material.

The movement of hazardous materials is an economic necessity for countless businesses and industries in the United States. For this reason, the volume and frequency of hazardous materials shipments present numerous opportunities for accidents to occur. Although the potential for a disaster is ever-present, the safety record for the shipment of these materials has been very good during the past decade. The total number of reported accidents involving the transport of hazardous materials has declined each year from 15,737 accidents in 1980 to 5,776 in 1984. Between 1984 and 1985 there was a slight increase in the number of these accidents nationally, but in 1986 the number of reported accidents dropped to 5,671 (Statistical Abstract of the United States, 1988). The number of fatalities that have occurred as a result of these accidents has remained consistently low.

The total number of reported injuries that have occurred each year as a result of hazardous materials transportation accidents also declined between 1975 and 1986, from 648 injuries to 315 (Statistical Abstract of the United States, 1988). In addition, the total reported financial damages resulting from accidents involving hazardous materials declined during the ten-year period from 1974 to 1984 although financial damages for particular modes of transport increased during this time period.

In spite of this safety record, there is a great deal of public concern regarding the transportation of hazardous materials because of the potential threat to public health and safety. Research has shown that people tend to be most concerned about the type of risks which they perceive are involuntary, uncontrollable, unfamiliar, manmade, have immediate consequences, and are catastrophic in nature (Slovic, Fischhoff, and Lichtenstein, 1980). The risks involved with the transportation of hazardous materials are often seen as having many of these characteristics which helps to explain public reaction in light of the accident statistics.

The task of ensuring that hazardous materials arrive safely at their destination presents a number of challenges to all those involved in this process. For instance, the responsibility for prevention of hazardous materials (hazmat) transportation accidents is jointly shared by federal, state, and local government officials. Officials at each of these levels of government have overlapping functions and responsibilities which contribute to a fragmentation of responsibility not only between these three levels of government, but also within and between various agencies, especially at the federal level. This makes program coordination difficult and can lead to interagency and intergovernment conflicts.

In addition to the administrative problems, there are a number of technical and political problems which compound the difficulty of ensuring the safety of hazardous materials shipments. For instance, the sheer volume and variety of hazardous materials shipped by air, water, rail, and highways present formidable challenges to inspection and enforcement personnel. At a time when the number of new hazardous materials entering the stream of commerce is growing rapidly and there is a need to increase inspection and enforcement activities, there have been reductions in the number of enforcement personnel at the federal level of government. Financial constraints have also affected the ability of state and local government officials to train and equip their personnel adequately. Officials at all levels of government of necessity are concerned about the tradeoffs between the costs and risks involved in preventing accidents from occurring. The costs of various planning, prevention, and training activities are relatively easy to calculate. It is a much more difficult task to calculate the probability that an accident will occur. Under these circumstances, decision makers have to weigh the merits of various levels of investment in emergency preparedness programs against the likelihood that hazmat accidents will occur.

RESPONSE TO THE PROBLEM

Federal, state, and local government officials have developed a variety of policies and programs in an attempt to ensure the safety of hazardous materials shipments throughout the United States. These efforts can be classified as prevention policies and programs, emergency response and training programs, and data collection and planning programs. The following section describes and discusses this intergovernment framework, paying particular attention to the roles and responsibilities of the various actors involved.

The transportation of hazardous materials has traditionally been a concern of the federal government. Federal preeminence in the transportation area has evolved largely as a result of the need to regulate interstate commerce and to avoid jurisdictional problems.[2] However, each level of government has a particular role to play with regard to the safety of hazardous materials shipments. The federal government has four major responsibilities: (1) regulation; (2) enforcement; (3) emergency response and planning; and (4) data collection. The U.S. Department of Transportation has primary responsibility for establishing and enforcing regulations in order to ensure the safety of hazardous materials shipments. The Federal Emergency Management

Agency (FEMA) is responsible for coordinating the federal government's assistance to states and localities, emergency response training, and planning activities. Data collection and dissemination responsibilities are shared by several federal agencies.

State governments vary in the roles that they play relative to the transportation of hazardous materials. Some states have extensive programs of regulation, enforcement, emergency planning, and training; whereas other states are still in the process of developing their own frameworks. Likewise, local governments vary in the scope of their activities. Some major cities and metropolitan areas engage in inspection, enforcement, and licensing activities similar to state and federal agencies. However, the primary function of local government continues to be that of responding to emergencies. The capacity of local governments to respond to transportation incidents involving hazardous materials varies greatly. Some localities have sophisticated emergency plans, well-trained response teams, and adequate resources for training and equipment. Many local governments, however, particularly those in small urban and rural areas, are ill-equipped to deal with a hazmat incident. In such cases, states often provide backup assistance to localities and coordinate emergency preparedness. Finally, industry also plays an important role in ensuring the safety of hazardous materials shipments through the programs that they provide their employees, clients, and contractors to learn how to properly handle and transport hazardous materials, and how to respond in an emergency.

Prevention Policies and Programs:
A Framework for Implementation

The prevention of accidents involving hazardous materials on the nation's highways, waterways, rail lines, and in the skies involves agency officials at each level of government. At the national level, twelve different federal agencies have some responsibilities with regard to the prevention of accidents and the enforcement of regulations involving the transport of hazardous materials. In particular, the Department of Transportation and the Nuclear Regulatory Commission "determine the context in which State and local agencies operate" (Office of Technology Assessment, 1986: 13). DOT regulates the transportation of hazardous materials through the cooperation and assistance of its Office of Hazardous Materials Transportation (OHMT), the Federal Highway

Administration (FHWA), Federal Railroad Administration (FRA), Federal Aviation Administration (FAA), and U.S. Coast Guard.

DOT's Office of Hazardous Materials Transportation has the overall authority and responsibility for promulgating and enforcing regulations regarding the shipment of hazardous materials and coordinating the department's hazmat activities. OHMT issues regulations designating and classifying substances which are considered hazardous, prescribes safety standards for containers and equipment, requires labeling, and outlines procedures for handling hazardous materials while they are in transit. While OHMT is responsible for the overall enforcement of these regulations, the day-to-day inspection of equipment and enforcement of regulations are carried out by the Federal Highway Administration, the Federal Railroad Administration, the Federal Aviation Administration, and the U.S. Coast Guard (Office of Technology Assessment, 1986). In those cases where a shipment of hazardous materials involves more than one mode of transport, OHMT assumes responsibility for enforcement. The Nuclear Regulatory Commission (NRC) and DOT have joint responsibility for the transportation of radioactive materials. Generally speaking, NRC has the lead role in setting standards for the design and performance of packages which contain radioactive and fissionable materials, and for the inspection of these containers. NRC is required to notify a state in advance of a shipment of certain types of radioactive material (e.g., spent fuel) within its borders and to provide adequate security to prevent acts of sabotage (Office of Technology Assessment, 1986).

State prevention programs generally emphasize inspection and enforcement of federal regulations although some states also issue regulations that are intended to enhance the federal requirements. This is especially true with respect to the routing of trucks and the prior notification of hazardous materials to be shipped through a state. Some localities are also involved in prevention and enforcement activities such as restricting the shipment of hazardous materials via various routes and the time of day when hazardous materials can be moved. In addition, some localities also require that hazardous materials shippers obtain a permit to travel through their community.

The Impetus for the Development of State Programs. The initiative for creating various state hazardous materials prevention programs came about as a result of a number of incidents involving radioactive materials which occurred in the early

1970s. As a result of a joint study by DOT and the Atomic Energy Commission (the predecessor of the Nuclear Regulatory Commission) to document the inadequacies in the movement of radioactive materials through states, the Department of Transportation through its Office of Hazardous Materials Transportation was given the responsibility to administer a number of programs to encourage the states to assume more responsibility for managing the transportation of hazardous materials. The State Hazardous Materials Enforcement Development Program (SHMED) was designed to achieve this goal. This program offered states grants to collect data, pass enabling legislation, and adopt federal regulations; develop and implement inspection programs; and establish enforcement procedures (Office of Technology Assessment, 1986).

The SHMED program has been judged as having had a significant impact on the development of the hazardous materials enforcement programs of the twenty-five states which participated in the program. Although the SHMED program emphasized the development of safety standards and regulations for highway transportation of hazardous materials, it did not ignore the necessity for regulatory programs aimed at rail, water, and air transportation. However, with the expiration of this program and its replacement by the Motor Carrier Safety Assistance Program (MCSAP), there are no programs specifically aimed at hazardous materials transportation by rail, water, and air.

Inspection and Enforcement: A State Perspective. As a result of the programmatic initiatives of the 1970s and 1980s, states have developed an inspection and enforcement capability. This capability is the result of states: (1) adopting enabling legislation and regulations in order to give them the requisite legal authority; (2) collecting data on hazardous materials shipments and the degree of compliance in order to assess the problems with enforcement; (3) establishing inspection and enforcement capabilities; and (4) establishing training programs. Because the following two sections of this chapter focus on the subjects of training and data collection as they relate to hazardous materials transportation accidents, the two subjects will not be covered here.

Effective inspection and enforcement programs are the backbone of successful hazardous materials transportation accident prevention programs. In many states, authority to carry out hazardous materials inspections is divided between the state highway patrol and the department of transportation. The former usually conducts roadside inspections and the latter oversee inspections at terminals. The most common type of violations found during roadside inspections include:

- failure to display the correct placard

- failure to block or brace hazardous materials containers

- leaking discharge valves on cargo tanks

- improperly described hazardous wastes

- inaccurate or missing shipping papers

- excessive radiation levels in the cab of the truck (Office of Technology Assessment, 1986: 22)

The failure to display the appropriate placard on a vehicle carrying hazardous materials and the failure to provide accurate information regarding the materials being shipped can result in serious safety problems for those who are first to respond to a hazardous materials accident.

There is a need for uniformity in the enforcement policies of the states if violations such as those described above are to be reduced. For instance, there is a great deal of variation among the states in terms of fines and penalties levied and prosecutions of hazardous materials transporation violations. "Fines for similar violations differ among the States . . . Texas has a $200 limit on fines, while Illinois may impose fines of up to $10,000 per day, per violation" (Office of Technology Assessment, 1986: 23). Likewise, some states provide for only civil penalties while other states allow enforcement agencies to impose either civil or criminal penalties. Finally, prosecutions of hazardous materials violators are often difficult because inspection officers are often poorly trained and do not follow correct procedures or provide adequate documentation for prosecution; and many judges and local prosecutors are unfamiliar with hazardous materials regulations and therefore dismiss cases or lower penalties as a result (Office of Technology Assessment, 1986).

Emergency Response and Training Programs

In spite of all these efforts to prevent transportation accidents from occurring, hazmat incidents are inevitable. When they do occur, those who arrive at the scene of the incident must be prepared to manage the problem. Typically, local police and fire officials are the first to respond because of their obligation to protect the health and safety of the public. However, federal and state officials also have a role to play in emergency response programs.

The Federal Emergency Management Agency (FEMA) is the lead federal agency which provides training for emergency responders. In addition, FEMA also develops and coordinates federal emergency response plans in support of state and local emergency response activities. Other federal agencies such as EPA and the Coast Guard share responsibility for providing technical information and advice to first responders and state and local governments. If state or local government officials cannot handle an accident or if they request federal intervention, EPA and the Coast Guard will assume control. In the event that a nuclear accident occurs, federal responsibility is shared by FEMA, NRC, and the Department of Energy.

Several federal agencies--NRC, the Coast Guard, FEMA, and EPA--conduct various types of emergency response training programs. The NRC program focuses on inspection and enforcement rather than on emergency response.[3] The Coast Guard program in Yorktown, Virginia, emphasizes the provision of basic hazardous materials emergency response training to its employees, state and local government officials, and industry participants. FEMA provides training in emergency response procedures at regional centers and at the National Fire Academy in Emmitsburg, Maryland. Finally, EPA offers a training course in response operations, equipment, and crisis decisionmaking. The diffusion of federal authority in this area is a major reason why it is difficult to develop an effective, coordinated federal response to emergencies.

Data Collection and Planning Programs

Prevention of hazardous materials transportation incidents can only occur if information is available for planning purposes. Public safety officials need to have information about the kinds of hazardous materials moving through their jurisdictions, the type of accidents that are likely to occur, and the geographical areas of highest risk. Unfortunately, many state and local governments do not gather this type of information until after a hazmat incident for which they were unprepared occurs.

The U.S. Department of Transportation, in conjunction with the Federal Emergency Management

Agency, has developed an innovative program to disseminate information to state and local emergency response personnel to assist them in planning for and responding to accidents involving hazardous materials. Any state or local emergency response official who has access to a personal computer and the appropriate communications devices (a telephone modem and communications software) can access the Hazardous Materials Information (HAZMAT) Exchange.[4]

The HAZMAT information system has provided information to approximately two thousand users since its inception in September 1987. Users can obtain information regarding training programs, planning techniques, upcoming conferences, current literature on relevant topics, changes in various laws and regulations as listed in the Federal Register, as well as information about whom to contact in the event that an accident occurs and assistance is needed.[5]

THE PITTSBURGH TRAIN DERAILMENT OF 1987: A CASE STUDY OF A HAZMAT INCIDENT

The following section describes a hazardous materials transportation accident which occurred in Pittsburgh during the spring of 1987. As the discussion of this hazmat incident indicates, the city's response to the emergency was successful due to prior planning efforts and an on-going emergency response training program. This particular incident illustrates the kinds of problems and issues that local authorities in one large urban community faced in responding to such an emergency, and it may provide insights for other state and local government officials faced with similar situations.[6] This case further emphasizes the need for policies and programs to: (1) prevent transportation accidents from occurring; (2) to assist decision makers in planning for emergencies; and (3) to train emergency officials to be able to respond to such incidents.

The Accident

On April 11, 1987, two Conrail freight trains collided in the Bloomfield area of Pittsburgh. The collision caused a thirty-three car derailment that triggered fires and the release of toxic fumes. This necessitated the evacuation of thousands of residents on the day of the accident and again early the following morning. The accident occurred as two of the westbound freight train's cars derailed and smashed into the eastbound train as they passed on a broad S-shaped curve. While the westbound train was not carrying anything classified as hazardous, a Conrail shipping manifest indicated that the eastbound train was carrying a variety of hazardous materials. Fortunately, however, only four of the thirty-three cars which derailed contained hazardous materials, and only one of these ultimately leaked.

Shortly after the train derailment occurred, city public safety officials arrived at the accident site.[7] They were they were faced with several serious problems: evacuating persons who were threatened by the release of toxic fumes from burning materials; controlling any leaking substances; and extinguishing the fire. In order to protect the health and safety of nearby residents, public safety officials knew that they first had to gain control over all aspects of the situation. Accordingly they established a command post atop a nearby bridge which overlooked the scene of the accident. Simultaneously, a hazmat team--dressed in protective clothing and wearing self-contained breathing units--approached the accident site to assess the damage visually.

The Problematic Nature of the Event

The situation which public safety officials faced was highly problematic and demanded a great deal of flexibility on their part. For instance, officials had to chart the progress of fire fighters, monitor weather conditions, and estimate the ever-changing threat to residents' health on a continuing basis in order to make necessary decisions. Fortunately, Pittsburgh had recently completed an Emergency Operations Plan (EOP) which outlined the roles and responsibilities of the various public safety officials in such situations.[8]

The fact that fire fighters could not immediately identify the contents of some box cars and tankers prohibited them from extinguishing the fire for fear that the chemical composition of the contents might trigger an adverse chemical reaction if it came in contact with water. Because of this delay, the fires continued to burn releasing smoke and fumes. Many residents reported a burning sensation in their eyes but it could not be determined whether this reaction was caused by the leaking chemical. Given these circumstances, it was decided that the residents of the immediate area needed to be evacuated.

The First Evacuation

The city had a generic evacuation plan in place at the time of the train derailment.[9] This plan called for the use of sirens and public address systems as well as door-to-door notification of residents to inform them of the need to evacuate. The plan also called for the use of public transportation (i.e. Port Authority buses) to move people out of the area quickly. In addition, the public safety department provided temporary shelter for evacuees which included food, clothing, medical assistance, recreational activities, nursery services, a kennel, and religious services.

An estimated ten thousand persons were evacuated that afternoon. Residents left the evacuated area primarily by automobiles--either their own or with friends, neighbors, or relatives.[10] Relatively few left by buses which were sent into the area. According to their plan, public safety officials primarily used loudspeakers to warn residents of the need to evacuate.[11] Most of those who evacuated during the day stayed with relatives or friends as opposed to going to the temporary shelters set up by the city.

Attempts to Control the Leak

Throughout the afternoon firefighters worked to control the blaze. By approximately 3:30 p.m. the fire was brought under control when the Conrail shipping manifests were obtained from the train's engineers-- identifying the contents of the various box cars and tankers--and it was determined that there were no leaking tank cars near the fire.[12] At this point, City Hazardous Materials Team members began working to seal the overturned tank car that was leaking phosphorus oxychloride. They finally managed to plug the leak at 5:15 p.m. by inserting a tennis ball into the vent pipe of the car. Soda ash and then sand were piled up over the soaked ground. City emergency management officials knew that the tank car would have to be set upright and the chemical siphoned out. Their plan was to perform that operation the following afternoon during daylight hours, and after residents had returned home from Sunday church services. The evacuated residents were permitted to return to their homes Saturday evening. They were told that they would not have to leave their homes again until Sunday afternoon, when the tanker car would be set upright and the contents siphoned out.

The Decision to Evacuate a Second Time

At 11:00 p.m. city officials learned that the overturned tanker car had begun to leak again. This fact, coupled with weather predictions for rain that evening, led city officials to the conclusion that it would be too risky for residents to remain in their homes overnight. Officials feared that the leaking phosphorus oxychloride would mix with the rain and release hydrochloric acid into the air, causing severe lung damage to anyone who breathed the substance. Therefore, at about 12:15 a.m. the city's public safety director, Glenn Cannon, ordered a second evacuation and brought in a crane to right the leaking tanker.

The original evacuation area was extended to include two adjacent communities--Lawrenceville and Garfield. The second evacuation began at 1:30 in the morning. Police with bullhorns cruised the streets, emergency vehicles sounded their sirens and officers knocked on doors alerting residents to evacuate. More than a hundred city buses were stationed at evacuation points to take residents back to the temporary shelters set up at the convention center and the city's Civic Arena for overnight stays. By 4:00 a.m., an estimated 15,000 persons had been evacuated from a one-square mile area surrounding the accident site.

By 4:30 a.m. Sunday the tanker car had been righted and removed from the track and the leak had been stopped. Approximately two hundred gallons of phosphorous oxychloride had leaked from the tanker car. On Sunday afternoon the remaining chemicals in the tanker car were pumped into two stainless steel tank trucks and the mayor declared an end to the emergency.

Health Impacts

While no serious injuries were reported as a result of the chemical accident, there were concerns among residents about the health effects of breathing various contaminants, the degree of soil contamination at the site and in residents' yards, and the air quality at the site. Initial qualitative testing of the air indicated that there were no harmful concentrations of toxic chemicals present. Air monitoring by the Pennsylvania Department of Environmental Resources showed no dangerous levels of toxic chemicals in the area.

Due to the fact that many neighborhood residents were concerned about long-term health and environmental effects of the train derailment, the University of Pittsburgh's Center for Hazardous Materials Research conducted a study of the environmental impacts of the train derailment.[13] The investigation indicated that the train derailment resulted in two independent events, only one of which "led to significant exposure of hazardous materials to the community" (Center for Hazardous Materials Research, 1988: ii). The study concluded that the burning of various paper products and plastic materials (especially polyvinyl chloride from phonograph records) posed "the most serious health and environmental threat because the combustion products of polyvinyl chloride include hydrogen chloride gas, a respiratory irritant that can be damaging to lungs at sufficiently high concentrations" (Center for Hazardous Materials Research, 1988: ii). However, because of the open air circumstances, the exposure levels within the affected areas would have produced only temporary discomfort in the average person.

The phosphorus oxychloride spill was confined to a relatively small area and, based on experiments performed by CHMR, it has been determined that the chemical was largely neutralized by the reactions with the moisture in the soil and air and the soda ash and water applied by emergency personnel.

Lessons Learned Regarding Hazmat Incidents

Most of the problems encountered by public safety officials in responding to the derailment underscore the importance of having an emergency operations plan (EOP) in effect and having personnel trained to implement it. Without such a plan, "the entire situation would have been handled differently."[14]

One of the problems faced by fire and emergency medical personnel at the train derailment site was insufficient information regarding the contents of the tanker cars; consequently they did not initially have a clear idea of the problem confronting them. Although federal law requires diamond-shaped hazard identification labels on all hazardous materials shipments, many of these labels had either been torn off in the collision or burned off in the ensuing fires. As a result of having an EOP, public safety officials had an established procedure for immediately notifying a number of organizations which are able to supply technical information on hazardous materials, including EPA, the Pennsylvania Department of Environmental Resources, the Allegheny County Health Department, and CHEMTREC.

Another major problem faced by public safety officials was evacuating the residents from the affected area. Pittsburgh's EOP outlined a set of procedures for evacuating persons under such circumstances. However, emergency management officials had to be flexible in their approach due to a number of factors which they were unable to control, such as weather conditions, the risk of explosion, and the necessity for a night evacuation. The timeliness of various decisions and the flexibility of the response was critical.

Another important point to note about the Conrail accident is the way in which public safety officials coordinated their response to the accident. The derailment pressed into service nearly all of Pittsburgh's 2,500 police, fire, and emergency medical service workers. Additional support was provided by emergency personnel from Allegheny County and surrounding municipalities as well as by state and federal emergency response officials. Coordination of an emergency response effort of this magnitude is a strong test of a community's emergency preparedness. In this instance, Pittsburgh met the challenge very well. One likely reason for the city's success in coping with the demands placed upon it by the emergency is the existence of a unified department of public safety with a director having considerable emergency management experience.

One weakness in terms of the city's planning efforts was the failure to make better use of the local media for dissemination of emergency information and instructions. At the beginning of the incident, local media officials were intent on transmitting the visual images of the accident--the wreckage, fires, and chemical clouds. City officials also did not make effective use of the media, particularly at the crucial stages of issuing an evacuation warning and at the conclusion of the emergency. One probable consequence was the failure to evacuate many residents, especially during the first afternoon evacuation. Many residents reported not knowing about the incident and/or the evacuation order, while a large number of others simply ignored the order. It is reasonable to expect that an official declaration by the mayor, carried by local radio and television, would have helped to both disseminate the message and persuade residents of the potential threat to their health and safety.

Accident Prevention Measures

A major concern of community residents and public officials is the avoidance of similar types of accidents. To this end municipal officials have called for greater control over rail shipments of hazardous materials through the community, including rerouting and tougher speed limits. The city council has called for stronger safety measures by the railroads, including testing of tanker cars carrying toxic materials for impact resistance, prohibition of transport of certain chemicals through the city, presentation of manifests by rail officials detailing the types of toxic materials being moved through the community, and reports of the condition of rail lines. Municipalities are limited in their authority to regulate rail transportation through their communities, however, so these safety measures will require federal legislation.

As a result of the Conrail train derailment, area legislators have introduced various railroad safety measures in Congress. As part of his inquiry into the Conrail incident, Pennsylvania Senator John Heinz has called for safety improvements in the operation of trains carrying toxic materials, including reduction of the number of cars, assignment of safety workers to cabooses, improved safety inspections, building more safety features into tanker cars, and rerouting trains from population areas where possible. Congressman Doug Walgren of Pittsburgh has also introduced a railroad safety bill which contains provisions aimed at addressing a number of the issues which came to light as a result of the accident (1987). These included, among other things:

1. A proposal to "deputize" the local police to help enforce federal speed limits (This would allow local police to use radar to enforce federal speed limits. This is a different strategy than relying on locally imposed speeding ordinances which have been overturned in court as being inconsistent with other federal statutes controlling interstate commerce.)

2. A requirement to license locomotive engineers

3. Federal penalties and suspensions for any individual who tampers with or disables a safety device

4. Regulations requiring the inspection, testing, and maintenance of signal systems at railroad crossings

5. Protection for employees who report safety violations by railroads

6. A study of automatic braking systems for all trains

The Conrail train derailment provides a dramatic illustration of the dangers presented by the transportation of hazardous materials through our country's urban areas. This incident highlights railroad transportation problems that require national attention. It also provides strong experiential support for the development of the emergency response capabilities of local communities facing the potential threat of hazardous materials transportation accidents.

A chemical accident such as the Conrail derailment leaves many issues to be resolved. Investigations into the cause of the accident are being undertaken by Conrail, the National Transportation Safety Board (NTSB), the Federal Railroad Administration (FRA), and the transportation committees of the U.S. House and Senate. Key questions to be resolved are the speeds of the two trains as they approached one another, the competence of Conrail crew members to be operating the trains, and whether Conrail officials were negligent in their operation of the trains.

AN EVALUATION OF EXISTING POLICIES AND PROGRAMS

In 1985, the congressional Office of Technology Assessment (OTA) undertook a national study of the transportation of hazardous materials to assist Congress in its reconsideration of the 1974 Hazardous Materials Transportation Act, which was due for reauthorization in 1986. In the course of its research regarding hazardous materials transportation, OTA found that state and local government officials are concerned about three basic issues: accident prevention and enforcement of regulations, emergency response, and collection of information for planning purposes. OTA concluded that there are a number of areas in need of improvement. Based on its assessment of the effectiveness of existing policies and programs, OTA has offered the following recommendations.

Prevention and Enforcement

There is a need for national standards establishing uniform state hazardous materials requirements and regulations. National standards would simplify and improve compliance by shippers, carriers, and state and local enforcement personnel. In addition, uniformity is also needed in the areas of licensing, permit or registration requirements, and shipment notification systems. Penalties should be imposed for

regulatory violations, including failure to report
hazardous materials incidents, and should be made
sufficiently burdensome to deter future violations.
Further, penalties should be consistent across
government and jurisdictional levels. Finally,
additional training and up-to-date information
regarding hazardous materials regulations for all
modes of transport need to be provided to state and
local enforcement personnel.

Emergency Response

In the area of emergency response, OTA has recommended
that: a program be developed to train first responders
nationwide in dealing with hazardous materials;
existing response programs be maintained; and national
guidelines for different levels of training and
national certification standards be developed. OTA is
also recommending that national equipment standards
and formal written mutual aid agreements with regional
and adjacent jurisdictions be implemented to protect
first responders from liability when they respond to
incidents for which they are not responsible and for
which they are not covered by their own insurance
programs.

Planning and Data Collection

OTA's recommendations in this area focus on improving
the availability and quality of data on hazardous
materials storage and commodity flow for routing and
emergency response planning; the development of a
reliable, comprehensive federal accident record
system; the development of a more clearly defined and
smoothly functioning federal authority for hazardous
materials transportation; and generally, a call for
improved interagency coordination at the federal and
state levels in order to simplify the work of regional
and local officials.

CONCLUSION

In this chapter we have presented a broad outline of
major issues in the transportation of hazardous
materials. Despite a favorable industry safety record,
hazardous materials remains a concern for public
officials and communities across the country.
Incidents such as the Conrail train derailment in
Pittsburgh illustrate the vulnerability of communities
to hazardous materials accidents. Efforts to develop
effective emergency preparedness for hazardous
materials transportation accidents often are hampered

by fragmented government authority, weak intergovernment and public-private coordination, and poor communication. Overcoming these problems continues to be the major challenge for emergency managers seeking to cope more effectively with the threat of hazardous materials transportation accidents.

NOTES

1. Some hazardous materials are transported via pipeline but they are not included in this discussion of transportation modes.

2. By all modes of transport.

3. The NRC training program is offered at the Technical Training Center in Chattanooga, Tennessee.

4. Users can "log on" to the system directly by dialing (312) 972-3275 or FTS 972-3275. Those users who do not have access to computer facilities or who are in need of assistance can call the following toll-free number Monday through Friday from 8:30 a.m. to 4:30 p.m. Central Time: 1-800-752-6367 (those calling from anywhere in Illinois must dial: 1-800-367-9592). The staff of the **HAZMAT** exchange will send a hard copy of information on any of the bulletin boards to those communities who do not have computer capabilities with which to access the system.

5. Personal communication, Tim Galvin, Argonne National Labs, January 26, 1988.

6. The material for this case study was obtained from newspaper accounts in the Pittsburgh Post-Gazette and the Pittsburgh Press, interviews with government officials, and a telephone survey of 255 area households conducted during the summer of 1987 by the University Center for Social and Urban Research at the University of Pittsburgh.

7. Pittsburgh created a department of public safety in 1985 in order to have an integrated approach to emergency management. The director of public safety is ultimately responsible for the activities of the police, fire, and emergency medical services personnel.

8. Interview with Glenn Cannon, public safety director, Pittsburgh, summer of 1987.

9. The city's evacuation plan had been developed in response to the discovery by public safety officials of an abandoned hazardous waste facility within the city limits that was considered to be a significant fire hazard.

10. According to 98 percent of respondents to a telephone survey conducted in the evacuated area in the summer of 1987.

11. According to 42 percent of respondents to a telephone survey conducted in the evacuated area in the summer of 1987.

12. Interview with Glenn Cannon, public safety director, Pittsburgh, summer of 1987.

13. The Center for Hazardous Materials Research conducted the study at the request of State Representative Frank J. Pistella and the research was provided as a public service to the citizens of the area.

14. Interview with Glenn Cannon, public safety director, Pittsburgh, summer of 1987. The director went on to say that the city did not have an approved emergency operations plan until 1986.

REFERENCES

Bureau of the Census, U.S. Department of Commerce (1988). Statistical Abstract of the United States (Washington, D.C.: U.S. Government Printing Office).

Center for Hazardous Materials Research (1988). An Investigation of the Environmental Effects Associated with the April 11, 1987 Train Derailment in Bloomfield, University of Pittsburgh.

National Conference of State Legislatures (1984). Hazardous Materials Transportation: A Legislator's Guide (Washington, DC: National Conference of State Legislatures).

Office of Technology Assessment, Congress of the United States (1986). Transportation of Hazardous Materials: State and Local Activities (Washington, D.C.: U.S. Government Printing Office).

Research and Special Programs Administration, U.S. Department of Transportation (1985). Annual Report on Hazardous Materials Transportation, Calendar Year 1984 (Washington, D.C.: U.S. Government Printing Office).

Slovic, Paul; B. Fischhoff; and, S. Lichtenstein (1980). "Facts and Fears: Understanding Perceived Risk," in Societal Risk Assessment: How Safe is Safe Enough?, edited by R. Schwing and W. Albers

University Center for Social and Urban Research (1987). "The Results of a Telephone Survey of 255 Households Conducted During the Summer of 1987 for Oak Ridge National Laboratories," University of Pittsburgh.

Walgren, Doug (1987). <u>Report to the 18th District from Congressman Doug Walgren: A Monthy Report</u>, Washington, D.C.

11

Nuclear Emergencies

Joan B. Aron

Nuclear power generation is a large-scale, advanced technology whose growing pains in emergency planning and preparedness activities provide a good example of shifting values and priorities. Before 1970, little attention was given to emergency planning at nuclear power plants or to the involvement of state and local governments in the emergency planning and response process. After 1970, as more and larger nuclear plants were built and operated, regulations were issued that required each licensee to develop emergency plans to assure protection of the public health and safety in the event of an accidental radioactive release. Even then, however, the most severe type of nuclear accident (involving disruption of the core) was regarded as extremely remote, so unlikely that it did not need to be covered by emergency plans (Committee on Government Operations, 1979: 4). Emergency planning was regarded as a secondary consideration and received only modest attention from the utilities, the affected public, and the regulatory bodies.

Federal responsibilities for assisting state and local governments in developing plans for responding to radiological emergencies were outlined in a Federal Register notice, "Radiological Incident Emergency Response Planning: Fixed Facilities and Transportation," December 24, 1975 (40 FR 59494). The notice was promulgated by the former Federal Preparedness Agency (FPA) of the General Services Administration and gave the "lead agency" role to the Nuclear Regulatory Commission and support responsibilities to the Environmental Protection Agency, Department of Energy, Department of

Transportation, the (then) Department of Health, Education and Welfare, the (then) Defense Civil Preparedness Agency (DCPA), and the (then) Federal Disaster Assistance Administration (FDAA) of the Department of Housing and Urban Development. (President Carter combined three of these agencies-- FPA, DCPA and FDAA, into a new Federal Emergency Management Agency [FEMA] on July 15, 1979. Current federal agency assignments in radiological emergency planning and response were developed by the new agency, FEMA, and published on March 11, 1982 [45 FR 10758].)

As lead agency, the Nuclear Regulatory Commission (NRC) relied on guidance which had been developed by its predecessor, the Atomic Energy Commission. NRC could encourage, but not require, states with nuclear plants to develop emergency plans; most states did not choose to do so. Consequently, only eleven states had secured NRC concurrence of their plans at the time of the Three Mile Island (TMI) accident on March 28, 1979. Local emergency planning efforts were equally uneven. Local authorities were often uninformed about their expected role in responding to a nuclear emergency and, in the few cases where emergency plans existed, the plans did not include the entire area that could be affected by a nuclear release (GAO, 1979: 7).

Prior to Three Mile Island, each applicant for an operating license was required to include in its final safety analysis report emergency plans for notifying state and local authorities of potential off-site releases, providing assessments of the off-site hazard, and recommending protective measures. The applicant was also required to develop an emergency organization and to provide emergency radiological health services for licensee personnel within the boundaries of the reactor site. Beyond the site boundary, the applicant was merely obliged to obtain written agreements from local and state authorities that the officials could and would provide emergency assistance for the public in the event of a reactor accident. Such assistance was supposed to include public notification, evacuation capability, and appropriate emergency response organizations and personnel. Historically, these agreements by states and local governments were voluntary and were not included as a regulatory requirement in the licensing process. Hence, formal agreements were not always in place at the time licensing decisions were made and the actual capabilities represented by the voluntary agreements were not tested.

GROWTH OF PUBLIC CONCERN

During the late 1970s, serious questions were raised by concerned citizens, environmentalists, the General Accounting Office, and others regarding the actual capabilities of states and local governments to respond to accidents at commercial nuclear facilities. David Dinsmore Comey, a mathematician and persistent critic of nuclear power, pointed out that NRC licensed plants in states where evacuation plans were "virtually nonexistent or clearly inadequate. A utility need only state that it has made all necessary arrangements with public authorities and provide a minimal outline of the proposed plans" (1975). The Natural Resources Defense Council (NRDC) asserted that "the entire area of emergency planning and site suitability have been sadly neglected at the Commissioner level" and proposed that NRC gain assurance that emergency plans would be properly implemented, that potential health consequences of accidents be considered in approving nuclear plant sites, and that population concentrations around operating plants be periodically reviewed to determine whether additional plans were warranted (1978).

The General Accounting Office (GAO) was critical as well. In March 1979, GAO found only limited assurance that persons living or working near nuclear facilities would be adequately protected in the case of a serious--although unlikely--nuclear accident and recommended that license applicants be required to enter into agreements with state and local agencies assuring the latter's full participation in annual emergency drills. GAO (1979: i) also recommended that, if states or local authorities were unable to provide assurance that they could implement off-site protective actions, a potential site should be eliminated from consideration during the licensing process. In response, NRC stated that it relied primarily on site characteristics and design features of nuclear facilities to protect public health and safety. Although NRC agreed that improvements were needed in state and local preparedness efforts, it did not consider state and local plans "essential" in determining whether nuclear plants could be operated safely (GAO, 1979: vii).

During this pre-TMI period, state officials sought further guidance for developing emergency plans. A joint NRC/EPA Task Force on Emergency Planning convened in 1978 concluded in a document entitled "Planning Basis for the Development of State and Local Government Radiological Emergency Response Plans in Support of Light-Water Nuclear Power Plants" that no specific accident sequence existed that could be used for emergency planning purposes. Instead, the report recommended that plans be developed to address a wide variety of accident scenarios and consequences. The report also recommended that emergency planning zones (EPZs) be established around each nuclear power plant for emergency planning purposes of about ten miles in radius for the plume exposure pathway, and about fifty miles in radius for a second concentric ingestion exposure pathway for milk and agricultural products. These recommendations were published for public comment and were incorporated into the commission's emergency planning rule in August 1980.

POST-TMI: A REDUNDANCY OF COMMISSIONS

On March 28, 1979, the most serious accident in American nuclear power history occurred at the Three Mile Island Nuclear Station in Dauphin County, Pennsylvania, about ten miles southeast of Harrisburg on an island in the Susquehanna River. The accident heightened public awareness of the potential consequences of nuclear power accidents and focused public attention and interest on the need for upgrading emergency preparedness by the utilities and federal, state, and local governments. The accident also stimulated the establishment of numerous investigating commissions and study groups to explore the causes and consequences of the accident and to make recommendations concerning future actions.

There was general agreement by each of the investigating commissions that serious deficiencies existed in the development, review, and implementation of emergency plans, in the definition and assignment of roles and responsibilities of the interested parties and government bodies, and in the interaction between them. The Kemeny Commission, named after its chairman, John G. Kemeny, president of Dartmouth College, was appointed by President Carter to investigate the accident and make recommendations. Among other things, the commission found that the quality of emergency plans among the many jurisdictions was highly uneven; that relationships among NRC, the utility, and state and local organizations were insufficiently coordinated to ensure an adequate level of preparedness for a serious radiological event; that public information was lacking; and that the roles of the commissioners were ill-defined. The Commission recommended "clear and consistent" emergency plans that laid out actions to be taken by public officials and the utilities in case of an accident, "flexible" plans based on various classes and types of accidents, expanded medical research on protective measures against radiation, public information and education programs, a study of risks in radiation-related evacuations, and coordination of federal technical support (Report of the President's Commission, 1979: 38-42).

The Rogovin Commission, named for Mitchell Rogovin, the attorney appointed to head NRC's Special Inquiry Group, agreed that improved emergency planning was warranted, arguing that future plants should be located in remote areas, that operating licenses be conditioned on approved and workable emergency plans, that minimum emergency planning zones be determined, that FEMA coordinate state and local planning efforts, and that NRC improve its emergency response function and assign a single director of its Executive Management Team to take charge during an emergency (Nuclear Regulatory Commission Special Inquiry Group, 1980: 129). The Subcommittee on Nuclear Regulation for the Senate Committee on the Environment and Public Works found that "effective emergency preparedness requires the assumption that serious accidents can happen and that adequate plans need to be made in advance to deal with them" (1980: 12). The subcommittee also agreed that such plans must consider a range of potential accidents and ensure availability of resources and procedures to deal with them.

NRC'S EMERGENCY PLANNING RULE (1980)

The TMI accident clearly showed that the protection afforded by proper plant siting and engineered safety features needed to be supplemented by assurance that the neighboring public could take protective actions during the course of an accident. The accident served as a catalyst in encouraging the development of emergency response plans and, stimulated by the various commissions that were appointed to investigate the accident, led to new responsibilities for the Federal Emergency Management Agency on the one hand and to the promulgation of a new emergency planning rule by the Nuclear Regulatory Commission on the other. In partial response to the Kemeny report, the president directed on December 7, 1979 that FEMA take lead responsibility for establishing and administering off-site emergency planning and response, for reviewing state emergency plans, and for coordinating federal agency assignments and responsibilities.

In July 1979, the commission initiated a rule making on the "Adequacy and Acceptance of Emergency Planning around Nuclear Facilities" which gave renewed emphasis to state and local participation and considered, among other matters, whether licenses for new or operating reactors should be conditioned on NRC approval of associated state and local emergency response plans. On August 19, 1980, the commission adopted a final rule requiring all power plant licensees and applicants for an operating license to submit comprehensive emergency response plans, together with the coordinated emergency plans of state and local governments, to NRC as a condition of continued operation of a nuclear plant or issuance of an operating license. No operating license could be issued for a reactor without a finding by NRC of reasonable assurance that adequate protective measures could and would be taken in the event of a radiological emergency. NRC's findings would rely in turn on a review of FEMA's findings and determinations as to whether off-site emergency plans were adequate and capable of being implemented, as well as its own assessment of the adequacy of the applicant's onsite emergency plans and their capability for implementation. If NRC determined that off-site preparedness at an operating plant did not provide adequate protective measures and if the deficiencies identified in FEMA's findings were not corrected within 120 days, NRC had to determine whether the plant should be shut down until the deficiencies were remedied, some other enforcement action was appropriate, or no enforcement action was needed. The decision on enforcement action was guided by such factors as the significance of the deficiency, the taking of adequate compensatory actions, or "other compelling reasons" for continued operation.

The emergency planning rule included the NRC/EPA recommendation of a ten-mile emergency planning zone and a fifty-mile ingestion pathway. Significantly, in the "Supplementary Information" section of the rule, NRC acknowledged the possibility that the operation of some reactors might be adversely affected through the inaction of state and local governments or by their inability to comply with NRC's rules. Nevertheless, the commission stated that it believed that state and local officials would serve as partners in emergency planning and preparedness and endeavor to provide fully for public protection.

RECENT POLICY ISSUES

Jurisdictional and Funding Problems

One of the early problems arising out of the new requirements in the emergency planning area underscored the marked fragmentation of jurisdiction and responsibility within the public sector. As a direct result of the expansion of the planning effort to encompass the approximately ten-mile radius emergency planning zone, the number of state and local governments involved in radiological emergency plans and exercises added up to about 400. As of September 30, 1982, 108 state and 255 local government plans had to be developed and tested for licensed and operating nuclear power plants. These numbers did not take into account the approximately 200 state and local plans affected by nuclear power plants then under construction. Richard T. Sylves (1984: 397) points out, for example, that in an unusual case, the fifty-mile ingestion pathway for Yankee Atomic Electric's Rowe Generating Station in Massachusetts embraced parts of five states, eleven Massachusetts townships, and six townships in Vermont. Review of plans and exercises for these jurisdictions imposed a severe burden on NRC and FEMA resources.

At the same time, many of the state and local governments lacked the resources and technical expertise to undertake the development and implementation of emergency plans. Since no federal funds were available to defray the costs of developing and maintaining these plans at the state and local level, these governments had to turn to the utilities for financial help. In some cases (seventeen states), state laws were passed requiring the utilities to pay for the development of emergency plans in either annual or one-time payments. For example, the California legislature passed a bill in 1982 requiring nuclear power companies to contribute $300,000 per reactor each year to the state and $100,000 to local governments for emergency planning. In New York State, utilities had to pay a tax of $250,000 per year for emergency planning for each reactor. In other cases, formal contracts existed between the states and local governments and utilities. Since emergency evacuation plans needed constant upgrading and improvement, local officials did not always consider funds received under state law or by agreement to be adequate (GAO, 1984: 15).

Some local governments refused to participate unless the utilities provided new equipment or additional personnel. In Missouri, for example, four local governments indicated they would develop plans for the Callaway nuclear plant site only if the utility provided funds for equipment and personnel. In still another example, St. Lucie County, Florida, requested the utility to pay an estimated $40 million for a bridge, sirens, a central communications center, a fire station, and tests of the emergency plan. The utility did not heed the request (New York Times, February 8, 1987). While some utilities and government observers regarded this as "political extortion" (Rosenbaum, 1987: 152) GAO found that "most of the utility, federal, state and local officials . . . agreed that the costs of offsite planning and preparedness are part of the costs of nuclear power which the utility and eventually the electric ratepayer or shareholder should bear" (GAO, 1984: 16).

Shared Governance

The presidential directive of December 7, 1979, which assigned responsibilities for off-site radiological preparedness to FEMA, directed NRC to coordinate its planning activities with the new organization. The two agencies cooperated in developing a joint Memorandum of Understanding (MOU), dated November 4, 1980 (and revised April 18, 1985), which established a formal framework for policy agreement on the conduct of agency missions. Both agencies also worked together in the preparation of joint guidance for assessing off-site and on-site emergency planning and preparedness. The standards that NRC and FEMA used in making determinations of the adequacy of the utilities' plans were based on the state-of-the-art knowledge in preplanning for technologically based accidents.

The MOU assigned responsibility to FEMA to take the lead in assessing off-site emergency plans and response, making findings on the adequacy of off-site plans available, and verifying that plans could be implemented on a continuing basis. NRC's responsibilities were to assess the licensee's emergency planning and preparedness, review FEMA's findings, and determine the overall state of emergency preparedness. FEMA reviewed state and local preparedness with the help of Regional Assistance Committees, interagency groups composed of representatives of the nine federal agencies with radiological response capabilities and responsibilities. Periodically (annually at first, semiannually after 1984), joint exercises were held with participation by the utility, states, and local governments to demonstrate their degree of preparedness for an accident. NRC assisted FEMA in off-site plan review through its participation as a member of the Regional Advisory Committee. The two agencies also met periodically to coordinate activities through the mechanism of the NRC/FEMA Steering Committee on Emergency Preparedness, on which both agencies had an equivalent number of votes.

Despite these elaborate efforts to delineate each agency's responsibilities, the shared involvement has not always been smooth. It is awkward for NRC, the agency with legal authority over power reactors, to be dependent upon and make regulatory judgments on the basis of information gathered by another non-regulatory agency. As GAO has pointed out, this was not always easy to obtain or timely when it became available (1984: 15). Moreover, FEMA has ten federal regions and NRC has five--with no congruence in federal boundaries. NRC regions often have to deal with several different FEMA regions whose professional judgments and assessments of state and local problems are not always consistent from region to region (May and Williams, 1986: 154). (For example, FEMA found the lack of agreement with a bus company for evacuation purposes at the Indian Point plant in New York State a major deficiency at that site but the same problem did not bar a favorable finding at eleven other plants.) Furthermore, FEMA's regional administrators are political appointees and more independent in program implementation--and less responsive to direction and control--than are those at NRC.

Over time, in this "uneasy marriage of nuclear regulators and civil defense planners," differences of opinions have developed (Sylves, 1984: 394). For example, the two agencies have not always agreed with respect to their assessments of emergency preparedness at the Perry plant in Ohio, the Shoreham plant in Suffolk County, New York, and the Seabrook plant in New Hampshire (Newsday, 1984). Such disagreements are not surprising in view of the agencies' different roles and constituencies. FEMA is primarily concerned with planning at the state and local level and is seen as an advocate of state and local governments. NRC, on the other hand, is concerned with the safety of nuclear reactors and is often perceived by the states and locals as an advocate of the nuclear industry.

Fragmented Responsibility

One of the principal points raised by the post-TMI investigating commissions concerned confusion at the reactor site during the accident resulting from the ill-defined roles and responsibilities of the individuals and agencies involved in managing the emergency. As Kemeny described it, "the response to the emergency was dominated by an atmosphere of almost total confusion. . . . Many key recommendations were made by individuals who were not in possession of accurate information, and those who managed the accident were slow to realize the significance and

implications of the events that had taken place"
(Report of the President's Commission, 1979: 17).
Kemeny was critical of the role played by the NRC
commissioners, among others, questioning whether a
collegial body was suitable for managing an emergency.
The Rogovin Commission agreed with Kemeny's view,
arguing that the agency should be reorganized along
the lines of a single administrator, that changes
should be made in the NRC's emergency response
function, and that decision making about protective
actions should be clarified (NRC Special Inquiry
Group, 1980: 115). The Senate Subcommittee on Nuclear
Regulation concurred, finding a lack of agreement
about commissioners' roles and responsibilities, a
lack of coordination among NRC offices, particularly
between the regional and headquarters staffs, and
confusion among state agencies, utilities, and NRC
about the responsibilities held by each in an
emergency situation (1980: 79).

As stated earlier, the president directed FEMA to
take lead responsibility for establishing and
administering off-site emergency planning and
response, for reviewing state emergency plans, and for
coordinating federal agency assignments and
responsibilities. The president also issued
Reorganization Plan No. 1 of 1980, which conferred on
the NRC chairman important powers to serve as the
principal executive officer of the commission and
transferred to the chairman all of the commission's
functions pertaining to an emergency at a licensed
facility, "including the functions of declaring,
responding, issuing orders, determining specific
policies, advising the civil authorities and the
public, directing, and coordinating actions relative
to such emergency incident" (45 FR 40561).

NRC also sought to clarify roles and
responsibilities in a new publication dealing with the
agency's Incident Response Plan. This document makes
it clear that, in the event of an incident at a
licensed facility, the licensee (in conjunction with
state and local authorities) bears primary
responsibility. Specifically, the licensee is
responsible for mitigating the consequences of the
incident, for providing protective action
recommendations to state and local governments, and
for notifying NRC. NRC monitors the incident to ensure
that appropriate off-site recommendations are made,
assists and advises the licensee, informs officials
and the public about the incident, coordinates federal
technical support, and obtains expertise and equipment
for the licensee as needed.

The Incident Response Plan makes it clear that authority and responsibility for managing NRC's emergency response efforts are transferred to a senior on-site manager as soon as possible after the senior representative arrives at the site and is prepared to accept responsibility. State and local authorities are responsible for taking actions to protect the public from the consequences of the incident, and FEMA coordinates all off-site nontechnical activities of federal organizations. In addition, a Federal Radiological Emergency Response Plan was published on November 8, 1985, and is periodically tested. This plan provides the mechanism for coordinating the federal response to all types of radiological accidents, including commercial nuclear power plants, and provides an integrated description of the authority and responsibility of each federal agency.

Inadequate Testing of Plans

Since 1980, the emergency planning and preparedness process has worked in most instances in a positive way. Nevertheless, some observers maintain that problems remain.

An early FEMA official, for example, described "generic weaknesses" in relation to many emergency planning functions: direction and control arrangements, public education and warning systems, coordination of medical facilities, accident assessment, contamination monitoring, and exercises (Jaske, 1983: 10). GAO (1984: ii) also identified weaknesses in the exercises that tested the adequacy of state and local preparedness, in the preparation of exercise scenarios, in the guidance furnished to state and local governments concerning their emergency plans, and in the implementation of the federal response plan. More recently, Walter A. Rosenbaum (1987: 152) has noted that many critics believe that NRC now enjoys too much discretion in determining the adequacy of site emergency plans and too often accepts plans that are seriously deficient. Rosenbaum also claims that NRC uses artificial and unrealistic scenarios and engages in insufficient testing of plans.

Notwithstanding these critical observations, nuclear emergency plans and equipment (such as sirens) have provided a basis for responding to other types of emergency situations, particularly chemical releases, and have proved to be workable and useful. It is believed that the deficiencies mentioned above reflect tractable problems that can be corrected over time should the agencies wish to devote the needed time and resources. Far more serious are the problems involving federalism issues--the division of powers between the federal government and the state. These will be considered next.

CONSTITUTIONAL ISSUES

Constitutional issues involving the appropriate division of emergency management responsibilities among federal, state, and local governments present more difficult problems. These issues typically involve the question of federal preemption over radiological health and safety versus constitutionally protected states rights and state police powers. Pursuant to the Atomic Energy and Energy Reorganization Acts, the federal statutes from which NRC derives its authority to license commercial nuclear power plants, the federal government possesses exclusive jurisdiction over the use of nuclear materials and the construction and operation of nuclear production and utilization facilities. The issue in the emergency planning case originates in the implementation of the 1980 emergency planning rule in which the issuance of licenses for new nuclear plants or the continued operation of existing plants was conditioned on the existence of adequate state and local plans. This meant, in effect, that state and local governments could veto or "hold hostage" the operation of nuclear plants through their refusal to develop emergency plans. And some have done just this.

The Shoreham plant, built by the Long Island Lighting Company (LILCO) in Suffolk County, New York, has been the most visible example of intergovernment conflict. In this case, the county determined during the latter stages of plant construction that workable evacuation plans could not be developed and refused to participate in emergency planning or response activities. Governor Mario Cuomo of New York supported the county's decision and stated that he would not overrule or superimpose a state plan upon the local authorities. Although LILCO submitted its own emergency plan in an effort to show that emergency response could be implemented without state or county support, both government bodies contended that the utility lacked legal authority to implement its plan without their cooperation. LILCO countered this view on preemption grounds, claiming that the federal government has exclusive jurisdiction over radiological health and safety and therefore preempts the traditional police powers exercised by the state and localities. LILCO also contended, as does NRC, that the state and county do what they can to protect their citizens and would follow the utility plan during a real emergency for lack of an alternative response plan. Governor Cuomo has developed an agreement which would enable LILCO to sell the plant to a state agency that would close the reactor and dismantle it. The agreement awaits legislative approval.

A somewhat similar situation exists at the Seabrook plant in New Hampshire, where emergency planning is the largest obstacle to an operating license that the owners face. Seabrook's ten-mile emergency planning zone encompasses seventeen towns in New Hampshire and six in Massachusetts. Although the governor of New Hampshire has been a staunch backer of the plant and has submitted emergency plans to FEMA, residents and town officials in Massachusetts doubt whether adequate preparation can be made for an emergency and have received the support of Governor Michael Dukakis. (Meanwhile, the utility has filed for bankruptcy protection from its creditors, the first major public utility to do so since the 1929 Depression.) Presently, emergency planning issues are being litigated and it is uncertain whether or when the plant will go into operation.

Still another example of federal-state disagreement can be drawn from the Ohio experience in which Governor Richard Celeste questioned the adequacy of emergency evacuation plans for two nuclear power plants, Davis-Besse and Perry 1 (August 1986), and appointed his own safety review panel to identify measures to improve emergency planning around the plants. Although Governor Celeste was unsuccessful in his effort to stop the restart of Davis-Besse and the full power operation of Perry 1, the panel's report, which called for use of the emergency planning issue as the basis for expanding the rights of states into the licensing process, posed another worrisome challenge to NRC and federal authority (Toledo Ohio Blade, 1987).

Congressional Action and Reaction

Congress enacted provisions dealing with emergency planning for nuclear power plants in the NRC Authorization Act for FY80 (PL 96-295). The act directed the commission to adopt standards for judging the adequacy of emergency plans and to establish regulations making the existence of an adequate emergency plan a prerequisite for issuance of a new operating license. In the same act, Congress reaffirmed its preference for a state or local plan that met all applicable NRC standards; in the absence of an adequate state or local plan, it permitted NRC to evaluate a utility-prepared emergency plan. The authorization provided that NRC could issue an operating license if it determined that a state, local, or utility plan provided reasonable assurance that public health or safety would not be endangered by operation of the facility. Congress reaffirmed its intent by adopting similar provisions in the authorization acts for FY82/83 and FY84/85 (PL 97-415, Sec. 5, and PL 98-553, Sec. 108, respectively).

Some members of Congress gave a similar message to FEMA. The conference report which accompanied the 1986 HUD-Independent Agencies Appropriations Bill (HR 3038) reflected the concerns of the House and Senate conferees that state or local government entities might refuse to participate in the preparation, exercise, or implementation of emergency preparedness plans and thereby veto the operation of commercial nuclear facilities. In the event of such inaction by states or local governments, the appropriations subcommittee instructed FEMA

> to presume that Federal, state and local governments will abide by their legal duties to protect public health and safety in an actual emergency. However, where state and local participation in the exercise or implementation of offsite plans is inadequate, the Committee intends for FEMA as a last resort to coordinate the supplemental assistance of federal agencies that are expected to provide requisite resources within their authorities. (Letter from Chairman of the House HUD-Independent Agencies Appropriations Subcommittee to Julius Becton, Director, FEMA, 1985).

Congress has continued to uphold federal authority against state action to prevent operation of a nuclear plant. In August 1987, the House of Representatives defeated a proposal by Representative Edward Markey (D-Mass.) that would have prohibited NRC from using FY88 or FY89 appropriations to license Shoreham or Seabrook unless the plants met existing NRC emergency planning requirements. The measure was targeted at a proposed rule change that would clarify NRC's authority to issue an operating license in the absence of state and local participation in emergency planning. The vote was acclaimed by the nuclear industry as affirmation of congressional support for nuclear power.

Stalemate

By 1986, the federal-state confrontation over emergency planning in New York and Massachusetts had deteriorated to a stalemate, with strong feelings on all sides. Samuel Speck (1986), former associate director of FEMA, suggested that states and local officials who objected to nuclear power might not only refuse to participate in the emergency planning process but "simply do a lousy job of offsite planning and exercising in a deliberate effort to show how bad they are, so that a finding of reasonable assurance could not be made." At the time, he saw few options to overcome the stalemate: (1) continue the status quo; (2) increase federal involvement in the form of a federal brigade or Special Weapons Assault Team (SWAT); or (3) remove emergency planning from the critical path of licensing a nuclear plant. In the event, he was not optimistic about preserving the nuclear option.

NRC too was becoming increasingly concerned by state intervention in the Shoreham and Seabrook cases. On March 6, 1987, the commission proposed an amended emergency planning rule to allow utilities to obtain an operating license under certain conditions even if state or local governments refused to participate. The conditions included a demonstration by utilities that any deficiencies in their plan could be remedied or adequately compensated by "reasonable" state and local cooperation, that a good faith effort had been made to obtain state and local cooperation, and that the utility plan compensated for state and local noncooperation and was filed with state and local governments. The proposed rule change rested on arguments of "fairness" and "equity," based on the notion that a utility could invest billions of dollars in a nuclear reactor and, once the reactor was constructed, could be frustrated in its effort to operate it because of local opposition.

Hearings on the proposed rule before NRC and Congress provoked unprecedented debate. One side saw it as a usurpation of constitutionally protected state police powers and a lessening of public health and safety requirements; the other side took the position that it "merely removes a specious licensing obstacle and protects the integrity of the licensing process" (Inside NRC, 1987). Typical of the comments were those of Governor Mario Cuomo of New York who called the proposed rule change "a blatant political fix" which flew in the face of traditional concepts of the state's power to protect the well-being of its citizens. He charged the commission with putting the interests of the nuclear industry and its investors ahead of public safety (New York Times, February 8, 1987). The Union of Concerned Scientists (UCS) and the Northeast Coalition on Nuclear Pollution believed the proposed rule change "essentially guts" the emergency planning rule. UCS, in particular, found the proposal the "functional equivalent of doing away with emergency planning" (Nucleonics Week, 1987).

James K. Asseltine, an NRC commissioner, said he believed that the proposal undermined the very foundation upon which emergency planning is based and, with a view toward Shoreham and Seabrook, stated that the commission's commitment to emergency planning only lasted as long as it did not get in the way of expeditious licensing of plants (Newsday, 1987). FEMA expressed serious concerns about the prospective rule's impact also, warning, among other things, that it incorporated a fundamental change in the way that off-site emergency planning would be evaluated by FEMA, would eliminate the need for full participation exercises both before and after licensing, would "seriously diminish" the value of exercises, would increase risk to population of affected emergency planning zones, and would not demonstrate the preparedness of state and local governments in a meaningful way (McLoughlin, 1987). Following a meeting with NRC representatives on October 9, 1987, however, FEMA advised NRC that it "remained committed to work cooperatively with NRC whichever way the decision came out" (Nuclear Regulatory Commission, 1987a).

At the same time, Chairman J. Bennett Johnston (D-La.) of the Senate Energy and Natural Resources Committee, ranking minority member James McClure (R-Idaho), and at least fifteen additional House members supported the proposed revision. The Atomic Industrial Forum also favored the change, on the basis that "it is a shame to let plants that are 99 percent finished just sit there and go to waste." Strong support of the rule was expressed by the U.S. Department of Energy, stating, among other things, that the amended rule "would . . . help to assure the availability of nuclear power to meet future energy needs" (Nucleonics Week, 1987).

The commission received 11,500 individual letters on the proposed rule, a record for NRC proceedings: about 5,400 in favor, 5,600 opposed, and 540 neutral. In addition, it received signatures on petitions with about 16,300 in opposition and about 27,000 form letters in opposition. The staff's analysis of the comments indicated that favorable comments were received from nuclear industry representatives, many citizens, some public interest groups, some state and local officials, and DOE. Those against the rule included many citizens opposed to operation of Shoreham and Seabrook, most state officials and agencies, and some public interest and environmental groups (Nuclear Regulatory Commission, 1987b: 25).

The commission's final rule, issued in November 1987, was based on what the commission saw as congressional intent embodied in the many appropriation acts, to provide the utilities with an avenue to submit their own emergency plans in cases where state and local officials, by refusing to participate, could block operation of a plant. The rule rested on the "realism" argument first articulated by the commission in the 1986 Shoreham proceedings which held that, in an actual emergency, state and local officials would act to protect their citizens and that it was appropriate for NRC to take account of this in evaluating the adequacy of an evacuation plan. In support of this view, the amended rule instructed a presiding licensing board to presume that state and local authorities would generally follow the utility plan. The NRC chairman defended the adopted rule, stating that "it is not a panacea for an particular plant. . . . [Nor does it] guarantee a license to any applicant (Nuclear Regulatory Commission, 1987a). The commission has voted to consider a utility-sponsored evacuation plan for the six Massachusetts towns situated within a ten-mile radius of the Seabrook plant in lieu of a state proposal. The states of Massachusetts and New York and the Union of Concerned Scientists have signified their intent to challenge the rule change in the courts.

Presidential Action

The president first intervened in the Shoreham situation in 1984, making a commitment to a former Republican congressman, William Carney, that "this administration does not favor the imposition of federal government authority over objections of state and local governments in matters regarding the adequacy of an emergency evacuation plan for a nuclear plant such as Shoreham." Since that time, the U.S. Department of Energy has been trying to develop options to help license the Shoreham and Seabrook plants (Journal of Commerce, 1988). On November 18, 1988, President Reagan issued an Executive Order giving the federal government broad new authority to prepare, coordinate, and contribute federal resources to evacuation plans for nuclear power plants in the event that states or local governments decline to participate. While the secretary of the Department of

Energy called the action "an important step forward in the process of licensing Shoreham and other nuclear power plants" (New York Times, November 19, 1988), many federal officials and observers believe that the order will have little impact on the troubled plants.

CONCLUSION

Given the current ferment about Shoreham and Seabrook, it is easy to lose sight of the very real improvement that has taken place in emergency planning and response at the nation's nuclear plants. The emergency planning process and the exercises have provided a level of assurance that people from private industry and public agencies at different governmental levels can work together in responding to emergencies. By and large, NRC, FEMA, the utilities, and the political jurisdictions have engaged in a cooperative effort to improve the process and make it function more effectively. Despite NRC's lack of direct regulatory authority over state and local governments, these jurisdictions have, albeit slowly in some instances, participated in the development of emergency plans and accepted responsibility for protecting the health and welfare of their citizens in radiological emergencies.

At the same time, the impact of the Chernobyl accident is strongly felt, and some state and local officials are seeking to expand their oversight of nuclear power plant operation. In 1986, the National Governors Association (NGA) Committee on Energy and the Environment approved a motion calling for state participation in nuclear safety, including the establishment of their own safety standards in cases where they believed federal standards to be lax. In February 1987, Idaho Governor Cecil Andrus was named to head an NGA task force on nuclear safety that would try to determine the proper role for the states in reactor safety and evacuation planning and, at their annual summer meeting in July 1987, the governors adopted a nuclear energy resolution calling for NRC to respond to a state's interest in setting stricter safety standards for nuclear plants (Wall Street Journal, 1986).

This view of the states as strong contenders in nuclear power policy making is not necessarily new; states have long since emerged as influential players in shaping federal policy and programs in nuclear energy. In place of the tidy demarcation of federal and state roles that characterized intergovernmental relations in nuclear energy prior to the 1970s, we now find a diffusion of lines of authority and spheres of jurisdiction in which the boundaries between federal and state concerns are narrowing and becoming less clearly defined (Aron, 1979: 469; Walker, 1981: 233). In 1979, states pursued regulatory activities that impinged on nuclear generation in rate regulation, environment controls, and land-use powers; in the 1980s, states are using the emergency planning issue as one more vehicle to expand state authority into nuclear operation in general. The passage of recent legislation by the State of Maine to establish a state nuclear safety emergency planning zone extending approximately one mile beyond NRC's emergency planning zone and providing for additional nuclear safety advisors at a nuclear plant is a recent case in point.

As with NRC's amended rule, there are divergent views on what the appropriate state role in emergency planning should be. On the one hand, it can be argued that off-site emergency planning authority has always been considered to lie within the purview of the state and such authority includes inaction as well as action. (However, the decision not to act is not without a penalty. Should a state decline to develop the required emergency plans, it does so knowing that it will have to forego the use of nuclear power to meet its citizens' energy needs.) State governments presently look upon emergency planning as a bona fide safety issue, with a direct bearing on the use of their police powers to safeguard health and safety. On the other hand, there are representatives of the academic community, industry, and journalism, who believe that the growing state assertiveness in this area threatens the national interest in maintaining an ample energy supply and that in energy, the overriding national interest lies in taking whatever steps are necessary to break our dependence on foreign oil (Chubb, 1987).

While arguments are made on all sides with respect to "national purpose" and the proper division of government responsibilities in radiological health and safety issues, it seems unrealistic to expect the states, on their own volition, to relinquish authority to a national interest that is designed to serve a different constituency at a different place and with a different set of policy choices. Although federal officials and industry representatives may be increasingly concerned about the new state assertiveness, it is unlikely that states will back off unless their legislative judgments and administrative determinations in this instance are overturned by the courts. Others have noted that the Burger court expanded authority of state police power in questions previously thought to be preempted by federal law; it is not yet known what the track record of the Rehnquist court will be (Walker, 1981: 141).

Meanwhile, there are a few points on which all observers can agree. First, it is clear that emergency planning and preparedness have been raised to an unprecedented level of public visibility. Second, the experience in developing and testing emergency response plans at more than sixty sites in thirty-one states has in many cases raised the level of capability of the states and localities for managing emergencies resulting from other potentially hazardous activities. In support of this point, a FEMA official notes that "the radiological emergency preparedness program has been a key element in stimulating the entire process of accident and disaster preparedness . . . [and] many of the concepts of preparedness planning and exercising for accidents involving radioactive materials will serve as core elements of future comprehensive emergency management for years to come" (Jaske, 1983: 10). One could also argue that the often contentious political environment in which nuclear emergency plans are formulated and implemented should provide a generous sampling of the political implications of emergency planning in general.

In conclusion, the difficulties noted here are not intended to obscure the important points. Notwithstanding current problems, there is ample reason to believe that emergency planning can be effectively implemented to protect public health and safety. In the case of new reactors--those not yet built--measures can be taken to avoid intergovernment confrontation of the Shoreham and Seabrook type. First, new criteria can be developed to site future nuclear reactors in areas distant from concentrations of population, where evacuation effectiveness can be maximized, as both the Kemeny and Rogovin Commissions have suggested. Further, it is conceivable that a commitment can be secured from a public service commission of the state in which a reactor is to be located that the certificate of public convenience and necessity issued at the time of construction includes state cooperation in emergency planning. Such actions would assure state participation in emergency planning prior to construction instead of when a plant is nearing completion, as is now the case. The mechanics of the emergency plan could be worked out subsequently once the plant is built. Finally, with existing reactors, much has been accomplished in successfully upgrading emergency planning and preparedness over the last decade. Should a serious accident occur, we are far better prepared than we were a decade ago to provide protective action for affected citizens.

REFERENCES

Aron, Joan B. (1979). "Intergovernmental Politics of Energy," Policy Analysis 5 (Fall).

Chubb, John E. (1987). "License Seabrook, Shoreham," New York Times (August 3).

Comey, David (1975). "Do Not Go Gentle into that Radiation Zone," Bulletin of Atomic Scientists (November).

Committee on Government Operations (1979). Emergency Planning Around U.S. Nuclear Powerplants, House Report No. 96-413 (Washington, D.C.: U.S. Government Printing Office).

General Accounting Office (GAO)(1979). Areas Around Nuclear Facilities Should be Better Prepared for Radiological Emergencies (Washington, D.C.: General Accounting Office, EMD-78-110).

___ (1979). Areas Around Nuclear Facilities (Washington, D.C.: General Accounting Office, EMD-78-110).

___ (1984). Further Actions Needed to Improve Emergency Preparedness Around Nuclear Power Plants (Washington, D.C.: General Accounting Office, GAO/RCED-84-43).

Inside NRC (1986). November 10; (1987) May 11; (1988) February 11.

Jaske, Robert T. (1983). "Emergency Preparedness-- Status and Outlook," Nuclear Safety 24 (January-February).

Letter from Chairman of the House and Senate HUD-Independent Agencies Appropriations Subcommittee to Julius W. Becton, Director, FEMA (1985), November 13.

McLoughlin, David, FEMA Deputy Associate Director, State and Local Programs and Support (1987). Letter to Samuel J. Chilk, Secretary, NRC, April 28.

May, Peter J., and Walter Williams (1986). Disaster Policy Implementation: Managing Programs under Shared Governance (New York: Plenum).

Natural Resources Defense Council (1978). Letter and Comments on NRC Proposed Emergency Planning Amendments, October 23.

Newsday (1987). April 29.

New York Times (1987). February 8, February 15, and March 1.

Nuclear Regulatory Commission Special Inquiry Group (1980). Three Mile Island: A Report to the Commissioners and the Public (Washington, D.C.: Nuclear Regulatory Commission, January 24).

____ (1987a). SECY Paper 87-257 "Emergency Planning Rule," October 13.

____ (1987b). Staff briefing on Emergency Planning Rule, October 22,25-28.

Nucleonics Week (1987). February 12.

Report of the President's Commission on the Accident at Three Mile Island (1979).(Washington, D.C., October).

Rosenbaum, Walter A. (1987). Energy, Politics and Public Policy, 2d Edition (Washington, D.C.: Congressional Quarterly).

Speck, Samuel W. (1986). "The Federal Perspective," American Nuclear Society topical meeting on radiological accidents, Bethesda, Md., September 15-17.

Subcommittee on Nuclear Regulation for the Senate Committee on Environment and Public Works (1980). Nuclear Accident and Recovery at Three Mile Island: A Special Investigation, June 12.

Sylves, Richard B. (1984). "Nuclear Power Plants and Emergency Planning: An Intergovernmental Nightmare," Public Administration Review (September/October).

Toledo Ohio Blade (1987). February 15.

Wall Street Journal (1986). September 19.

12

Air Disasters

Margaret Baty

During the early years of aviation it was not uncommon for a pilot to experience a number of mishaps during his flying career. Due to the slower speeds of the aircraft, injuries to the pilots were often minimal. And, because earlier models carried very few passengers, the number of airplane victims was also very small. The general public considered those who flew "daredevils" and stunt pilots.

The first fatality to occur in a powered airplane occurred on September 17, 1908. Orville Wright was in Virginia demonstrating the Wright biplane to the U.S. Army Signal Corps and had taken Lieutenant Thomas Selfridge on board for a demonstration ride. During the course of the flight one of the propeller blades failed; the plane made a crash landing from a height of seventy-five feet. Lieutenant Selfridge died and Orville Wright suffered serious injuries (Taylor et al., 1979).

An aviation disaster which dramatically influenced the public's view of air safety was the Hindenburg catastrophe in 1939. The loss of so many lives in an air device left an indelible impression on many. The accident was reported live on the radio, headlines blared across the nation, film crews were on the spot instantaneously (they were prepared to film the approaching craft). These films were later shown in movie theaters nationwide. Several factors were responsible for making this accident unique: the publicity encompassing the event, the number of fatalities and serious injuries, and the speed of the occurrence.

Since that time, aviation accidents have made good headlines for the press. As air travel became a more widely accepted means of transportation for the average person, the public more than ever wanted to know the causes of accidents. Information pertinent to aviation accidents is made available to the public through the Public Affairs Office of the Federal Aviation Administration and through formal written reports from the National Transportation Safety Board.

In the early years of aviation, the Aeronautics Branch and later the Bureau of Air Commerce were charged with the task of promoting air commerce, maintaining air safety, and investigating air accidents. This dual role meant that when a disaster did occur not only was the Aeronautics Branch or Bureau of Air Commerce investigating the components of the aviation industry involved (manufacturers, air carriers, and pilots), but supposedly their own agency as well. It was not until a crash occurred in 1935, taking the life of a prominent U.S. senator, that questions arose regarding the feasibility of the present aviation checks and balances system (Komons, 1978).

Today, the Federal Aviation Administration (FAA) is providing safety recommendations based on the accident investigations of the National Transportation Safety Board (NTSB), an independent agency of the FAA (aviation's certifying body). From these suggestions often come revisions and additions to the FAA regulations. Aviators have been known to say that the regulations they follow were written in blood.

THE HUMAN ELEMENT

Accidents do not simply happen; they are caused. In transportation accidents humans are often cited as the primary cause. Human error, usually referred to as "pilot error," is a leading determining agent in aviation accident reports. One individual described the human element as "the nut behind the wheel."

According to statistics, there was an estimated total of 709,118 active pilots in the United States in 1986. The total was down slightly from 1985 when the estimated number was 709,540. And, in 1980 there were 827,071 registered pilots. Aviation showed a steady decline between 1981 and 1986, with a slight exception from 1983 to 1984, as far as the pilot population was concerned (Federal Aviation Administration, 1986). FAA figures also indicated that the age of the average pilot is between thirty and thirty-nine years of age (Federal Aviation Administration, 1986).

To fully understand the large numbers of people involved in the total National Airspace System, here are some nonpilot population numbers (based on 1986 data):

1. Mechanics--284,241

2. Ground instructors--59,443

3. Dispatchers--9,025

4. Control tower operators--22,036

5. Flight navigators--1,512

6. Flight engineers--46,323

Even these figures do not account for all persons involved in aviation (e.g., weather specialists, refueling operations personnel, etc.). And, though FAA has its safety programs, federal regulations, inspections, and careful monitoring of the various phases of air travel, accidents still happen.

THE FEDERAL ROLE

When an aircraft accident occurs several individuals and agencies take part in the investigative process. The government agency charged with the responsibility of determining the probable cause of any transportation accident is the National Transportation Safety Board (NTSB), initially a branch of the Department of Transportation (DOT). DOT was established by Congress with the Department of Transportation Act of 1966 to meet the following objectives:

1. To assure the coordinated, effective administration of the transportation programs of the federal government

2. To facilitate the development and improvement of coordinated transportation services to be provided by private enterprise of federal, state, and local governments, carriers, labor, and other interested parties toward the achievement of national transportation objectives

3. To stimulate technological advances in transportation

4. To provide leadership in the identification and solution of transportation problems

5. To develop and recommend to the president and the Congress for approval national transportation policies and programs to accomplish these objectives with full and appropriate consideration of the needs of the public, users, carriers, industry, labor, and the national defense

The National Transportation Safety Board was made an independent government agency by the Transportation Safety Act of 1974. NTSB is responsible for the investigation of civil aircraft accidents and it is the duty of the board (Federal Aviation Act of 1958, Title VII and the Transportation Safety Act of 1974) to:

1. Make rules and regulations governing notification and reporting of accidents involving civil aircraft

2. Investigate these accidents and report the facts, conditions, and circumstances relating to each accident and its probable cause

3. Make recommendations to the administrator of the Federal Aviation Administration that, in NTSB's opinion, will tend to prevent similar accidents in the future

4. Make reports public in a form that NTSB deems to be in the public interest

5. Determine what will best reduce or eliminate the possibility of accidents or their recurrence by conducting special studies and investigations on matters with regard to safety in air navigation and accident prevention

The Safety Board has the authority to take possession of the wreckage and prevent or direct its removal, pending completion of the investigation. The investigator-in-charge will examine facts, conditions, and circumstances of the accident. After all information has been reported to the NTSB headquarters in Washington, D.C., and any necessary laboratory tests are completed, the board will publish a report indicating probable cause. (Such reports are available from the NTSB Accident Inquiry Section, Washington, D.C. 20594.)

NTSB Team Concept

Investigation of catastrophic aircraft accidents by NTSB is normally conducted utilizing a team approach. The formal team investigation, involving wreckage recovery, security, field investigation, public hearings, and report writing, is conducted under the direction of an NTSB investigator. The groups include investigation, operations, and airworthiness specialists (U.S. Department of Transportation, 1982).

Board technical specialists head the investigation groups. These group chairpersons may be assisted by technical specialists representing the state of registry, the operator, crew organizations, manufacturers, and other selected experts who can contribute to the investigation. The primary function of each group is to examine all facts within their specialized area. A secondary function of the group is the apprising of other team members of specific group findings. Frequently one group uncovers information which will serve as a lead to another group. Apprising team members of investigative findings is accomplished through a daily progress report meeting.

These teams are most frequently referred to as "Go Teams" and are composed of as many as ten members of NTSB (Triplett, 1987: 48). They are on call twenty-four hours a day, to be on location at an aircraft accident site when the call comes. NTSB has ten field offices located throughout the United States with an average of ten air investigators per site.

Operations Groups

The operations area of an aircraft accident investigation includes operations in general, air traffic control, human factors, witness information, meteorological conditions, cockpit voice recorders, and performance. The operations investigation is best conducted by assigning separate groups. Each group headed by a chairperson can then concentrate on a specific portion of the operations investigation. Coordination is effected among group chairpersons to ensure investigative coverage in areas where more than one group may have a responsibility. For example, the operations group may coordinate their questioning of the crew with the Witness, Human Factors, or Cockpit Voice Recorder Groups (U.S. Department of Transportation, 1982).

The General Operations Group is responsible for investigating flight planning, dispatching procedures, airport data, possible psychological factors affecting crew performance, probable flight path and profiles, crew history, training, competency, and crew interviews. The Weather Group is responsible for collecting relevant meteorological data, synoptic situations, surface weather observations, pilot reports, upper air information, radar weather observations, forecasts, weather briefing services, and satellite observations.

The Performance Group is responsible for investigating aircraft design factors, operational capability, stability/control, aerodynamic characteristics, fail-safe systems, performance limitations, and certification.

The Human Factors Group is responsible for investigating crashworthiness factors, pathological factors, cockpit and cabin environmental hazards, energy absorption modes, postcrash factors, psychological factors (crew), physiological factors, and toxicological factors.

The Air Traffic Control (ATC) Group is responsible for determining status of ATC facilities, reviewing tower tapes, interviewing ATC personnel, studying ATC flight handling, determining whether ATC personnel or facilities were at fault, and reviewing ATC procedures.

The Witness Group is responsible for questioning persons who may have information concerning the accident, obtaining witness statements, preparing a witness location chart, establishing a probable flight path based on witness observations, interpreting lay witness observation, and applying witness information to the accident.

The Cockpit Voice Recorder Group is responsible for documenting recorder damage, shipping tapes to readout facilities, auditioning original tapes and making recording, and transcribing pertinent tape data for the public record.

Airworthiness Groups

The airworthiness area, like the operations area, can be most effectively investigated using the separate group system. Each group investigates a given technical specialty. Group chairpersons coordinate to ensure investigative coverage in areas where more than one group may have responsibility. For example, the structures, systems, and powerplants groups would coordinate their activity in examining the wing structure wreckage on a large jet aircraft (U.S.

Department of Transportation, 1982). The airworthiness area of an aircraft accident investigation includes a study of structures, systems, powerplants, maintenance records, and flight recorders.

The Structures Group is responsible for examining the airframe and flight controls and accounting for all parts, plotting the wreckage distribution, and preparing a mockup or a partial layout of the wreckage when necessary.

The Systems Group is responsible for examining the various aircraft systems (hydraulic, electrical, fire detection and prevention, oxygen, deicing, pneumatic, and air conditioning), documenting cockpit instrumentation and control readings, accounting for system components and ensuring system continuity, and determining system operational capability prior to impact.

The Powerplants Group is responsible for examining the fuel system, conducting the on-site powerplant investigation, removal of powerplants from the site for further study and teardown, determining operational capability of powerplants prior to impact, and examining powerplant accessories.

The Maintenance Records Group is responsible for reviewing the aircraft maintenance records, documenting compliance with specified maintenance practices, studying the history of the aircraft for possible accident causes, and documenting compliance with airworthiness directives.

The Flight Recorder Group is responsible for identifying voices, analyzing sounds, preparing transcripts, establishing speed control, and reviewing shipping instructions for on-scene investigators.

In comparatively minor general aviation accidents, one or two FAA investigators conduct the airworthiness and operations phases of the investigation. Occasional technical assistance may be required from participants and other specialists in the airworthiness or operations areas. Additional assistance is available from aircraft manufacturers.

FAA's Role

FAA's responsibility to promote the safe flight of civil aircraft in air commerce is defined in the Federal Aviation Act of 1958. FAA's specific responsibility in the investigation of all accidents involving civil aircraft is to determine whether:

1. There is a violation of the Federal Aviation Regulations

2. The performance of FAA facilities or functions is involved

3. The competency of FAA-certified airmen, air agencies, air taxis, commercial operators, air carriers, or airports is involved

4. The Federal Aviation Regulations (FARs) are adequate

5. The airport certification safety standards or operations are involved

6. The air carrier/airport security standards or operations are involved

The key word to describe FAA's role in air disasters is "prevention." Through the certification process for airmen, airports, airlines, and aircraft FAA strives to prevent air accidents from occurring. When an incident or accident does take place, FAA will often take recommendations submitted by NTSB, after investigation is completed, and implement them through new regulations, requirements for certification, or new safety programs or procedures.

The general aviation accident prevention program, officially established in 1977, is one example of FAA's attempt to improve air safety through the use of prevention tactics. The general concept of the program was to reduce the accident rate of general aviation through the combined efforts of FAA, the aviation industry, and the general aviation public by improving the attitude, knowledge, and proficiency of airmen and reducing environmental hazards. The program developed a network of "accident prevention counselors," a series of workshops, clinics, and seminars, a liaison with aviation organizations to identify potential safety problems, and participation in aircraft accident investigations (FAA, 1977).

AIR DISASTER INVESTIGATIVE PROCEDURES

Any time an aircraft accident occurs, with resultant damage to the aircraft or injury to persons, the National Transportation Safety Board must be notified. This does not necessarily mean that an investigation by NTSB will take place. Due to the number of accidents that occur nationwide and the small number of investigative teams available, many accidents are never investigated by NTSB. In fact, NTSB gives the Federal Aviation Administration the authority to investigate accidents involving small aircraft (those weighing 12,500 pounds or less).

The responsibility of the FAA investigative team is to determine whether a violation of a Federal Aviation Regulation occurred. Although they are required to submit a report to NTSB of their findings, the final responsibility for determining the probable cause of any aviation accident is ultimately that of NTSB.

The law prohibits the utilization of any part of the formal report of an NTSB accident investigation to be used in a court of law as evidence. It is possible, however, to request the presence of an investigator as a witness. But even in these instances, due to the time constraints of the investigative team members, these requests are not often met.

Some individuals in aviation question the reliability of FAA-conducted investigations of air accidents. A certain conflict of interest enters into their deliberations. It was this conflict that prompted the origination of NTSB in the first place. How could an agency, charged with the safety and certification of an industry, be trusted to conduct an impartial investigation of an accident involving their standards?

The purpose of an aircraft accident investigation is to identify those events comprising the accident, determine the causes, and make recommendations to prevent similar accidents from occurring. Two emergency plans are required for an accident investigation. The first is the immediate effort to save lives and reduce the amount of damage. The second is the investigation of the accident itself. Careful procedures in the first plan will aid in the results of the second. Many accident investigations have been rendered almost totally useless by the carelessness of some in the initial phase of the investigation (Ellis, 1984).

An important first step at the scene of the accident is to secure the area. It is essential that the aircraft remain intact as found. Gathering scattered parts and pieces into one area may seem helpful but in reality hampers the investigators' ability to determine cause. Perishable evidence is generally collected first, such as samples of fuel, leaking fluids, and so forth. Photographs of the accident scene play an integral role in the investigation. While the pictures are taken, careful notes will be made as to the layout of the area, general description of the scene, and measurements of the various components of the aircraft. Parts of the wreckage are tagged and identified.

Collection of data other than that previously mentioned becomes a secondary concern. Investigators must try to obtain accurate accounts from witnesses as soon as possible. Information tends to be more accurate the closer to the time of the actual accident it is received, and it is better to get an individual's own perceptions before he or she have had an opportunity to discuss the accident with others. Other pertinent data would include the procurement of weather data, the status of navigational aids, FAA communication facilities, and the status of the airport.

Next, the data must be analyzed. Usually members of the investigative team will meet on a daily basis to exchange and compare information. For example, do the instrument indications match the expectancies of the investigator looking into the engine, or do they coincide with the reports of eyewitnesses?

Finally, a written report is prepared. The report has four basic components: a description of the accident, investigation and analysis, conclusions, and recommendations. In most instances, there will be several findings or conclusions which will be summarized into a probable cause. The recommendations must be as specific as possible because they are expected to help prevent future occurrences.

LEGAL IMPLICATIONS

An increasing number of aircraft accidents has resulted in litigation against FAA and NTSB, both representing the "deep pockets" favored by litigants seeking monetary damages. Suits brought against FAA for its alleged part in contributing to aircraft accidents amount to billions of dollars annually.

Sometimes the judgments brought against FAA result from the lack of familiarity of the courts with the areas of control and responsibility that FAA holds. Accusations are oftentimes made by relatives of the deceased as to the qualifications of a pilot. Should a pilot certificate have been issued or was the pilot medically able to hold a particular type of medical certificate? Should the controller have warned the pilot of an impending situation involving another aircraft or a weather phenomenon in the vicinity of his craft? These kinds of questions along with many others are raised in such law suits.

Legal implications are also evident in other facets of aircraft accident investigation, such as the failure of an operator to report an accident, concealing information relevant to the accident investigation, unauthorized removal of accident wreckage, autopsy authorization, wreckage custody, and investigative jurisdiction.

Interesting implications arise when an aircraft manufactured in one country, operated by a company in another, carrying passengers from several nations, crashes in yet another country's territory. In these instances the International Civil Aviation Organization (ICAO) often becomes involved. Obviously the legal implications in such an aircraft accident investigation are many and varied.

THE INTERNATIONAL CIVIL AVIATION ORGANIZATION

The International Civil Aviation Organization (ICAO) was formed on December 7, 1944, under the terms of the Convention on International Civil Aviation. The principal aim was, and still is, to develop the principles and techniques of international air navigation and air transportation so as to provide a safe, efficient, and peaceful means of international air travel.

ICAO is composed of an assembly (made up of 150 nations or "contracting states") and a council or governing body (a combination of 33 contracting states). One representative from each contracting state makes up the assembly. Council members are elected by the Assembly and serve a three-year term. Their responsibility is to establish appropriate committees coinciding with the objectives of the organization and to procure information relative to international air service, present problems or new ideas to the assembly, investigate infractions of standards already in existence, and develop more efficient and effective methodologies of international air travel.

The goals of ICAO, according to Article 44 of the Chicago Convention, are to:

1. Insure the safe and orderly growth of international civil aviation throughout the world

2. Encourage the arts of aircraft design and operation for peaceful purposes

3. Encourage the development of airways, airports, and air-navigation facilities for international civil aviation

4. Meet the needs of the peoples of the world
    for safe, regular, efficient, and economical
    air travel

5. Prevent economic waste caused by
    unreasonable competition

6. Ensure that the rights of contracting states
    are fully respected and that every
    contracting state has a fair opportunity to
    operate international air lines

7. Avoid discrimination between contracting
    states

8. Promote safety of flight in international
    air navigation

9. Promote the development of all aspects of
    international civil aeronautics

ICAO has done much since its inception to standardize aviation procedures around the globe. It accepted English as the international language of aviators and controllers. It recently reflected a standard approach and landing guidance system, the U.S./Australian-developed Microwave Landing System. And ICAO has been instrumental in solving a disparity of problems related to national sovereignty and aircraft accident investigation.

AVIATION ACCIDENT STATISTICS

Certain phases of flying itself are more dangerous than others. The majority of aviation accidents take place during the takeoff and landing stages (FAA, 1986). Several factors account for this phenomena: the close proximity of the aircraft to the ground (leaving little room for error or for reaction to a problem), the slow speeds of aircraft during these stages, and the possibility of distraction during these more complex segments of flight.

Earlier in this chapter pilot error was cited as the leading cause of aviation accidents. Statistics indicate that 80 percent of accidents from 1977 to 1982 were due to pilot error. From 1977 to 1981 the second leading cause was weather. In 1982 weather was surpassed by terrain as the second leading cause of aircraft accidents. Even when fatal accidents are looked at separately, pilot error causes approximately 90 percent of aviation accidents.

AIR DISASTER BUDGET TRENDS

Aviation disasters are considered for the most part to be a concern of the federal government. State and local agencies are involved generally in the location and security of a wreckage site and in the removal of bodies from the scene. But budget items earmarked specifically for aviation disasters are not to be found. Even within FAA's own budget there is no mention of air disasters or accidents as this is contrary to the agency's philosophy. Instead, it notes only those monies spent on accident prevention programs.

In FY87 Congress gave FAA through DOT a budget allowance of $4.842 billion. Of that amount, approximately $318 million was allotted to flight standards operations. It is within this part of the budget that accident prevention and investigation monies are spent (FAA, 1976).

In general Congress has been very supportive of FAA when it has come to annual budgetary allocation, increasing the budget by 50 percent from 1981 to 1986 (Congressional Quarterly Almanac, 1986). This has been especially true since the air traffic controllers' strike of 1981 coupled with FAA's insistence on bringing the workforce up to the standards held before the strike. The increase in the amount of air traffic since the deregulation of the airline industry has also been a significant factor in budgetary considerations. FAA's National Airspace Plan is designed to increase air safety over the next twenty years while costing billions of dollars.

The National Transportation Safety Board, as an independent agency, receives its support directly through Congress. Although NTSB receives an annual budgeted amount to carry on its operations, it has the option of returning to Congress for additional money, depending on the number and severity of air accidents. In 1986 the Reagan administration opposed the proposed "Independent Safety Board Act Amendments" due to budget concerns rather than safety issues.

CONCLUSION

Policies and programs regarding air disasters have experienced few changes throughout the history of aviation. The most significant event occurred when the federal government established the National Transportation Safety Board and granted it absolute rights over aircraft accident investigations. NTSB determines probable causes of air disasters and usually recommends safety procedures to the Federal

Aviation Administration to prevent similar accidents. The FAA is the other agency involved in air disasters through its role as regulator, monitor, and safety officer.

Overall aviation boasts a tremendous safety record and is truly the safest means of transportation available today. But, unfortunately, where moving objects and humans interact there remains the possibility of air disaster.

REFERENCES

Congressional Quarterly Almanac (1986). Independent Safety Board (35 D).

Dole, Elizabeth H. (1986). Annual Report on the Effect of Airline Deregulation on the Level of Air Safety, report of the secretary of transportation to the U.S. Congress (Washington, D.C.: U.S. Department of Transportation).

Eddy, Paul, Elaine Potter, and Bruce Page (1986). Destination Disaster (Times Newspapers).

Ellis, Glenn (1984). Air Crash Investigation of General Aviation Aircraft (Capstan Publications).

Federal Aviation Administration (1976). The National Aviation System Challenges of the Decade Ahead (Washington, D.C.: U.S. Department of Transportation/Federal Aviation Administration).

___ (1977). General Aviation Accident Prevention Program (Washington, D.C.: U.S. Department of Transportation/Federal Aviation Administration).

___ (1986). FAA Statistical Handbook of Aviation, Calendar Year 1986 (Washington, D.C.: U.S. Department of Transportation/Federal Aviation Administration).

Komons, Nick A. (1978). Bonfires to Beacons (Washington, D.C.: U.S. Department of Transportation).

Taylor, John W. R., Michael J. H. Taylor, and David Monday (1979). Air Facts and Feats (New York: Sterling).

Triplett, William (1987). "The Go Team," Air and Space Magazine (September): 48-57.

U.S. Department of Transportation (1982). Aircraft Accident Investigation General Principles and Procedures, Authorities and Responsibilities (Washington, D.C.: U.S. Department of Transportation/ Transportation Safety Institute).

13

Structural Failures

Ronald John Hy

In the past few years there have been several failures of long-span structures in the United States. Recent structural failures include collapses of the roof of the Hartford (Connecticut) Civic Center after several days of snow, the steel and aluminum dome over the C. W. Post Center of Long Island University under accumulated snow drifts, the scaffolding used in construction of the Willow Island (West Virginia) power plant, the roof of Kansas City's Kemper Arena, the wooden arches at Chicago's Rosemont Horizon Arena, the Harbour Cay Condominium (Florida), the walkway over the lobby of the Kansas City Hyatt Regency Hotel, and the Teton Dam and Hord Canal Bridge failures. The preponderance of such failures, it should be noted, has been with long-span rather than short-span structures.

The major difference between a long-span and a short-span structure is that many long-span structures have fewer structural elements, meaning that if one of the structural elements fails, there are fewer alternative paths of load resistance than in most short-span structures. Since the load cannot be shifted to other structural elements, collapse occurs. If, for example, a beam is resting on two piers, one at each end (long-span), and one of the piers fails, the beam will collapse. But, if the beam is resting on four piers (short-span) and one of the piers collapses, the beam probably will not fail—although its ability to perform its specified function will be seriously impaired.

Another characteristic of long-span structures is that they generally house a large number of people at one time; therefore, when they fail, a tragedy occurs. Consequently, special care in the design, construction, and maintenance as well as provision of alternative means of supporting structural loads, an increase in safety concerns, and more intensive inspections are needed for these types of structures.

GOVERNMENT POLICIES

From the earliest of times, Americans have depended upon government to develop and implement policies which protect their well-being. For the most part, these policies consist of three distinct types of actions. The first and most simple action is to do nothing and let individuals assume their own safety risks. Under this course of action individuals are responsible for going where they wish, living where they want, and doing what they desire. If persons, for example, want to live in a floodplain, they should be allowed to do so. But, having made that decision, these persons should not expect the government to provide for their safety and well-being if a flood occurs.

This policy is not widely accepted because most people have insufficient information about the degree of risk—which admittedly is an inexact undertaking—and its consequences and thus can endanger themselves unwittingly when they are unprotected by the government. Moreover, the government finds it difficult not to accept some responsibility to help disaster victims. Consequently, this type of action (or inaction) has been supplanted by a more popular type of governmental action commonly referred to as "mitigation" or "risk containment."

Risk containment focuses on establishing standards which usually are dictated by the largest failure experienced by a type of structure erected in a given region (e.g., building codes). This form of structural mitigation historically has proven to be quite successful in preventing structural failures. While established standards may protect admirably against occurrences at or below the accepted standards, they fail to protect the public from occurrences which exceed those standards. This is invariably what happens in a building failure in which building codes or standards have been met.

Inasmuch as it is impossible to prevent all structures from ever failing, governments have felt that they must develop some supplementary responses in the event that structures do fail. To supplement this form of government action, yet another set of actions are used, namely preparedness, response, and recovery procedures. This type of action is undertaken after a failure occurs. Translated into its simplest terms, government develops disaster policies and provides disaster aid mainly because it has the personnel, fiscal resources, and power to deal with the aftermath of a serious failure.

FUNCTIONAL FAILURES/STRUCTURAL COLLAPSES

Structural failures occur when a structure loses its ability to perform its intended functions because of the lack of maintenance or improper use and/or because of design or construction errors. (In this chapter, we will not deal with structural failures due to wind, earthquakes, snow, floods, overloads, fires, and explosions since these factors will be discussed in other chapters.) To be sure, not all structural failures are alike. There actually are two types of structural failures. Functional failure occurs when a structure does not collapse but lacks the capacity to perform one or more of its intended functions. Examples are leaking roofs and deteriorating parking structures. Functional failure normally does not constitute a hazard to human life and is amenable to correction.

The second type of failure is structural collapse which occurs when part or all of a structure comes apart or undergoes large permanent deformation. As a result, it loses all capacity to perform intended functions. Although there are many more functional failures than collapses, the latter, unfortunately, are more dramatic and receive greater media coverage because they frequently involve death and injury.

Dams

Dams differ somewhat from buildings, roads, and bridges. There are approximately six hundred dams in this country. Yet a large number of states have either inadequate dam legislation or insufficient funding to ensure safe dams. Most of these structures are virtually ignored once built as is the changing environment around them. Like other structural failures, dam failures can be classified as either functional or collapse. Also, like other structural failures, most dam failures are functional; collapses seldom occur.

As previously mentioned, problems with dams stem from the lack of rigid standards, despite the fact that periodic inspection and surveillance are known to contribute greatly to dam safety. The absence of inspections facilitates functional failures and allows them to go unnoticed. For instance, seepage occurs through or beneath water impoundment structures. Such seepage is quite normal and thus expected. These seepage patterns, however, need to be monitored as the structure ages. Rapidly advancing technology is available and can provide valuable insight into internal or subsurface conditions. But, information from this technology must be reviewed critically by competent design personnel. To further assist in averting structural failure, recognition must be given to the time needed to correct latent defects and changing geological conditions, such as cavities in rock formations which tend to occur after extended periods of successful operation. Increased surveillance is necessary to prevent periodic dam failures.

Bridges

Bridges are also important structures which deserve special mention. As with dams, most of these structures are ignored once they are built. Bridge failures, like others, can be classified as either functional or collapse. By far, most failures are functional, though collapses do occur occasionally. (While few bridges actually collapse, it is estimated that over 50 percent of the bridges over twenty feet long are rated as deficient and in need of repair.) This situation suggests that most bridge failures stem from a lack of rigid standards, unsystematic inspections, and inconsistent enforcement, all of which allow failures to go unnoticed.

Functional and collapse failures generally result from construction design flaws and/or shortcuts which make bridges susceptible to erosion. Inadequate maintenance and inspection procedures allow functional failures to go undetected until collapses occur. It should be noted, however, that most functional failures are detected and fixed before they become collapses.

Although several factors contribute to both functional and collapse bridge failures, the most common causes are construction shortcuts, floods and underwater rush, and weather. Construction design flaws and shortcuts, for the most part, take place underwater via corrosion and chemical reactions. Ambiguous plans and specifications also contribute to these structural failures. Thus, designs and inspections must address these long-term processes.

Floods and underwater rush obscure bridge footings and piers, causing erosion and scouring. Erosion is the chemical process which destroys by degree the fragility of the material used to construct bridges (concrete, asphalt, and steel). Scouring occurs when rushing water disrupts the gravel and silt around the footings. As rushing water hits the footings, it sets up eddy currents. These whirlpool currents work up the gravel and silt and transport them downstream, creating a hole at the base of the footings which undermines the structure.

Weather, particularly cold weather extending over a period of time, is yet another cause of older bridge failures. Bridges built shortly after World War II are especially susceptible to cold weather because they often were constructed of low-grade steel. Low temperatures can cause low-quality steel to break instead of stretch. For example, studies of bridge collapses due to cold weather indicate that the steel broke "cleanly," suggesting fragility.

Proper designs and inspections are the two fundamental ways to detect problems. Appropriate designs usually rely on ripraping, placing heavy rocks around the footings to prevent soil erosion from undermining the structures. Suitable inspections while easy to contemplate are difficult to implement. Inspections quite often cannot guarantee against failures due to defective design and construction. And authority is fragmented. Inspections are essentially a state function. The National Transportation Safety Board and the Federal Highway Administration, for example, have only oversight responsibilities and little practical leverage over states or state agencies. Nevertheless, inspections are the chief way to mitigate functional or collapse failures.

Causes of Failures

Functional failures frequently result from the introduction of new or modified technology. For instance, rapid deterioration of parking facilities is usually the consequence of deicing salts. Collapses, on the other hand, are normally due to improper application of existing technology rather than to the inadequacy of technology. They are the consequence of a combination of events which are unique to each project rather than repetitive in future projects. It is not often that such failures can be attributed to a single cause inasmuch as buildings deteriorate, occupancy requirements shift, and fire-proofing and energy requirements change.

Collapses are almost always the result of a breakdown in the fragmented system of checks and balances used in construction projects. Design and detailing errors are often translated into actual construction because no one reviewed them carefully. Other areas that contribute to structural failures include a myriad of factors, such as technical, legal, materials, management, contracting, economic, organization, procedures, financial, and quality control methods.

Ever-increasing construction costs have also brought pressure to bear on owners to accelerate the time needed for design and construction of projects. This in turn has placed greater pressure to short-circuit some traditional steps in order to meet accelerated schedules. With construction loan rates ranging from 10 to 20 percent financing also siphons off thousands of dollars daily. To control costs, architects are pressured to use the lightest, most economical material available. While improved technology enables architects and engineers to streamline buildings with lighter, less costly materials, and to develop innovative designs, it also reduces safety margins because of the lack of redundancy.

Contractors are pushed to build as quickly as possible. Construction often begins before all designs are completed and checked. Harried engineers also cut costs by allowing suppliers to develop specifications, which leads to trouble if the manufacturer's engineers are not trained for this task.

Other major causes of both types of structural failures are as follows:

1.   Improper design

2.   Inadequate drawings for material procurement and construction

3.   Nonconforming materials

4.   Nonconforming construction

5.   Loading in excess of design capacity

MITIGATION AND PREPAREDNESS

Unlike most disasters discussed in this book, structural failures are addressed primarily by mitigation and to a lesser extent by preparedness rather than by response and recovery. Mitigation, it should be recalled, entails implementing a risk reduction program, whereas preparedness involves developing a plan to save lives and reduce damage almost immediately after a structure fails.

When developing mitigation and preparedness procedures and mechanisms, governments must first be aware of the uniqueness of the construction industry. In the first place, in the construction business a "new" organization consisting of architects, engineers, builders, owners, insurers, and subcontractors is formed each time a facility is constructed or renovated. This organization has no time to establish, let alone implement, efficient and effective lines of communication. Second, because of the temporary nature of the organization that is put together no single group or person is ultimately responsible for quality control, even though there is a need for more exacting and coordinated quality control and analysis of dynamic behavior during design and construction phases--especially for long-span structures such as bridges, dams, hotels, and sports arenas. In addition, structural engineers who are responsible for the design do not as a general rule perform all of the design work. Frequently, most of the design details are implemented by steel or precast concrete fabricators. Yet structural engineers are the only persons who are capable of inspecting work and detecting potential failures.

Mitigation

Structural policies normally have not been crisis-reactive, though each structural failure frequently has resulted in a reassessment of mitigation and preparedness procedures. Most structural policies, in fact, are intended to provide an engineered reduction in risk, even if they involve greater economic costs than monetarily calculable benefits. Moreover, most of these policies are quite rational, taking into account a vast array of technical, social, administrative, political, legal, and economic factors.

Although the federal government is involved, structural mitigation and preparedness procedures commonly are implemented at the state and local level via building codes and zoning ordinances.

Building Codes. In the area of structural policies, the emphasis undeniably has been on mitigation and risk containment. Implementation of these procedures, generally speaking, has taken the form of establishing and implementing state and local building codes. Such codes and standards have been quite effective in mitigating structural collapses, though they are unable to prevent collapses due to natural phenomena like earthquakes and tornadoes. Building codes, however, have been less effective in controlling functional failures because they cannot keep up with new and modified technology.

A building code is a series of standards and specifications designed to establish minimum safeguards in the erection, renovation, and construction of buildings. These safeguards are intended to protect persons who live and work in buildings from hazards and to constitute regulations to further protect the public's health and safety (Schreiber and Clemmer, 1982: 166).

Building codes deal with the three main parts of a building: (1) the substructure (the part of the building below the ground), (2) the superstructure (the part above the ground), and (3) the infrastructure (the interior of the building, primarily the plumbing and electrical systems). The substructure and superstructure support the load weight of the building. The load weight consists of the weight of the building (dead load) and the weight of the infrastructure, including furniture, equipment, stored material, and occupants (live load). In some regions of the country building codes also address wind load, snow load, and earthquake load.

A building code is actually a series of standards dealing with building, plumbing, electrical, heating, safety, sanitation, lighting, ventilation, and fire prevention. The primary reason that almost every American city and most counties have such codes is public safety. Walls need bracing and anchoring to prevent them from collapsing. The size of nails, thickness of beams, strength of trusses, thickness of shingles, and numerous other construction details are regulated by building codes. Electrical codes regulate wiring, while heating codes regulate ducts, chimneys, and furnaces. Other codes regulate occupancy space, amount of light, and fire prevention--all in the name of public safety. (Codes, it must be remembered, apply not only to the construction of new structures, but also to the renovation of old structures which owners can be forced to stop using until defects are corrected.)

Cities and counties either write their own building, electrical, and plumbing codes, or they adopt codes suggested by various national associations. Normally localities adopt some, but not all, of the standards suggested in the model codes. The principal reason is that such standards, while generally applicable, fail to address the environment unique to each locality. The major model building codes are listed in figure 13.1.

As previously mentioned, the federal government is becoming increasingly concerned with building safety. Figure 13.2 summarizes some of the federal agencies that regulate building professionals. In fact, sometimes the federal government's concern for building safety has preempted state and local authority. These overlapping areas of concern normally are handled in the following manner (Reznikoff, 1979: 19):

1. Federal laws on the same subject supersede state and local laws

2. State and local laws not in conflict with federal laws remain valid

3. State and local laws prevail when they are more stringent than federal laws

Figure 13.1

Major Model Building Codes

	Model Building Codes	Fire Prevention Codes
NBC	National Building Code, American Insurance Association, Engineering & Safety Service	American Insurance Association Fire Prevention Code
UBC	Uniform Building Code, International Conference of Building Officials	Uniform Fire Code
BOCA	Building Officials and Code Administrators International	BOCA Basic Fire Prevention Code
SBC	Southern Building Code Congress International	Southern Standard Fire Prevention Code

Building Classifications and Geographical Region. Building codes vary according to several factors such as building classification and geographical region. Buildings are classified on the basis of types of occupancy (building use), occupancy load (minimum number of persons expected to be in a building at any given time), and degree of hazard (amount of combustible material per square foot of floor space). Standards differ according to types of occupancy. For instance, standards are more stringent when the occupants of a building are physically disabled, elderly, or children. Occupancy load standards increase with the capacity of the building--the larger the building capacity, the more stringent the standards. Finally, the degree of hazard affects standards. Low-hazard buildings such as churches and hospitals have different standards than do high-hazard buildings like paint shops and service stations.

Figure 13.2
Federal Agencies That Regulate Building Professionals

Federal Departments	Duties	Acts of Congress	Date
DOC Dept. of Commerce			
NBS National Bureau of Standards	Testing of materials. Promotes enforcement and adoption of uniform building codes.	Public Law 177 Act to establish NBS	1901
FEMA Federal Emergency Mgmt. Agency	Incl. Civil Defense and Federal Disaster Adm. and U.S. Fire Administration.	Reorganization Plan No. 3	1978
USFA United States Fire Adm.	Service, education, training. Supports state and local fire safety training (National Fire Academy). Maintain a fire data system.	Federal Fire Prevention Act	1974
HEW Dept. of Health, Education, & Welfare	Fire safety standard for health-care facilities.		
PHS Public Health Service	Sets standards for private and public nonprofit hospitals/ nursing homes.	Hill Burton Act Title IV of Public Health Service Act	1974
SSA Social Security Adm.	Medicare & Medicaid. Requires compliance with fire safety standards.	Social Sec. Act Title 18-19	1965
HUD Dept. of Housing and Urban Develop.	Enforces standards for one-and two- family dwellings and nursing care- type housing.		
FHA Federal Housing Adm.	Establishes and enforces minim. building standards.	Housing and Community Development Act	1974

Federal Departments	Duties	Acts of Congress	Date
FAA Federal Aviation Adm.	Enforces standards for safety in aircrafts and airports.	Federal Aviation Act	1958
FRA Federal Railroad Adm.	Sets standards for equipment and operations of trains/railroads.		
CPSC Consumer Product Safety Comm.	Enforces and regulates standards for products sold to consumer. Collects injury data. Conducts public educational programs. Administers the Flammable Fabrics Act.	Consumer Product Safety Act Public Law 92-573 Flammable Fabrics Act	1972 1967
EPA Environmental Protection Agency	Enforces & regulates standards in regard to air, water, and noise pollution. Publishes reports on criteria for noise levels.	Noise Control Act PL 92-574- HL-11021	1972
FTC Federal Trade Comm.	Enforces standards for: 1. Misleading advertising of products 2. Misleading labeling of goods 3. Assists CPSC in enforcing the Flammable Fabrics Act.	Wool Products Labeling Act Textile Fabric Products Identification Act Fur Products Labeling Act	1939 1951 1951
GSA General Services Adm.	Provides supplies and buildings for federal agencies. Performance standards. Systems approach to design.	Federal Property and Adm. Services Act Section 206	1949

Figure 13.2 (continued)

Federal Departments		Duties	Acts of Congress	Date	Federal Departments		Duties	Acts of Congress	Date
DOL	Dept. of Labor	Enforces mandatory standards for safety and health of employees.			FSS	Federal Supply Service	Buys supplies and contracts for services for federal agencies.		
OSHA	Occupational Safety and Health Adm.	Estb. 1970. Develops and enforces mandatory standards for safety educational and training programs for state and federal programs.	Title 29-USC Section 651	1970	PBS	Public Building Service	Responsible for supervising the design, construction, operation, and maintenance of federal buildings.		
DOT	Dept. of Transportation	Enforces standards and regulates construction of private and commercial vehicles. Conducts research.	Nat'l Traffic Motor Vehicle Safety Act / Transport. Safety Act	1966 / 1974	VA	Veterans Adm.	Regulates and sets standards for VA hospitals and healthcare facilities. Conducts research-flammable fabrics. Sets standards for tests methods.		

Note: The identities and functions of federal agencies can change without notice. Their function depends on current need.

Source: Reznikoff, 1979: 20.

Region of the country also affects building codes. Buildings in New Orleans, which are subject to hurricanes, and buildings in San Francisco, which are subject to earthquakes, are built to different specifications than are buildings in Kansas City. For example, the building code could suggest that buildings must be able to resist winds with a design velocity of 120 miles per hour. Then, too, the code might also stipulate detailed requirements for anchorage, fasteners, and connections to maintain structural integrity under high wind pressures.

Building Permits. Before construction or renovation begins, building professionals normally are required to purchase or otherwise receive a permit and to submit a detailed plan to the city or county building department. Sometimes the owner of the building pays for the permit. At other times, the building professional pays for it. And, still at other times, the city or county will waive the fees for a building permit so that the building is built and added to its tax rolls.

Building permits are granted by building departments after careful assessment of the plans and specifications. Then at periodic intervals during construction or renovation a building inspector investigates whether the work complies with the specification standards. An inspector, therefore, must know the code thoroughly in addition to being familiar with the specifications. Work that violates the code is stopped and brought to the attention of the builder.

Most building standards are set by cities and counties and are legally based on powers granted to them by the constitutions of their respective states. But states also pass laws dealing with public safety. It is the duty of the building department to ensure a building's safety. At any point in the construction or renovation the building inspector can halt work on the project and force the building professional to pay fines or face jail terms. (Local governments, through the delegation of police powers vested in the state, have the authority to implement building codes.)

Enforcement of codes, however, is one of the weaknesses in structural mitigation since it depends upon having a sufficient number of qualified inspectors. Because of the continually increasing volume of development, the number of inspectors normally is insufficient to handle the workload. In many of the structural failures complaints were lodged citing the lack of qualified and/or overworked inspectors.

Local inspections run the gamut from excellent to very poor. Budgets are typically inadequate due to insufficient fees or government uses of fees for purposes other than building department services. Thus, many local building departments operate with inadequate funding, staffing, and employee salaries. The personnel attracted to such departments often are barely adequate at best. Despite this bleak situation, building departments are important contributors to mitigation procedures and mechanisms. For instance, they review structural plans. Such checking cannot be careless. If a crucial design error is not detected, it will become an integral flaw in the structure.

Materials Testing. Closely associated with building codes is materials testing, another set of mitigation procedures designed to ensure safety. Certain materials that are used must be tested before, during, or after construction or renovation. The amount of testing is governed by the specifications. Some materials must be accompanied by test reports. Premixed concrete, for instance, often comes with a report showing the exact mix. Some bulk materials must be accompanied by a certification form from a laboratory showing their chemical and physical properties. The American Society for Testing and Materials (ASTM) is a nationwide organization that suggests standards for materials and testing procedures (Watson, 1964: 43). It publishes many volumes of standards widely used by all industries.

Code Uniformity. One of the most confusing aspects of structural mitigation is the lack of uniformity among codes and standards. The number of codes in use and their varying standards lead to confusion and inconsistency. For example, some types and grades of wood are required to meet a standard of 1,800 pounds per square inch (psi) in one city, while in another city the same wood must meet a standard of only 1,600 psi.

Although there have been major efforts to standardize the codes, that approach is not promising because the simple fact is that the codes have evolved through modification to meet local needs. Figure 13.3 illustrates the overlapping code authorities that must be satisfied and that make it virtually impossible to have code uniformity.

To reconcile differences among federal laws, codes, and standards, state codes and standards, county building and fire regulations, municipal building and fire codes, city and county zoning ordinances, and insurances interests is quite unlikely given the lack of cooperation and coordination that surely exists.

Zoning. A brief word needs to be mentioned about zoning because it is so closely linked to building codes. While building codes are used as a mitigation mechanism to prevent structural failures, zoning ordinances, to a lesser extent, are used to contain risk. Zoning ordinances are utilized most frequently to control population density, land use, minimum building and lot sizes, prohibition of signs, and landscape requirements. However, zoning also deals with the types of buildings that can be built in certain areas.

Zoning not only regulates the types of structures that can be built, but it also controls safety considerations such as the height of buildings in relation to the environment, the width of streets, the size and depth of structural foundations, the proportion of the lot that a structure may cover, setback and sideline provisions, and an array of other factors dealing with structural safety. Examples of such zoning standards include minimum elevations above the hundred-year flood height for the first floor of a structure in flood zones and minimum beachfront setbacks to protect structures from coastal erosion. Zoning ordinances, like building codes, are based on the police power that the state has delegated to local governments and as such are enforced by local building departments via on-site inspections and the issuances of building permits. Departments can issue building permits only for new structures or for the renovation of old ones which conform to zoning ordinances and building codes.

Zoning, if it is to promote and mitigate public safety, must be related to future needs, trends, current resources and materials, and potential resources and materials. It must, in short, be grounded on comprehensive knowledge that reveals a complete understanding and coordination of engineering principles, structural designs, and materials.

Figure 13.3
Overlapping Code Authorities

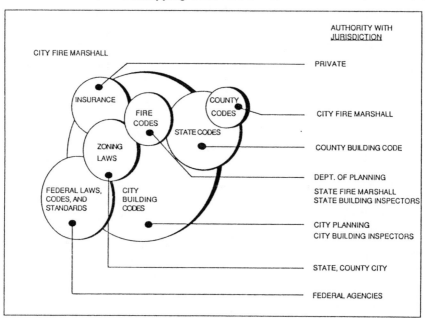

SOURCE: Reznikoff, 1979: 22.

Preparedness

Preparedness involves those activities that develop operational capabilities for responding to an emergency, such as operation plans, operating centers, communications, public information, mutual agreements, resource management plans, and training and exercises. Evidence, however, indicates that improvements in preparedness have met with mixed results, primarily because emergency management in general has been given low priority in the competition for scarce resources and even scarcer time with other required municipal and county activities (Clary, 1985: 27). In an overarching sense, preparedness must allow persons to deal with conflict in times of crises for the purpose of facilitating the integration and implementation of preparedness activities. Elimination of this crisis atmosphere obviously is the principal reason for preparedness.

Because of the overwhelming success of structural mitigation, there is no overpowering need for well-developed preparedness procedures. When structural failures do occur, they are usually the result of other types of disasters such as fires, earthquakes, or hurricanes. Recent structural failures include the bombing at Harvey's resort hotel in 1980 by an extortionist and fires at the MGM Grand Hotel in Las Vegas, the Stouffer Hotel in Harrison, New York, in 1980, and the Las Vegas Hilton in 1981. None of these was a structural failure per se. In recent years the only large-scale structural failure was the collapse of the skywalks at the Kansas City Hyatt Regency Hotel in 1981.

Thus, preparedness procedures specifically designed for structural failures seldom exist; they almost always are piggybacked onto general disaster procedures as developed by the city and the county. Recall also that most structural failures are functional and not collapse, and preparedness procedures are not needed for functional failures. Consequently, there has been relatively little effort to tie the concern for structural failures to preparedness (see chapter 16). Despite having preparedness procedures "on the books," most localities lack the experience and expertise to deal with structural failures. (While this situation is unfortunate when a failure does occur, it is also a testimony to the success of structural mitigation, meaning that localities do not get "hands on" experiences because few collapses actually occur.) As a result, common sense, and in some cases the lack of it, generally is used in providing medical and other emergency services.

The Kansas City Hyatt Regency Experience. The collapse of the skywalks at the Hyatt Regency Hotel in 1981 illustrates the essential components of sound structural preparedness procedures. The response to the disaster was immediate. Hotel staff and medical personnel attending social functions at the hotel or staying there as guests quickly moved the crowd away from the debris. Persons not buried in the rubble were removed. A first aid station (and later a triage) was established to assess the extent of injuries, ascertain priorities of treatment, and furnish treatment whenever necessary.

Paramedics, police, and fire fighters from the city and the surrounding area responded rapidly. An estimated 250 police, 250 fire fighters, and over 100 paramedics were joined by volunteers from hospitals, civic organizations, and other groups. Ambulances, cabs, hearses, and helicopters were used to transport the most seriously injured. Private automobiles transported the less seriously injured.

Then, too, construction workers volunteered to remove concrete, glass, and other material covering those trapped beneath. Hospital emergency plans were implemented, bolstered by off-duty personnel. The Red Cross issued calls for blood donors and established a telephone center to answer inquiries and identify the victims.

The news media, as might be expected, suggested that the curious and sightseers not cluster around the disaster site. They also provided up-to-date information as well as mobilized support and volunteers. For instance, the media transmitted information about the kinds of personnel needed and told blood donors to wait until morning to give blood because of the traffic jam at the blood bank.

However, as with any disaster, not all the procedures were implemented smoothly. William L. Waugh (1988: chapter 16) lists five major problems that occurred in the Hyatt disaster response:

1. Communication among doctors, paramedics, and ambulance personnel was inadequate because they lacked walkie-talkies, two-way radios, and bullhorns, although some were later borrowed from the police and fire units.

2. Medical supplies, particularly oxygen, splints, and drugs were in short supply initially, although that problem was solved when supplies arrived from other jurisdictions.

3. Life Flight helicopters were withdrawn before all the critically injured were transported.

4. Distribution of patients among area hospitals was inefficient and too few casualties were sent to the trauma center at the Kansas University Medical Center.

5. Although the initial response times were good, ambulance response times became too slow because of the one-way flow to and from the hotel entrance.

Kansas City's reaction to this structural failure clearly shows the way preparedness procedures actually function. And an examination of their procedures suggests the types of activities that should be part of any structural preparedness plan. The key elements of preparedness obviously are cooperation, coordination, and communication, all of which are essential if "turf" concerns are to be reduced or eliminated and services are to be delivered as efficiently and effectively as possible.

Liability

Structural mitigation and preparedness are promoted primarily by the government's desire for public safety. Another factor contributing to mitigation and preparedness is the increasing number of liability law suits and the concomitant fear of bankruptcy. The constant possibility of a liability law suit leads to a concern for structural safety.

This is a decade of increasing liability law suits. For instance, between 1978 and 1980 there was a marked increase in both the severity and frequency of claims--from 36 percent in 1978 to 45 percent in 1980. Today, almost half of the building professionals who are insured can expect to be sued. The average cost of settling claims has risen from $15,000 in 1975 to $40,000, according to Shand, Morahan, a large insurer of architects and engineers. The claims against those connected with the Hyatt Regency collapse, for example, exceed 3 billion dollars. As a result, building costs have escalated and, more importantly, most of the insurance companies in this field are reluctant to insure due to the volatility of this market.

Proponents of such suits argue that they are long overdue. They contend that building professionals have enjoyed virtual immunity from responsibility for their actions and decisions. Proponents also contend that law suits have made building professionals exercise a higher degree of care than they would have without such legal accountability. Incompetent professionals, they argue, should be prevented from continued practice, if they cannot do the job correctly and safely.

Opponents of such lawsuits, on the other hand, feel that the rapidly increasing threat of liability hampers professional practice. They believe that law suits have forced building professionals to become conservative and less imaginative in trying new materials, products, and designs, which may also be less expensive, more functional, and safer. Opponents also point out that lawsuits have increased the costs of buildings and other structures astronomically.

The following four factors represent the legal basis for most liability law suits (Reznikoff, 1979: 14):

1. Professional negligence, which is the foundation for most liability law suits, involves an error of omission. Whenever building professionals expose others to unreasonable risk because of known defects, they can be sued.

2. Misrepresentation entails not keeping the usual promises that are an inherent part of competency. That is, a competent building professional can be assumed to be aware of and compliant with building and fire codes. Failure to comply with federal, state, and local codes may be construed as professional negligence.

3. Breach of contract involves implied responsibilities, such as the understanding that building professionals will use accurate measurements, new materials, and so forth.

4. Liability for design defects essentially is concerned with injury and damage resulting directly from the drawings, designs, or specifications. The professional can be held responsible if the injury or designs can be shown to be the primary cause of structural failure.

Such liability lawsuits indirectly, if not directly, contribute to building safety by requiring the government and building professionals to be more concerned with public safety than they might otherwise have been. More to the point, fear of bankruptcy and crippling insurance premiums have brought a return to other safety standards.

In the Kansas City Hyatt Regency disaster, for example, the liability cases finally ended in 1985, some four years after the collapse, although the licenses of the engineers who designed the skywalks were not revoked in Kansas until 1987. The investigation looked into the design and fabrication of the skywalk supports. The court settled millions of dollars in law suits by federal, state, and city agencies as well as several professional construction and architectural organizations, not to mention personal claims.

The Missouri Office of Disaster Preparedness, Consumer Protection Office, and Department of Mental Health assisted in the investigations. The Federal Bureau of Standards tested building materials and the Occupational Safety and Health Administration checked records to see if there was advanced knowledge of design flaws. In 1985 the Administrative Hearing Commission judge upheld the decision of the state engineering licensing board against the structural engineers involved in the hotel construction (Waugh, 1988: chapter 16). For the most part, the investigation concluded that the building codes were sufficient to protect public safety, but that the design flaw (the size of the washer supporting the skywalks) was such that it easily escaped detection.

The primary result of the liability law suits was to increase the inspection force and to analyze more carefully computer models which "test" structural safety. Moreover, for all practical purposes, the litigation doomed the future use of skywalks in other buildings. (The only Hyatt hotel with similar skywalks was at Chicago's O'Hare International Airport, and there the skywalks were fastened to the superstructure and thus were an integral part of the building--not hanging from the roof as was the case in Kansas City.)

CONCLUSION

Mitigation and preparedness are the keystones of structural failure policies. All levels of government are involved, though local governments are more involved than others. City and county governments normally work with the private sector to develop mitigation and preparedness procedures to provide for public safety and protection as well as cooperation and coordination should a failure occur. State and federal government agencies are also involved, but to a lesser extent.

Too often emergency management is related to failures, thus focusing on response and recovery. But, in the area of structural policy, mitigation has been extremely successful. Actually, the most severe structural failures (collapses) have occurred during construction or renovation and not after completion of the project. Consequently, mitigation and preparedness procedures must address this situation, too. Although collapses have occurred, they are few and far between. And most of them are usually the result of other disasters such as fires and earthquakes.

Unlike other emergency management policies discussed in this book, structural policies do not compete favorably with other local issues for time and attention. Every local official deals with building codes and zoning ordinances on an almost daily basis. To be sure, there is always a need for more and better-trained inspectors. But building and zoning departments normally get their share of the tax dollar.

As mentioned before, the overwhelming success of the mitigation and preparedness facets of structural policies are quite astounding. There nevertheless is always room for improvement. A systematic analysis of past structural failures would go a long way in preventing past mistakes from being repeated. Up to now, however, such an analysis has not been forthcoming. There seem to be two primary reasons for this lack of research. First, many materials and system failures go unnoticed, especially functional failures. Second, court proceedings and years of protracted litigation normally prevent information concerning probable causes from being released to the public.

To improve the effectiveness of structural mitigation and preparedness procedures and thus decrease the number and severity of failures, governments need to establish:

1. Authority to investigate and assess data

2. Procedures to gather ephemeral data (data that may be destroyed by rescue or renovation teams)

3. Investigatory organizations with laboratory and intellectual resources to conduct investigations

4. Periodic inspections by qualified personnel (especially for dams, bridges, and roads)

The following points are also suggested as ways of improving structural mitigation and preparedness procedures:

1. Keep detailed records of all inspections.

2. Make sure that any changes are implemented according to codes, standards, and specifications.

3. Get information from approved or qualified laboratories.

4. Use reputable national standards.

5. Analyze computer tests carefully, especially for structural designs.

6. Require written proof of all test results, including documentation.

7. File the complete set of project drawings, schedules, and specifications.

8. Make sure that drawings and specifications conform to code and zoning requirements.

9. Work constantly with all jurisdictions in developing and updating community preparedness and response plans.

10. Participate in community simulations whenever possible.

Simply put, structural policies must plan and prepare for the unexpected by trying to prevent the unpredictable. The basic obstacles are lack of competent technical personnel and adequate financing. Careful design, construction, and maintenance; provisions for alternative means of supporting structural loads; and more intensive inspections are needed to increase mitigation and preparedness.

REFERENCES

Clary, Bruce (1985). "The Evolution and Structure of Natural Hazard Policies," Public Administration Review 45 (January).

McCandless, Carl (1970). Urban Government and Politics (New York: McGraw-Hill).

Reznikoff, S.C. (1979). Specifications for Commercial Interiors: Professional Liabilities,

Regulations, and Performance Criteria (New York: Watson-Guptill).

Schreiber, Arthur, and Richard Clemmer (1982). Economics of Urban Problems (Boston: Houghton Mifflin).

Watson, Donald (1964). Specifications Writing for Architects and Engineers (New York: McGraw-Hill).

Waugh, William L., Jr. (1988). "The Hyatt Skywalk Disaster," in Crisis Management, eds. Michael Charles and John Choon Kim, pp. 115-29 (Springfield, Ill.: Charles C. Thomas).

14

Public Health Emergencies

Caffilene Allen

Emergencies, whether they occur naturally or are the result of human error, have major impacts on public health. Earthquakes destroy safe drinking water systems. Ash spewed from volcanic explosions can cause respiratory illness or even death. Chemicals released into the air through explosions or some other means of contamination can cause various kinds and levels of poisoning. And, of course, the adverse health effects of radiation from nuclear fallout or accident have been extensively chronicled in the various media.

Quickly responding to public health emergencies is nothing new for such public health agencies as the federal Centers for Disease Control (CDC) in Atlanta. CDC has long had a cadre of epidemiologists who can be assigned to anywhere in the world to diagnose and treat illnesses, discover their cause, and implement control measures. What is relatively new, however, is the nature of the cause of the illness. Historically, CDC has focused on infectious diseases. Though these still receive a major emphasis, public health professionals increasingly are beginning to recognize that environmental hazards are responsible for significant public health problems. It has become evident that public health policy needs to be expanded to include these emerging environmental issues.

PUBLIC HEALTH AND EMERGENCY MANAGEMENT

Public health policy relating to emergency management is still being formulated, but some major steps have been taken toward its development. The first step is to determine which agencies are responsible for which problems. As appendix A illustrates, various federal agencies have been designated by the U.S. Public Health Service as lead public health agencies for different types of emergencies. CDC, for example, has been designated as the lead agency for radiation, chemical, toxic waste, air pollution, and biological emergencies. (Lead agencies outside of the Public Health Service are also noted in the appendix.)

To create a central focal point for activities relating to environmental hazards, the Center for Environmental Health and Injury Control (CEHIC) was established within CDC. Within CEHIC, the Emergency Response Coordination Group (ERCG), the Division of Environmental Hazards and Health Effects (DEHHE), and the Division of Environmental Health Laboratory Sciences (DEHLS) were given the responsibility of managing public health problems caused by natural and man-made disasters.

The head of the Emergency Response Coordination Group has the unique position of being employed by two federal agencies. Not only is he responsible for coordinating the response activities for all CDC for any of the areas listed in the guide, but he also has the same responsibility for the Agency for Toxic Substances and Disease Registry, another Public Health Service agency (see appendix B for a description of this new agency). The Emergency Response Coordination Group (ERCG) determines the extent of danger to the public health from a release, or threatened release, of a hazardous substance. It also provides consultations upon request from state, local, or federal officials on health issues relating to exposure to hazardous or toxic substances and, in cases of public health emergencies caused or believed to be caused by exposure to toxic substances, provides medical care and testing to exposed individuals, including, but not limited to, tissue sampling, chromosomal testing where appropriate, and epidemiological studies.

While ERCG is more involved with emergencies while they are happening, the Division of Environmental Hazards and Health Effects within CEHIC/CDC focuses more on events before and after an emergency occurs. For example, after an evacuation has taken place, DEHHE personnel might question residents about the ease of evacuation--whether adequate transportation was available, whether traffic jams occurred, and whether adequate information about procedures for evacuation was effectively communicated. DEHHE personnel would then work with communities to help them improve or assess their current evacuation procedures. Upon request, DEHEE personnel also evaluate other types of emergency response systems and sometimes provide assistance by conducting surveillances of adverse health effects.

In the 1970s, CDC was involved in emergency response activities long before they were formally defined as such within the Division of Environmental Health Laboratory Sciences of CEHIC/CDC. Today that support is still being provided, though on a much larger scale. Laboratory personnel may accompany the epidemiologists into the field to assist in the procurement and handling of critical environmental and biological samples or assist local laboratories in obtaining adequate data. DEHLS personnel at CDC in Atlanta analyze the samples sent from the field to help determine the cause of the illness. CDC personnel, both in Atlanta and at the site of the outbreak, then confer with local health officials to decide which control measures, if any, should be implemented.

Problems Related to Emergency Response

In large measure, the management of public health emergency programs is similar to the management of other kinds of emergency response. The technical nature of public health issues, however, can exacerbate the problems already endemic to emergency management.

Communications. Effective communication is essential. Correctly conveying needed information in a timely manner to those affected by a crisis may save thousands of lives and may save thousands more from needless suffering. Accomplishing such a task, however, can be difficult. For example, if a local fire fighter has been told to evacuate the population "two miles downwind" from a hazard, what does "downwind" mean? It means, of course, that the wind is blowing away from the hazard, but many may interpret the message otherwise. In simulation exercises designed to test the efficacy of emergency preparedness measures, many who misunderstood the message evacuated population toward the hazard rather than away from it (Kent Gray, personal communication, 1987).

When communications about emergency response include the various levels of government in the United States, as well as those of foreign governments, the chances for miscommunication increase. For instance, a call to CDC about a public health problem in Sierra Leone, Africa, led to contacts with numerous levels and types of government officials. The World Health Organization (WHO) was contacted with a request for possible information concerning the incident. Four days later, a communication was received by the CDC that stated that, after numerous inquiries, WHO personnel in Cameroon were unable to obtain any information concerning a public health problem in that nation. Cameroon? Somewhere along the way, the name of the nation had been changed and the public health inquiry had been sent to the wrong place. Four days and extensive personnel time had been lost. The health officials in Cameroon had been unnecessarily alarmed over a public health problem for which they were not responsible.

What are the essential elements of effective communication? Barry Johnson, associate administrator of the Agency for Toxic Substances and Disease Registry, cites five elements involved in successful health risk communication:

1. The source of the message must have credibility

2. The message must be accurate, truthful, up-to-date, and based on current scientific knowledge

3. The receiver of the message should be involved as much as possible in the shaping of the message

4. The message must be delivered in words free of government jargon and in a way in which the sender speaks <u>with</u> (not <u>to</u>) the audience

5. The outcome of communication should be evaluated to assess its effectiveness in order to improve future communications.

Preparedness. An essential element of effective emergency response involves the preparatory actions that take place before an emergency occurs. By being adequately prepared, health workers can reduce a "crisis" to an "unplanned event" (Kent Gray, personal communication, 1987).

This means that systems for handling the "crisis" have already been set up and tested so that an actual occurrence is taken in stride. Of course, the success of any such system depends to a substantial degree on its ability to respond to the unique aspects of a specific situation.

To test the degree of preparedness, simulations of actual emergencies are sometimes carried out. In Chicago in June 1987, for example, about six hundred

people were involved in a simulation of emergency
responses to a nuclear attack. Numerous agencies at
all levels of government actively participated in
exercises designed to test how well the emergency
response systems of the various agencies meshed.
Deficiencies were identified and corrected, and
misunderstandings were cleared up. Effective
simulations can save valuable time during an actual
emergency when a few second can have a substantial
impact on the outcome of emergency operations.

Evacuation. Public health workers have a
particular interest in successful evacuations since
they can result in an excess of public health problems
among the persons refusing to leave a contaminated
area. Therefore, public health workers focus much of
their effort on helping to assure success through
studying actual evacuations and developing guidelines
based on their findings.

Effectively communicating information about
evacuation is crucial during a public health
emergency. How readily people will respond to an order
to evacuate varies. In Nanticoke, Pennsylvania, for
instance, well over 90 percent of the population
evacuated after a fire occurred in a nearby metal-
plating plant. In North Dakota, however, an order to
evacuate after an explosion in a pesticide plant was
not well heeded by local residents (Sue Binder,
personal communication, 1987). The explanation for the
different reactions may be that the residents of
Nanticoke, because they lived in the vicinity of a
potentially hazardous facility, had been previously
prepared for the possibility of an evacuation.

What other factors make a difference in whether a
person is willing to evacuate? Seeing actual physical
evidence of a disaster occurring and developing health
problems that seem related to the disaster are two of
the principal factors. Another major factor that
influences a person's decision to evacuate is the
action taken by neighbors. If a person sees his or her
neighbors leave the area, then he or she will also be
more likely to leave (Marty Rosenman, personal
communication, 1987).

Timing. <u>When</u> to communicate information about
steps to take in a public health emergency is another
problem, especially when communicating information
about man-made environmental hazards. In the chemical
leak explosion in Bhopal, India, that claimed an
estimated 2,500 lives, creating what has been called
the worst man-made public health disaster in history,
many people died because they did not realize that
breathing through a wet towel would lessen the effects
of the pesticide. Many more died because they ran out

of their homes and <u>toward</u> the plant (Bowonder et al., 1987). Knowledge about correct evacuation direction might have prevented some of these deaths.

Clearly, trying to communicate information in a chaotic crisis situation is difficult. But when should information be communicated? Manufacturers want to assure townspeople that their plant is safe. To inform people in advance about what to do in case of an explosion or a poisonous gas leak could lead to misgivings that could result in the plant's being shut down. How does one communicate information needed to protect the public's health without creating additional public health problems caused by residents living in constant fear about being too close to a dangerous plant or without causing panic? There are no simple answers, but involvement of residents in government decisions that might affect their health and safety is essential.

Authority. <u>Who</u> communicates information plays a crucial part in determining whether public health efforts are successful. The person telling thousands of people to evacuate their comfortable homes to live in makeshift housing for an indefinite period of time must be perceived as having sound judgment and enough technical knowledge to assess accurately the situation.

Judgment. Sound judgment is a requisite for officials who must decide if a public health emergency exists and what measures should be taken to cope with such an emergency. In many ways, deciding whether evacuation is necessary or is the best method for handling the problem is as much of an art as it is a science. Environmental hazards are unpredictable. Hurricanes often threaten to wreak havoc along a coastline and then, at the last minute, change direction and subside harmlessly out in the ocean. Similarly, the effects of many chemicals are simply not known. For instance, some may be highly carcinogenic or they may not be. Should an evacuation be ordered if massive amounts of such a chemical are released into the air?

It is tempting to endorse evacuation in a debatable situation. But evacuation itself poses some risk to public health. Chances for traffic accidents involving distraught individuals trying to get away from the hazard are increased. Masses of people thrown together in makeshift living quarters create the perfect setting for the spread of contagious diseases. Added to this is the reluctance of people evacuated once for an emergency that did not happen to evacuate again. The danger exists that such people, having responded once to a false alarm, may refuse to evacuate during an actual emergency.

Just as ordering an unnecessary evacuation may result in the creation of health problems, so incorrectly labeling a situation as a public health crisis can cause unnecessary fear and suffering. In Guyana, for example, information spread to the general public that thallium, a highly toxic rodenticide, had been discovered in their food supplies. As a result, some citizens sent their children out of the country. Upon closer examination, however, the problem turned out to be not one of poisoning but of laboratory error. The analytical methods being used by the Guyana laboratory for the analysis of both food and biological samples were highly susceptible to interferences, which resulted in the reporting of many false-positive thallium readings (Blackman et al., 1987).

Flexibility. Adequate response to public health emergencies requires an enormous amount of flexibility. Public health personnel involved in emergency response are on call twenty-four hours a day and must be ready to respond to a call (which often means actually traveling to the site) from anywhere in the world within a matter of minutes. Civic obligations and other personal concerns must be secondary when the threat of death or serious illness is imminent in a given population.

To assure adequate flexibility, an extensive network of professionals highly trained in a variety of disciplines must be established and maintained. Physicians, toxicologists, epidemiologists, engineers, and statisticians are among those needed to establish an effective emergency response network. As much as possible, all members of a network need to be cross-trained to assure continuity in needed skills. It is also important that no one member of the team have unique skills; if one member is unable to function, another should be able to supply the missing expertise. As a consequence, a solid network will necessarily have to be composed of several physicians, epidemiologists, and so forth.

Health. It is a paradox of their profession that public health workers, by doing their jobs, often place their own health at risk. This is especially true of emergency response personnel. Simply working within the vicinities where explosions have occurred and might again occur is hazardous. Traveling to countries where contagious diseases are still common poses another threat to health, as does the political unrest that still simmers in many places. Public health can be an intensely political issue in some nations.

CONCLUSION

Clearly, while substantial steps have already been taken toward implementing a sound public health policy relating to emergency response, much more remains to be done. Additional information is needed about the most effective methods for communicating information about health emergencies. Assessments of the best methods for achieving optimal interagency coordination are also needed. More studies about evacuation, including its effects on health, need to be done. Issues relating to the health of public health workers also need to be addressed. In many ways, emergency response to environmental threats can perhaps be viewed as the "new frontier" of public health.

REFERENCES

General

Blackman, N., et al. (1987). "No Evidence for General Thallium Poisoning in Guyana," Lancet (May 9): 1084-85.

Bowonder, B.; J. X. Kasperson; and R. E. Kasperson (1985). "Avoiding Future Bhopals," Environment 27 (September): 6-37.

Interviews

Sue Binder, M.D., Division of Environmental Hazards and Health Effects, Center for Environmental Health, Centers for Disease Control, 1987.

Kent Gray, Chief, Emergency Response Coordination Group, Centers for Disease Control/Agency for Toxic Substances and Disease Registry, 1987.

Marty Rosenman, Ph.D., consultant, 1987.

APPENDIX A

Technological Hazard Response Guide

(Adapted from the Disaster Response Guides prepared by the U.S. Department of Health and Human Services, U.S. Public Health Service, Office of Assistant Secretary for Health, PHS Office of Emergency Preparedness, Rockville, Maryland)

This Technological Hazard Response Guide is designed to serve as a ready reference for use by Public Health Service managers in marshalling a PHS response to the various hazards discussed herein.

The following paragraphs represent short overviews of the five sub-guides which comprise this response guide. The chart included here as figure 14.1, at the end of Appendix A, schematically depicts the PHS response to all five types of technological hazards.
PHS may be involved in many emergencies because of the many diverse regular program authorities and responsibilities, especially those of the Centers for Disease Control, Agency for Toxic Substances and Disease Registry, and Food and Drug Administration. Therefore, some PHS organizations may be involved in incidents before the matter comes within the realm of these guides.

A. PHS Plan for Radiation Emergencies

1. "Radiation Emergency" refers to any occurrence which results in the loss of control of radioactive materials resulting in a direct or indirect hazard to life and health.

2. Lead Agencies outside of PHS:
Federal Emergency Management Agency (FEMA)
Department of Energy (DOE)
Nuclear Regulatory Commission (NRC)
Department of Defense (DOD)

3. Lead PHS Agency:
Centers for Disease Control, supported by the Agency for Toxic Substances and Disease Registry, the Alcohol, Drug Abuse, and Mental Health Administration (ADAMHA), the Food and Drug Administration (FDA), the Health Resources and Services Administration (HRSA), and the national Institutes of Health (NIH) and the PHS Office of Emergency

Preparedness (OEP)/OASH, the PHS coordinating component for emergency preparedness.

4. Guide for PHS Response (See figure 14.1)

B. **PHS Plan for Acute Chemical Emergencies**

1. "Acute Chemical Emergency" refers to any acute situation involving potential direct or indirect exposure of significant segments of civilian populationn to one or more toxic chemicals at levels which constitute a threat to public health.

2. Lead Agencies outside of PHS:
    Federal Emergency Management Agency (FEMA)
    Environmental Protection Agency (EPA)
    Department of Labor/Occupational Safety and
       Health Administration (DOL/OSHA)
    National Response Team/Regional Response
       Team (NRT/RRT)
    Department of Transportation

3. Lead PHS Agency
    Centers for Disease Control (CDC), supported by ATSDR, ADAMHA, FDA, HRSA, and NIH.

4. Guide for PHS Response (see figure 14.1)

C. **PHS Plan for Toxic Waste Crisis**

1. "Toxic Waste Crisis" refers to situations when significant segments of the general population are found to be exposed to toxic chemicals from toxic waste sites at levels which constitute a direct or indirect threat to public health.

2. Lead Agency:
    Public Health Service (PHS/DHHS)

3. Lead PHS Agency:
    CDC for all cases except those involving recombinant DNA.
    NIH for all cases involving recombinant DNA.
    ADAMHA, FDA, and HRSA also have significant roles.

4. Guide for PHS Response (see figure 14.1)

Figure 14.1
Guide for PHS Response

Type of Incident

Response Steps	Radiation Emergencies	Acute Chemical Emergencies	Toxic Waste Crisis	Air Pollution Emergencies	Biological Emergencies
A. Decide if emergency exists	ASH	ASH	ASH	ASH	ASH
B. Notify all Appropriate PHS Components	CCC *(OEP/HRSA)	CCC (OEP/HRSA)	CCC (OEP/HRSA)	CCC (OEP/HRSA)	CCC (OEP/HRSA)
C. (1) Gather technical information about source	FDA (NIH)	CCC (NIH)	CCC (NIH)	CCC (NIH)	CCC (NIH)
(2) Tentatively identify and describe nature, location and extent of potential health problems	CCC (FDA/NIH)	CCC (FDA/NIH)	CCC (FDA/NIH)	CCC (FDA/NIH)	CCC (FDA/NIH)
(3) Establish and conduct appropriate surveillance to obtain ongoing information on which to base decisions	CDC/FDA	CDC/FDA/NIH HSRA	CDC/HRSA FDA	CCC (FDA)	CCC (FDA)
D. Reassess, decide whether to continue in crisis mode	ASH	ASH	ASH	ASH	ASH
E. Develop and implement PHS activities to protect public	CCC	CCC	CCC	CCC	CCC
(1) Determine response capacity of local community	HRSA/FDA	HRSA/FDA	HRSA/FDA	HRSA/FDA	HRSA/FDA

Figure 14.1 (continued)

Type of Incident

Response Steps	Radiation Emergencies	Acute Chemical Emergencies	Toxic Waste Crisis	Air Pollution Emergencies	Biological Emergencies
(2) Provide medical personnel to assist in triage/ treatment	HRSA	HRSA (CDC)	HRSA (CDC)	HRSA	HRSA (CDC)
(3) Advise FEMA of need for additional health resources	HRSA	HRSA	HRSA	HRSA	HRSA
(4) Provide or assist in locating needed medical supplies	FDA (CDC)	HRSA (CDC,FDA)	HRSA (NIOSH,FDA)	HRSA (NIOSH,FDA)	FDA (CDC)
(5) Provide assistance in evacuation *medical care *health surveillance	HRSA CDC	HRSA CDC	HRSA CDC	HRSA CDC	HRSA CDC
(6) Prevent exposure via food chain and other sources	FDA	FDA	FDA	FDA	FDA
(7) Advise on protection of workers and clean-up personnel	CDC/NIOSH	CDC/NIOSH	CDC/NIOSH	CDC/NIOSH	CDC/NIOSH
(8) Provide technical assist/advice on decontamination *people *environment	FDA	CDC/NIOSH	FDA	FDA	CDC/FDA

Figure 14.1 (continued)

Type of Incident

Response Steps	Radiation Emergencies	Acute Chemical Emergencies	Toxic Waste Crisis	Air Pollution Emergencies	Biological Emergencies
(9) Advise on funding and administer funds for crisis counseling services and mental health training materials for disaster workers	ADAMHA	ADAMHA	ADAMHA	ADAMHA	ADAMHA
(10) Assist in collection of appropriate biological specimens	CDC HRSA/FDA	CDC HRSA/FDA	CDC HRSA/FDA	CDC HRSA/FDA	CDC HRSA/FDA
(11) Provide health information to public via FEMA or other spokesman	CDC (FDA/HRSA)	CDC (FDA/HRSA)	CDC (FDA/HRSA)	CDC (FDA/HRSA)	CDC (FDA/HRSA)
(12) Assist in training of medical personnel	CDC (FDA,HRSA)	CDC (FDA,HRSA)	CDC (FDA,HRSA)	CDC (FDA,HRSA)	CDC (FDA,HRSA)
(13) Assist in formulating damage and casualty estimates	CDC (HRSA)	CDC (HRSA)	CDC (HRSA)	CDC (HRSA)	CDC (HRSA)
(14) Provide health advice to state/local officials	CDC (FDA)	CDC (FDA)	CDC (FDA)	CDC (FDA)	CDC (FDA)

Figure 14.1 (continued)

Type of Incident

Response Steps	Radiation Emergencies	Acute Chemical Emergencies	Toxic Waste Crisis	Air Pollution Emergencies	Biological Emergencies
(15) Prevent further spread from source	**	CDC (FDA)	CDC (FDA)	CDC (FDA)	CDC (FDA)
F. Decide when protection, treatment and prevention objectives are achieved	CDC (FDA/HRSA)	CDC (FDA/HRSA)	CDC (FDA/HRSA)	CDC (FDA/HRSA)	CDC (FDA/HRSA)
G. Conduct research relating to long-term effects of exposure	CDC (NIH)	CDC (NIH)	CDC (NIH)	CDC (NIH)	CDC (NIH)
H. Conducts evaluations, issue reports with recommendations	CDC (HRSA)	CDC (HRSA)	CDC (HRSA)	CDC (HRSA)	CDC (HRSA)

*Lead organizations for each listed first; supporting organizations in parentheses.
**In radiation emergencies, the radiation source will likely be under control of one or more of the following agencies: DCD, DOE, DOT, NRC.

APPENDIX B

Agency for Toxic Substances and Disease Registry

The Agency for Toxic Substances and Disease Registry (ATSDR) was created in 1980 by the Comprehensive Environmental Response Compensation and Liability Act (commonly known as the Superfund Act). ATSDR was officially established as a public health agency within the Public Health Service of the U.S. Department of Health and Human Services in 1983. ATSDR now also receives operating authority from the Resource Conservation and Recovery Act as amended in 1984 and the Superfund Amendments and Reauthorization Act of 1986.

ATSDR works closely with state, local, and other federal agencies to reduce or eliminate illness, disability, and death resulting from exposure of the public and workers to toxic substances at spill and waste disposal sites. The Superfund Amendments and Reauthorization Act mandate an emergency response program within ATSDR that is required to: (1) provide consultations upon request on health issues relating to exposure to hazardous or toxic substances on the basis of available information to the administrator of the Environmental Protectional Agency; (2) determine the extent of danger to the public health of a release, or threatened release, of a hazardous substance; and (3) in cases of public health emergencies caused or believed to be caused by exposure to toxic substances, provide medical care and testing to exposed individuals, including but not limited to tissue sampling, chromosomal testing, epidemiological studies, and any other assistance appropriate under the circumstances.

In addition to activities related to emergency management, ATSDR is required to determine the extent of danger to the public health from a release or threatened release of a hazardous substance by conducting a health assessment of the situation. A health assessment is the evaluation of data and information on the release of hazardous substances into the environment in order to assess any current or future impact on public health, develop health advisories or other public health recommendations, and identify studies or actions needed to evaluate, mitigate, or prevent human health effects. When conducting a health assessment, ATSDR considers such factors as:

1. The nature and extent of contamination at a particular site

2. The existence of potential pathways of human exposure

3. The proximity of human populations to the site or release

4. The potential for adverse health outcomes resulting from the exposure to the substances under investigation

ATSDR also:

1. Establishes and maintains disease and exposure registries

2. Establishes and maintains an inventory of information on health effects of toxic substances

3. Maintains a listing of areas closed or otherwise restricted to the public because of toxic substance contamination

4. Consults with private and public health care providers in the provision of medical care and testing

5. Conducts survey and screening programs to determine relationships between exposure and illness

6. Conducts health assessments of currently regulated landfills and surface impoundment sites

7. Assists the Environmental Protection Agency in identifying hazardous waste substances to be regulated

8. Issues periodic reports, including peer-reviewed assessments

15

Civil Defense

Loran B. Smith

In January 1985, the <u>Public Administration Review</u> published a special issue dealing with the subject of emergency management. Of the twenty-one articles included in that issue, none dealt specifically with the topic of managing the disaster caused by nuclear war. This omission appears to be symptomatic of much of the emergency management literature. A quick review of the literature published in the past five years reveals a plethora of articles dealing with floods, hurricanes, tornadoes, and nuclear accidents. But there is very little information regarding the role of civil defense in protecting citizens in the event of a nuclear exchange.

The omission of civil defense topics from the emergency management literature apparently is deliberate. Emergency management specialists seem to be seeking to divorce their field from any association with civil defense programs. In their view, civil defense has a "contaminating" effect upon emergency management programs. First, civil defense detracts from the image that emergency services agencies wish to convey--that of civilian professionals capable of dealing with a wide range of emergency needs. Second, the association with civil defense programs makes it difficult to convince state and local officials of the needs of other types of emergencies. As long as civil defense programs are primarily funded by the national government, state and local officials have little incentive to focus on other functions of emergency management which require additional local funding. Finally, to many people, "civil defense" conjures up the image of military officers engaging in war planning--a perception that reduces public and political support for emergency management programs (May, 1985: 45). For these reasons, civil defense is viewed by many emergency management specialists as deleterious to their interests.

In addition, the potential scope, magnitude, and consequences of nuclear warfare make it quantitatively and qualitatively different from any other type of disaster likely to confront emergency management specialists. In every other type of disaster, the death toll, no matter how great, is usually psychologically manageable. In almost every other type of disaster, the ultimate management goal has always focused on recovery; the belief that when the crisis has passed, citizens may return to their normal lives. In contrast, a disaster caused by a nuclear war is likely to leave a death toll in the millions, possibly hundreds of millions--numbers which we are psychologically unable to grasp, much less accept. The feeling also exists that there is absolutely nothing we can do about a nuclear war if it occurs; normal recovery is impossible and that alone removes one of the major incentives for emergency management. Thus, the stark contrast between a nuclear war and other types of disasters provides another rationale for the separation of civil defense and emergency management programs.

All this suggests that civil defense programs are very controversial. The futility of trying to save people from heat, blast, and radiation today only to expose them to cold, starvation, and disease tomorrow has been a very effective argument against civil defense programs. Yet a full-scale nuclear exchange is not the only nuclear possibility for which civil defense must be prepared. Civil defense must also be able to cope with nuclear terrorism, a limited nuclear exchange, and, given the increase in the number of countries in possession of or having the potential to develop nuclear weapons, the prospect that a nonsuperpower nuclear war could generate fallout threatening the United States.

Thus, civil defense programs are a calculated risk; a gamble with the lives of the American people. Recognizing this responsibility, Congress has mandated that insofar as possible, emergency management programs should be integrated with civil defense programs. This "shotgun marriage" has obviously irritated emergency management professionals if for no other reason than it makes a discussion of civil defense programs relevant to the aims of emergency management so long as they are integrated with other emergency management programs and procedures.

This chapter will concern itself solely with the emergency management of disasters caused by nuclear warfare. It will discuss civil defense programs, assess the effectiveness of these programs, and analyze the major problems facing civil defense policies and programs. This chapter takes no position on survivability in a full-scale nuclear exchange. It does, however, recognize that civil defense policies must be prepared for other nuclear war scenarios.

HAZARD/RISK DISASTER POLICY FOR NUCLEAR WARFARE

As mentioned in the initial chapters of this book, it has become popular to analyze emergency management policies and programs through investigation of four related functional phases that are associated with foreseeable disasters: mitigation, preparedness, response, and recovery.

These four phases of emergency management provide a convenient tool for analyzing civil defense policies and programs. Given the uniqueness of the challenges created by any sort of nuclear war, one should not be surprised to find that the almost total emphasis of civil defense planning has been placed on mitigation, and to a lesser extent, preparedness policies. Indeed, the Federal Emergency Management Agency (FEMA), the locus for civil defense planning, has recognized that its response and recovery efforts have been quite inadequate which, in turn, has weakened the credibility of all civil defense programs (FEMA, 1986: 5).

RECENT NUCLEAR HAZARD POLICY

Civil defense mitigation policies take two forms: (1) actual facilities and equipment which can either warn citizens of an impending attack or shelter them from the effects of such an attack; and (2) plans which can be implemented in the event of an attack which will further protect citizens. The first category includes the Emergency Broadcast System (EBS), air-raid sirens, and fallout shelters. The second category includes plans for crisis relocation (evacuation), emergency operating centers (EOCs), and the continuity of government.

The oldest and most publicly visible aspects of civil defense have been hazard warning measures and the yellow and black signs designating fallout shelters. A nation of radio listeners and television viewers has become familiar with the periodic tests of the Emergency Broadcast System. Similarly, residents of urban areas in the tornado belt of the Midwest have learned to rely on sirens to warn them of an approaching tornado. Even fallout shelter signs, while declining in number, have been noticed by most Americans. High visibility, however, does not guarantee effective implementation. Thus, a closer look at civil defense activities in this area seems warranted.

In seeking to protect civilians from any sort of disaster, the first item of business is to develop an adequate warning system. At an early stage, civil defense planners decided to rely upon radio and television and, where feasible, outdoor warning systems (sirens, whistles, horns, or bells) to alert the population. Originally, this system was to be activated through a leased landline that connected civil defense headquarters with 2400 points throughout the nation. By 1979, two major limitations of the system became apparent. First, many segments of the population could not be effectively alerted on a twenty-four-hour-a-day basis as they lived in locations where outdoor warning systems were either inadequate or nonexistent. Second, serious questions were raised about the survivability of the landline network in a nuclear attack. Moreover, the broadcasting abilities of EBS stations could be effectively eliminated, even in areas not directly targeted, by electromagnetic pulse (EMP) damage (FEMA, 1980: 10).

In response to these limitations, FEMA has urged state and local governments to make greater efforts to upgrade their outdoor warning systems--an exhortation little needed in areas where flash floods, tornadoes, and other sudden natural disasters have given residents experience in the value of such warning systems. FEMA has also started to develop a "hardened" communication system relying on each state's Emergency Operating Center which can activate local EBS and outdoor warning systems. Finally, FEMA has sponsored a Broadcast Station Protection Program which is intended to provide fallout and EMP protection for stations in the EBS. By the end of 1981, six hundred stations were provided with fallout protection and 105 stations were protected against EMP damage (FEMA, 1982: 4). In 1982, however, the Broadcast Station Protection Program became a victim of budget cuts which severely limited further progress. For example, in 1984, FEMA could report that it had provided protection and equipment for only fifteen EBS stations and the upgrading of fifty in the previous year (FEMA, 1984: 5).

Once a warning has been issued, civil defense has the responsibility of protecting the civilian population. Since the 1960s, one of the more visible methods of doing that is to provide shelters. The shelter program had its origins during the Truman administration. When the Federal Civil Defense Administration was established by President Truman in January 1951, the executive order creating the agency also recommended the implementation of a shelter program. Due to cost factors, however, little was done during the early 1950s. It should be noted that during this period, shelters were conceived as essentially bomb shelters similar to the bomb shelters used in Great Britain during World War II. Radioactive fallout did not become a concern until after 1954 when a hydrogen bomb test in the South Pacific caused several crew members of a Japanese fishing boat to develop radiation sickness with the subsequent death of one of the crew. Public awareness of the dangers of radiation was popularized in Nevil Shute's 1957 novel, and subsequent motion picture, On the Beach (Winkler, 1984: 17).

This new danger resulting from nuclear war generated considerable public and government pressure for the development of fallout shelters. President Eisenhower, however, remained unconvinced about the value of shelters and was concerned about the high cost of a massive shelter program. Moreover, the credibility of the ruling strategic doctrine of the day, massive retaliation, would be undermined by a massive shelter program (Fitzsimons, 1968: 40; Winkler, 1984: 19).

In May 1961, President Kennedy told the nation that fallout shelters were good insurance. He asked Congress for and received $207.6 million for a fallout shelter program. Most of the money was spent stocking existing shelters in subways, tunnels, corridors, and basements with food (large tins of "survival biscuits"), plastic-lined water drums, sanitation kits, medical supplies, and simple radiation instruments. By March 1964, 57 million shelter spaces had been located but sufficient food and supplies had been stocked for only 20 million shelter spaces (Fitzsimons, 1968: 43). Although President Kennedy had intended to expand his 1961 initiative into an ambitious five-year shelter program, his White House and Defense Department advisers convinced him that political costs (both domestic and international) and financial costs would be too great. As a result, the fallout shelter program was reduced considerably (Pittman, 1968: 61; Winkler, 1984: 20).

For the next twenty years the fallout shelter program was limited to conducting shelter surveys which sought to locate buildings which could be employed as fallout shelters. As for the shelters stocked in the 1962-64 period with food and supplies, many became forgotten over the years. In New York City, many of the shelters were burglarized by junkies looking for hypodermic needles. In the late 1970s, local authorities were told to remove food and other shelter supplies which had either spoiled or outlived the period of safe use.

By the late 1970s, technological developments in weapons design forced civil defense planners to recognize that the then existing fallout shelter system was inadequate. Too many shelters were located in cities where they would be destroyed in the fireball or the blast of a nuclear explosion and too few shelters were located in suburban or rural areas. As a result, civil defense expanded its shelter surveys for the purpose of identifying fallout shelters--not blast shelters--in these other areas (FEMA, 1980: 8).

The shelter surveys were completed in 1984. The program surveyed a total of 1,680,047 buildings and found that 540,400 contained 394.2 million shelter spaces providing fallout protection (FEMA, 1985: 9). The total cost of the shelter survey program originally begun in 1962 was $690 million--in 1988 dollars (Becton, 1986: 6).

It is important to recognize that the shelter surveys only identified buildings which provided adequate fallout protection. Civil defense planners took no steps to stock these shelters with food, water, or other supplies. As a matter of fact, these shelters are bare shells. Civil defense procedures today rely upon persons to bring their own food, water, and clothing to the shelter with them. The experts assume that the rapid decay of radioactive fallout will allow citizens to return outside after a period of two to three weeks so that massive amounts of food and water need not be stored (FEMA, 1987: 37).

As previously noted, the Emergency Broadcast System, outdoor warning systems, and fallout shelter designations are the most visible aspects of civil defense's mitigation policies. But, there are other mitigation policies chiefly composed of emergency plans which can be activated immediately prior to a nuclear exchange, of which the average citizen is unaware. These policies include plans for crisis relocation (evacuation), emergency operating centers (EOCs), and the continuity of government.

CRISIS RELOCATION PLANNING

Civil defense planners originally considered evacuation as a viable alternative to shelters. During the Truman administration, there was an on-going policy debate over the relative merits of shelters versus evacuation, a debate resolved by the president in favor of shelters. The development of the thermonuclear bomb forced a reassessment of the shelter policy. The Eisenhower administration reopened the original debate and this time the debate was resolved in favor of evacuation. The magnitude of the H-bomb's impact made evacuation an easy choice. One of the assumed benefits of the Interstate Highway Act was that it would facilitate the evacuation of large cities. But evacuation as a policy suffered a crippling blow when the disastrous effects of radioactive fallout began to be recognized. Unless the population could be protected from fallout, evacuation was useless. Thus, civil defense reemphasized fallout shelters during the Kennedy years (Windler, 1984: 17).

For over fifteen years, the emphasis of a low key civil defense program rested with identification of fallout shelters--most of which were located in urban areas. By 1978, technological developments in nuclear weapons systems once again forced a reevaluation of civil defense policy. During the Carter administration, a civil defense plan was prepared that combined evacuating the public from likely targets of Soviet missiles with identification of fallout shelters in the areas to which people were to be evacuated. Because the word "evacuation" had certain negative connotations, the planners decided to use the words "crisis relocation." The Reagan administration adopted the plan as its own and sought $4.2 billion from Congress to finance it (Reed, 1982: 554).

Although President Reagan's proposal made some provision for the construction of blast shelters in urban areas, the emphasis on evacuation made it clear that civil defense planners had written off the population of major urban areas in the event of a nuclear war. In fact, civil defense anticipated that any city with a population above 50,000 with significant military, industrial, or economic importance would need to be evacuated (FEMA, 1985: 12). If one adds to this list any area containing military facilities which are likely to be targeted in a nuclear war, civil defense planners estimate that 3,135 separate evacuation plans would need to be prepared (FEMA, 1983: 5).

The underlying assumption of crisis relocation planning was that a period of rising international tensions and a deteriorating diplomatic situation would give a four- to five-day warning of a possible nuclear exchange. During that period, civil defense officials could implement evacuation plans. Refugees would be sent to designated "host" communities in low-risk areas where they would be housed in public shelters. The evacuation plans called for refugees to take food, clothing, and other needed supplies with them as many of the host communities would be unable to provide these items. In the event of a nuclear attack, the plans called for refugees to stay in the fallout shelters for two to three weeks. After that time, the refugees could then assist in the rebuilding process (FEMA, 1980: 7; FEMA, 1987: 33, 47, 50-51).

Although Congress scaled down President Reagan's civil defense proposal, crisis relocation planning (CRP) was initiated. The actual preparation of the plans was done by state agencies under contract to FEMA; the evacuation plans were not concocted by federal bureaucrats in Washington, D.C. as many critics were later to imply (FEMA, 1980: 7). By the end of 1982, 37 percent of the needed evacuation plans covering about 25 percent of the risk area residents were completed (FEMA, 1983: 5). But many cities refused to participate in the program. The governing boards of these jurisdictions rejected CRP on the basis that it was unworkable, provocative to the Soviet Union (which might initiate a nuclear attack when it learned of the evacuation plans), and lead citizens to believe that a nuclear war was survivable. By 1985, CRP had been rejected by about 120 jurisdictions representing 90 million people. Among the areas rejecting evacuation planning were New York City; Cambridge, Massachusetts; Sacramento County, California; Marin County, California; Houston, Texas; Boulder, Colorado; and Greensboro, North Carolina (Reed, 1982: 555; Stuart, 1982: A20; New York Times, 1985).

The criticisms of crisis relocation planning became so intense that, by 1985, FEMA officials no longer used the phrase in its publications or press releases. The intense opposition of many local communities coupled with congressional opposition killed CRP as a primary civil defense program. Moreover, the Reagan administration decided to back a new form of civil defense program which offered more political advantages and fewer political liabilities--the Strategic Defense Initiative or "Star Wars" program (New York Times, 1985).

While crisis relocation planning may be dead, evacuation is still in the lexicon of civil defense planners. Present mitigation policies still call for evacuation of high-risk areas--at least those areas which have an evacuation plan. In its 1987 publication, Preparedness Planning in a Nuclear Crisis, FEMA makes it quite clear that individuals living in high-risk areas are unlikely to survive and that evacuation is the only viable option for such individuals (FEMA, 1987: 45-47).

In addition to the mitigation policies already mentioned, FEMA has developed several other plans which may be considered mitigatory in nature. These plans include: (1) developing state and local emergency operating centers (EOCs); (2) ensuring the continuity of government; (3) revitalizing the National Defense Executive Reserve; and (4) establishing a National Disaster Medical System and the National Defense Stockpile. In brief, each of these plans attempts to provide for the protection and availability of personnel, services, and materials in the event of a national emergency. For example, the National Disaster Medical System plans to augment state and local medical resources in a mass catastrophic situation (FEMA, 1985: 12). Two of these plans, the development of EOCs and the continuity of government, are central to the implementation of the rest and, therefore, deserve closer investigation.

EMERGENCY OPERATING CENTERS

Emergency operating centers (EOCs) are intended to be decentralized headquarters for emergency management. If communications and control from federal officials are severed, most of the three thousand state and local EOCs would still function and perform a range of communications, warning, and response functions. In other words, the network of state and local centers would still be able to function if federal civil defense headquarters succumbs to blast or EMP damage. Moreover, the network allows those closest to the scene of a disaster to respond to local problems.

Yet few EOCs are actually prepared to deal with a nuclear war. While all states but Florida have a state EOC, twenty-six state headquarters lack sufficient food, an independent source of water, emergency electrical power, or fallout protection. Of the remaining state EOCs, thirteen are located in areas likely to be targeted in the event of an attack and only nine of those have a backup EOC and plans for relocating in a crisis. Thirty-two states lack two-way radio communications with their local jurisdictions (FEMA, 1986a: 13; FEMA, 1986b: 3).

The situation appears to be even worse at the local level. While 86 percent of the local jurisdictions have some sort of direction and control facility, 95 percent of these local EOCs lack survivability characteristics. More than 80 percent of these local EOCs lack two-way radio links between their command centers and emergency broadcast stations, response units, and neighboring jurisdictions (FEMA, 1986a: 13; FEMA, 1986: 3).

The evidence indicates that FEMA has a long way to go before it can effectively decentralize its communication and control functions. Most state and local EOCs would either not survive or not function during a nuclear war. Most of the EOCs which managed to survive the first few days after a nuclear exchange would be unable to perform their functions due to a lack of food, water, and other supplies being readily available. It seems obvious that state and local officials, in designating and equipping EOC sites, were concerned only with managing natural disasters or relatively localized man-made disasters (toxic spills, nuclear power, and plant disasters) they did not consider the emergency management requirements for a nuclear war.

CONTINUITY OF GOVERNMENT

While some would consider FEMA's role in providing for the continuity of government to be a strategic measure, it is also a civil defense policy. In order to meet the requirements of preparedness, response, and recovery, citizens must be assured that a legitimate government continues to exist even in the midst of a nuclear war. Only such a government can authoritatively exercise power. More importantly, the existence of a legitimate government would have a salutary effect on citizen morale.

FEMA is charged with the responsibility of identifying presidential successors and federal employees with emergency duties, keeping track of the whereabouts of these individuals through the Central Locator System, and making plans for the evacuation of these individuals in the event of an impending nuclear attack. In addition, members of the National Defense Executive Reserve (NDER), a group of senior business executives and other civilian specialists, would be activated and evacuated whenever possible (FEMA, 1980: 8; FEMA, 1982: 2). It is hoped that evacuation and dispersal will ensure the safety of at least some key members of the government who could then proceed with the response and recovery functions (McGrath and Lord, 1982: 31).

FEMA tests its evacuation and dispersal plan for federal officials at regular intervals. The tests have generally been successful although some breakdowns in communication and operational failures have occurred. Like many school fire drills, the plans have never been tested under actual emergency conditions so that no one can guarantee their effectiveness. Moreover, the plans might be modified or even thwarted by other considerations. For example, President Carter and President Reagan both decided that the president must stay at the White House in a crisis situation as a premature presidential evacuation might be interpreted by the Soviets as a prelude to a first strike by the United States. Other federal officials might come to the same conclusion although it is anticipated that the vice president will be removed to a place of safety in order to preserve the U.S. command structure after a nuclear attack (Mohr, 1982: A18).

As previously noted, civil defense policies and programs have concentrated almost exclusively on the mitigation function of emergency management. Some of these plans have been field-tested in FEMA's REX-ALPHA series of exercises. Similarly, portions of the civil defense program have been implemented in response to local emergencies such as floods and tornadoes. Still, no one knows how prepared the United States is to protect its civilian population in the event of a nuclear attack. Likewise, no one is certain about the ability of national, state, and local civil defense efforts to respond in a transattack period. There are plans available which can be implemented but no one can guarantee that those plans will, in fact, be implemented nor can they guarantee the cooperation of the civilian population. The total lack of experience with nuclear warfare makes any preparedness and response plans little more than optimistic guesswork.

Much of the same can be said for the recovery aspect of civil defense. In 1963, a special study group (called the "Project Harbor" group) convened by the National Academy of Sciences found that plans for a postattack recovery were totally inadequate (Wigner, 1966: 48; and Fitzsimons, 1968: 43). If anything, the situation is even worse today. Although FEMA's citizen's guide to civil defense admits that "no one knows exactly what life in the United States would be like after a nuclear attack," it then confidently asserts that "the U.S. would go on to reorganize and reconstruct itself." The citizen's guide concedes some aspects of the nuclear winter theory might be accurate but considers these aspects to be temporary. At the same time, the guide speculates that "Americans could be forced back to pioneer living standards. . . ." Significantly, the guide makes no mention of government strategies, plans, or proposals to deal with postattack recovery (FEMA, 1987: 119).

A cynic, reading between the lines of the citizen's guide, might conclude that the government has no postattack recovery plan or that widely scattered groups of survivors would have to fend for themselves. In fact, government does have a recovery plan, but it is simply not credible. Critics maintain that, even under the most optimistic circumstances, government recovery plans will not work because of the destruction of transportation and communication abilities. FEMA admits that its entire civil defense efforts have been hampered because it has been unable to convince people that a postattack recovery is possible (FEMA, 1986: 5).

The real problem, of course, is that the threat of nuclear war, unlike any other type of disaster discussed in this book, does not fit neatly into the mitigation, preparedness, response, and recovery aspects of emergency management. Every other type of disaster is geographically specific, it is confined to a relatively small area of the country. Every other type of disaster, even major catastrophes, directly affect only a small portion of the population. Because every other type of disaster involves only a relatively small portion of the population, every other type of disaster retains the essential government, social, and economic infrastructure which facilitate a response to that disaster. Finally, every other type of disaster offers the promise of recovery, the hope and assurance that the public and private sectors will do all that they can to restore things to normal. Even at the high water mark of a flood or at the darkest moment of a tornado, people can talk about rebuilding.

None of these factors necessarily apply to a nuclear war. But, on the other hand, none of these factors are necessarily excluded. The nation's experience with nuclear weapons testing has only limited utility in predicting what will happen in a nuclear war. Much of the threat to the civilian population depends upon the number, size, and targets of enemy missiles, at what altitude these missiles explode, whether the day is sunny or cloudy, whether the day is windy or calm, whether it is summer or winter, and so forth. The evidence suggests that a full-scale nuclear war, under the right conditions, might very well obviate the need for any of the aspects of emergency management. But, as noted previously, some sort of limited nuclear exchange or attack under less than optimal conditions offers some hope for survival. As long as there is the potential for survival, civil defense must plan for the mitigation, preparedness, response, and recovery from this type of disaster even though it lacks sufficient information and experience to do such planning with any degree of precision.

CIVIL DEFENSE ISSUES

Civil defense policies and programs are surrounded by controversy. This discussion has already suggested that one of the issues confronting civil defense is the adequacy of its plans and programs. More fundamental, civil defense has always had to confront the issue of its legitimacy. To put the issue more concretely, there are a large number of people who question whether this country should have any civil defense program. As long as the legitimacy issue remains unresolved, civil defense programs will remain inadequate. This section will discuss the legitimacy and adequacy questions with the intent of showing the relationship between the two.

Those individuals and groups who question the need for any civil defense program base their arguments on one or more of the following propositions. The first proposition is that a nuclear war is not survivable, and therefore any civil defense program is at best a waste of money and at worst a cruel hoax. This proposition assumes that the American death toll immediately following a nuclear exchange will exceed 140 million (McGrath and Lord, 1982: 31). In the following weeks, additional millions will die from injuries sustained in the attack or from the interruption of life-support medication. After that, starvation and epidemic disease will take a high toll. According to the proponents of the nuclear winter theory, even if one sought protection in a well-supplied fallout shelter prior to a nuclear exchange, long-term survival would be problematic. If a nuclear winter does occur, there would be no plant growth for months, no harvest of wild fruits, and few wild animals to kill (Greene et al., 1985: 138). What do the survivors eat for the year to two years which may be required for substantial plant growth to reoccur? Moreover, any food the survivors find (and, in fact, the fuel which they burn for warmth and cooking), will probably be contaminated by radiation which can lead to death, sterility, and birth defects. These possibilities force many people to conclude that a nuclear war, even with the best civil defense system that can be devised, is not survivable. Thus, these individuals consider any attempt at civil defense to be illegitimate. Instead, they concentrate efforts on reducing or eliminating nuclear weapons stockpiles held by the superpowers. For them, ending the arms race is the only sure civil defense (Greene et al., 1985: 138, 145, 165-70).

The second proposition used by opponents of civil defense is that a vigorous (and effective) civil defense system is a provocation to the Soviet Union. This proposition maintains that a strong civil defense would provide a first-strike credibility to the United States. Such a development will, at minimum, fuel another arms race but it will also increase the likelihood that a nuclear war will occur (Payne, 1966: 3; Winkler, 1984: 21).

To understand this argument, one must realize that the nuclear balance between the United States and the Soviet Union is stabilized by something called mutual assured destruction (MAD). MAD is essentially a balance of terror; each side is assured that if it launches a first strike, the victim nation possesses sufficient retaliatory weapons to annihilate the aggressor's population (Dye, 1984: 215). If the United States, however, embarked upon a massive civil defense program, it would be signaling that the civilian population might survive the Soviet Union's retaliatory measures. That would give the United States the opportunity to attack first (a first strike) and "win" a nuclear war. In response to this development, the Soviet Union could only increase its level of nuclear armaments in the hope of targeting civil defense facilities. More ominously, however, the civil defense buildup might encourage the Soviet Union to attack now while it still has a first-strike advantage rather than wait until the United States achieves a credible first-strike option. In this view, any destabilization of the MAD system, such as a civil defense initiative, increases the possibility of nuclear war.

The third proposition contends that civil defense is not a cost-effective means of spending defense dollars. Not surprisingly, the major advocates of this proposition are the Department of Defense and defense contractors. Historically, the Department of Defense and civil defense have been viewed as competitors for tax dollars. While military officers have often made public statements in support of civil defense, their commitment has generally evaporated when it came time to discuss appropriations (Cater, 1961: 33). It was no coincidence that, shortly after President Kennedy transferred civil defense functions to the Department of Defense, his 1962 civil defense initiative was scuttled by, among others, his military advisers (Fitzsimons, 1968: 42). It appears that the only thing the Department of Defense and civil defense have in common is the word "defense" (Payne, 1966: 8).

Essentially, the Department of Defense believes that the development and deployment of a weapons system is a much more efficient and effective means of protecting the civilian population. There is some evidence to support this position. Most important, the deployment of additional second-strike weapons strengthens our retaliatory capacity and reinforces the assumptions made under the doctrine of mutual assured destruction. In recent years, however, the Department of Defense has supported the development of a defensive weapons system which has been publicized as a civil defense system and, like other civil defense programs, has been criticized for its potential to provide the United States with a first-strike credibility. This defensive system, of course, is the Strategic Defense Initiative, otherwise known as "Star Wars" (New York Times, 1985).

Before considering other civil defense issues, it should be noted that one factor in the military defense versus civilian defense dichotomy has been the activity of defense contractors. These contractors constitute a significant lobbying force for Department of Defense programs simply because there is a lot of money to be made from weapons contracts. In contrast, there is relatively little money to be made from civil defense programs. This factor may be significant in explaining the Reagan administration's switch from emphasizing a massive civil defense program to emphasizing the Strategic Defense Initiative. Although the latter would cost more money, it also would (and, in fact, did) receive more political support. Given the political and economic power of the Department of Defense and its defense contractors, "Star Wars" was a more achievable program than any traditional civil defense program.

POLITICAL ISSUES

This discussion has previously identified some of the weaknesses in the civil defense programs involving warning, evacuation, shelter, and continuity of government. To some extent, these inadequacies can be blamed on a lack of leadership, poor planning, insufficient funding, structural disorganization, and general apathy among citizens regarding the subject. But these are only the symptoms, not the causes, of the malaise that affects civil defense. The primary cause is political in nature, often stemming from the legitimacy arguments discussed above but also originating from differing perceptions of government priorities. Since it can do little to resolve the legitimacy issue, FEMA has, in recent years, sought to confront the political issues, the two most critical of which are the support of state and local governments and civil defense's lack of a political constituency.

SUPPORT OF STATE AND LOCAL GOVERNMENTS

The structural framework of emergency management in the United States requires close collaboration between FEMA and state and local governments. FEMA is essentially a planning, training, and disbursing agency; it develops policy guidelines, trains local officials in emergency management procedures, and disburses technical and financial assistance for emergency planning and disaster recovery. The operational aspects of emergency management are performed by state and local governments. As previously noted, the crisis relocation planning effort, for which federal officials were so severely criticized, was actually performed by state and local officials operating under contracts with FEMA. The same can be said for almost every aspect of emergency management: the chief responsibility for mitigation, preparedness, response, and recovery rests with state and local governments which may request technical or financial assistance from FEMA. The system seems to have worked well--except in the area of civil defense. Several elements have combined to strain the relationship between FEMA and state and local governments in the area of civil defense.

The first element of tension was the establishment of FEMA itself. Prior to 1979, civil defense was an entirely separate and unique function of government. Even during those periods when the civil defense function was managed by the Department of Defense, it had never been seriously linked with other areas of emergency management. With the establishment of FEMA, however, five separate agencies and several orphan functions were combined within one agency.

The only thread linking these agencies and functions was their involvement in one or more of the four aspects of emergency management. In attempting to unite these diverse units into a cohesive whole, Congress and FEMA decided to focus on attack preparedness through improving the ability to deal with peacetime disasters. This "all-hazards" approach developed into a program of its own called the Integrated Emergency Management System (IEMS), which can be described as a generic approach to emergency management (see chapter 2 in this book). Instead of emphasizing civilian defense from a nuclear attack, IEMS emphasized "population protection planning" that would take into account the functional elements common to any emergency regardless of whether it was a peacetime natural disaster or a nuclear war. This approach was complemented by the 1981 amendment of the

Civil Defense Act which permitted use of FEMA assets for peacetime disasters as well as for attack preparedness.

The creation of FEMA and its new approach to emergency management cut across the traditional pattern of established relationships which had previously existed. More significantly, it meant that if state and local governments wanted federal money to plan and prepare for disasters, such plans would also have to consider the needs of civil defense, such as evacuation plans, shelter surveys, and EOCs. This was an entirely novel situation and many state and local governments vigorously resisted. While FEMA asserted that crisis relocation planning, shelter surveys, and the like were equally needed and applicable to both a natural disaster and a nuclear attack, many critics thought that IEMS was a front for civil defense planning. In so doing, the critics activated the legitimacy issue.

This issue came to a head during the 1980-1984 controversy over crisis relocation planning. About 120 units of government refused to participate in drawing up evacuation plans for their areas. Most of these governments based their decision on the proposition that nuclear war was not survivable. Many of the governments that did participate in civil defense planning did so under the same rationale as New York governor Mario Cuomo, who said that civil defense was futile but refused to interfere with state civil defense efforts because he did not want to lose the federal money (Oreskes, 1984: B1; New York Times, 1985).

Once the controversy became public, it also expanded in scope. Many local officials, who could once spend federal civil defense money on almost anything, resented FEMA's guidelines. Other officials linked the cutbacks in natural disaster aid with the all-hazards approach and concluded that FEMA's IEMS was a front designed to emphasize nuclear war planning and postattack civil defense. By 1986, it was clear that much of the cooperation between FEMA and state and local governments had broken down (Moore, 1987a: 933).

Instead of compromising, FEMA decided to fight. During 1986 and 1987, FEMA director Julius Becton constantly repeated the theme that the all-hazard approach was mandated by Congress and did not constitute a change in FEMA policy. In a report to the Senate and House Committees on Armed Services, FEMA defended its policies by noting that 1981 amendments to the Federal Civil Defense Act, while permitting civil defense funds to be used in preparing and responding to natural disasters, required that such expenditures be consistent with, contribute to, or not detract from attack-related civil defense preparedness. The report also suggested that it was time for the federal government to enforce its policy by withholding funds from any jurisdiction which refused to participate in all-hazard planning. In 1987, FEMA decided to do just that. Both Oregon and Washington refused to participate in a FEMA test of their civil defense responses following a nuclear attack. As a matter of fact, Washington had a state law which prohibited such exercises. Notwithstanding, FEMA threatened to withhold over $1 million dollars to each state unless the tests were conducted (FEMA, 1986a: 1, 4; Moore, 1987b: 934).

This controversy has severely impaired the effectiveness of civil defense. As previously noted, the major responsibility for mitigating, preparing, responding, and recovering from a disaster rests with state and local governments. These governments have generally done an effective job in coping with natural disasters and, while they may complain about FEMA's recovery policies, they would also recognize that FEMA has made some valuable contributions to their emergency management programs. Now, however, the mood is one of confrontation rather than collaboration. In the fight over the all-hazards policy, state and local governments are not without their allies in Congress. As a result, until the partnership is restored and some common ground agreed upon, civil defense policies will continue to be inadequate.

LACK OF A POLITICAL CONSTITUENCY

The controversy over the all-hazards approach points out another reason why civil defense programs are inadequate: they lack a political constituency. Throughout most of its forty-one-year history, civil defense has been at or near the bottom of government priorities. Congress, the president, and state and local governments have treated civil defense in much the same way that drug companies view the production of orphan drugs for extremely rare diseases. Many public officials have said something about the subject, but few have acted upon their words. Civil defense has never been the beneficiary of major interest groups lobbying the government or the public on its behalf--and for good reason, the benefits are future-oriented and uncertain, the liabilities enormous, and, probably most important, the profits too small. This studied neglect has been broken only in those times, such as the Cuban Missile Crisis, when people actually confronted the possibility of a nuclear war. But once the crisis passed, public and political attention focused elsewhere.

In a sense, one can interpret the entire post-World War II history of civil defense as a search for political support. In that history, the civil defense function has endured at least ten reorganizations and ten name changes. An astute political observer can easily recognize the signs of an unwanted and unappreciated function. Created and granted status as an independent agency in 1951, the Federal Civil Defense Administration lost the appropriations battles to the Strategic Air Command which insisted that it had a fool-proof civil defense system. FCDA's successor, the Office of Civil and Defense Mobilization (OCDM), had no better luck in convincing Congress that civil defense should have a higher priority. As a matter of fact, during the 1950s, Congress regularly slashed, on the average, 74 percent of the executive's appropriations requests for civil defense (Cater, 1961: 32; Payne, 1966: 8; Winkler, 1984: 17).

In 1961, civil defense supporters had reason to feel optimistic. President Kennedy made it known that he supported a strong and vigorous civil defense program. He also recognized that civil defense needed to develop stronger political support. One of his strategies was to shift responsibility for civil defense to the Department of Defense. Given the antagonism between military and civilian defense, Kennedy's reorganization seemed to defy logic, but it was actually a shrewd maneuver. As an independent agency, the appropriations for the Office of Civil and Defense Mobilization came under the jurisdiction of Albert Thomas (D-Texas), chairman of the Subcommittee on Independent Offices of the House Appropriations Committee and a staunch opponent of civil defense. By moving civil defense to the Department of Defense, jurisdiction was transferred to the Subcommittee on Defense chaired by George Mahon (D-Texas) who was a supporter of civil defense. The strategy worked for one year and during that year President Kennedy launched a major civil defense effort. But in 1962, Representative Thomas regained control of civil defense appropriations, and President Kennedy's military and civilian advisers urged him to retreat from his planned civil defense initiative (Cater, 1961: 33; Fitzsimons, 1968: 43).

Within a year after Kennedy's assassination, civil defense was transferred from the assistant secretary of defense to the Office of Civil Defense under the secretary of the army. In 1972 another reorganization created the Defense Civil Preparedness Agency (DCPA) within the Department of Defense, but the move did nothing to improve either the effectiveness of civil defense or its level of political support. The only remaining vestige of Kennedy's attempt to revitalize civil defense was the Office of Emergency Planning (renamed the Office of Emergency Preparedness in 1968) which was originally created as a staff agency in the Executive Office of the President in order to placate Frank B. Ellis, the last director of OCDM and a strong political supporter of President Kennedy. The office was intended to "coordinate" civil defense functions assigned to other agencies and to keep the president informed of developments. Instead, it merely served to confuse the chain of command. With the establishment of DCPA in 1972, the office was abolished (Cater, 1961: 33).

One can speculate whether the creation of the Federal Emergency Management Agency was another attempt to develop a political constituency for civil defense. By linking civil defense with the more politically popular natural disaster planning and preparedness programs and by mandating an all-hazards approach to emergency management, the potential exists to increase the effectiveness of civil defense without forcing Congress to deal with any specific civil defense program. The controversy over crisis relocation planning and the subsequent retreat from that program indicates that, if FEMA was created with the partial intent of developing support for civil defense, it has not been successful.

CONCLUSION

One point that has been stressed throughout this discussion is that a nuclear war is unlike any other disaster. A flood, a tornado, or even a meltdown at a nuclear power plant may cause hundreds of deaths but the average person can be confident in the ability of national, state, and local governments to handle the crisis. But a nuclear war--even a limited nuclear exchange--engenders no such confidence. Warning systems have been "hardened," fallout shelters designated, evacuation plans developed, and emergency command centers established. But, are these measures sufficient to protect the civilian population in a nuclear war? Hardly anyone, including FEMA, thinks so.

The future of civil defense programs is not encouraging. The ideological and political problems that afflict civil defense programs are deeply rooted and will not be resolved in the near future. It also appears that FEMA's attempt to circumvent ideological and political problems through the all-hazards approach has not been effective; state and local governments continue to resist full implementation of civil defense programs. In other words, very little has changed since 1946; civil defense programs are still underfunded, controversial, and hopelessly inadequate and will remain that way in the foreseeable future. Clearly, the history of civil defense provides a guide for its future.

REFERENCES

Becton, Julius W., Jr. (1986). "Emergency Management-- Where We are Now. What May Lie Ahead," address delivered at a plenary session of the World Future Society, New York, New York, July 15.

Cater, Douglass (1961). "The Politics of Civil Defense," Reporter 25 (September 14).

Dye, Thomas R. (1984). Understanding Public Policy, 5th ed. (Englewood Cliffs, N.J.: Prentice-Hall).

Federal Emergency Management Agency (FEMA)(1980). A Report to the President on Comprehensive Emergency Management, 1979 (Washington, D.C.: U.S. Government Printing Office).

_____ (1982). Annual Report, 1981 (Washington, D.C.: U.S. Government Printing Office).

_____ (1983). Annual Report, 1982 (Washington, D.C.: U.S. Government Printing Office).

_____ (1984). Annual Report, 1983 (Washington, D.C.: U.S. Government Printing Office).

_____ (1985a). Annual Report, 1984 (Washington, D.C.: U.S. Government Printing Office).

_____ (1985b). Protection in the Nuclear Age (Washington, D.C.: U.S. Government Printing Office).

_____ (1985c). In Time of Emergency: A Citizen's Handbook (Washington, D.C.: Federal Emergency Management Agency).

_____ (1986a). Report for the Senate and House Committees on Armed Services on National Civil Defense Program (Washington, D.C.: Federal Emergency management Agency).

_____ (1986b). "FEMA Report Shows Severe Weaknesses in Nation's Civil Defense Abilities," Federal Emergency Management News No. 86-52 (July 8).

_____ (1987). Preparedness Planning for a Nuclear Crisis: A Citizen's Guide to Civil Defense and Self-Protection (Washington, D.C.: U.S. Government Printing Office).

Fitzsimons, Neal (1968). "Brief History of American Civil Defense," in Who Speaks for Civil Defense? ed. Eugene P. Wigner (New York: Charles Scribner's).Greene, Owen, et al. (1985). Nuclear Winter (Cambridge, England: Polity).

May, Peter J. (1985). "FEMA'S Role in Emergency Management: Examining Recent Experience," Public Administration Review 45 (January).

McGrath, Peter, and Mary Lord (1982). "Does Civil Defense Make Sense?" Newsweek 99 (April 26).

Mohr, Charles (1982). "Preserving U.S. Command after a Nuclear Attack," New York Times (June 29).

Moore, W. John (1987a). "After The Deluge," National Journal 19 (April 18).

___ (1987b). "Back to the Atomic Cafe," National Journal 19 (April 18).

New York Times (1985). "Civil Defense Relocation Plan Said to be Dropped" (March 4).

Oreskes, Michael (1984). "Civil Defense Planning Futile, Cuomo Says," New York Times (May 15).

Payne, Fred A. (1966). "The Basic Case for Civil Defense," in Civil Defense, ed. Henry Eyring (Lancaster, Pa.: American Association for the Advancement of Science).

Pittman, Stewart L. (1968). "Government and Civil Defense," in Who Speaks for Civil Defense? ed. Eugene P. Wigner (New York: Charles Scribner's).

Reed, Michael (1982). "Coast-to-Coast Protests Greet Reagan's Civil Defense Buildup," National Journal 14 (March 27).

Stuart, Reginald (1982). "Some Local Officials Refuse to Plan Mass Relocation in an Atom Threat," New York Times (May 12).

Wigner, Eugene P. (1966). "The Possible Effectiveness of Civil Defense," in Civil Defense, ed. Henry Eyring (Lancaster, Pa.: American Association for the Advancement of Science).

Winkler, Allan M. (1984). "A 40-year History of Civil Defense," Bulletin of the Atomic Scientists 40 (June-July).

16

The Utility of
All-Hazards Programs

William L. Waugh, Jr., and Ronald John Hy

Following a decade that opened with the spectacular eruption of Mount St. Helens and closed with a catastrophic oil spill in Alaska, a very destructive hurricane in the Caribbean and the Carolinas, and a strong earthquake in northern California, there should be few topics as compelling as disaster or emergency management. One might expect policy makers to respond with legislation to reduce the likelihood of damage and to improve the responses during the next major disasters. One might expect a ground swell of public support for such programs, that they would be popular campaign issues.

However, while television brought these disasters into millions of homes all over the world, as it did the great earthquakes in Mexico City and Armenia, the nuclear accident at Chernobyl, drought and famine in northern Africa, cyclones and flooding in Bangladesh, and chemical disaster in Bhopal, India, the political response has been less than overwhelming. Although tragedy is news and the public tends to respond with sympathy and assistance, interest wanes as the months pass. The question is whether these disasters have been enough to encourage communities and officials to design and implement more effective emergency management programs. Will we see some improvement in our emergency management policies and programs following the recent disasters? Also, will the current policy momentum created by the recent disasters encourage the development of more generic, all-hazards approaches to emergency management? Those are difficult questions to answer.

When Mount St. Helens erupted, we were unprepared, without a well-defined and effective set of emergency management programs for volcanic hazards. We were better prepared with wildfire policies and programs during the dramatic fires in Yellowstone National Park in 1989. The impact of policy changes brought about by public pressure to extinguish the fires, rather than to let them burn, is still uncertain. Interestingly, the Yellowstone appears to be recovering quickly from the fires, much as the proponents of the natural role of wildland fires had suggested. Federal regulation of the airline industry mandates precautions, but airline safety is currently being assessed and new programs focusing on everything from aircraft design and maintenance to security against terrorism are being put into place following a series of tragic aviation disasters in the 1980s. Responsibility (and liability) for the Exxon Valdez oil spill is being debated as environmental damage in the Prince William Sound is being weighed and pressures are building for increased domestic oil production. Nonetheless, there are signs that the recent disasters are helping overcome the inertia experienced by emergency management programs in the 1980s.

Problems with response and recovery efforts are being examined in South Carolina following Hurricane Hugo's devastating landfall. It is uncertain how well the coastal land-use regulations will fare as political pressures increase for development. Certainly there are lessons to be learned from the response and recovery efforts. To be sure, the continuing expense of storing clothing and other assistance sent by well-meaning people in other states has increased awareness of the need to determine just what kinds of assistance are needed. From this and other recent disasters, agencies have learned to solicit money and canned food (as well as such things as medicines, beds, tents, diapers, and water), rather than than clothing, to avoid being deluged with unneeded items. Charleston officials also learned that surprisingly large numbers of their residents owned chainsaws, which facilitated the clearance of fallen trees from many residential streets.

Similarly, programs designed to lessen the impact of and respond to major earthquakes are being evaluated in the aftermath of the Loma Prieta earthquake of October 1989 and in anticipation of the expected "great quake" along the Hayward fault. Officials in cities like Oakland are now at least aware of the problems of providing shelter to the urban poor who cannot easily find housing even after the initial recovery period. Many months after the disaster, victims were still being sheltered in public school facilities. Officials have had to contend with the growing problems of prostitution and drug dealing in and around the shelters, distinguishing between those made homeless by the earthquake and those who were homeless already (a distinction that is important in determining the kinds of aid for which they qualify), and providing appropriate assistance to a variety of ethnic groups that have special needs. Despite the expectation among federal officials that victims from low-income and ethnic areas could be evacuated to and sheltered in more affluent and resilient neighborhoods and suburbs, the political obstacles to such moves are tremendous. In short, disaster response and recovery efforts have tended to become entangled in the response to broader social problems and have been made more complex by the multicultural population and existing socioeconomic cleavages.

The chapters here demonstrate that effective emergency management programs are still elusive. It remains to be seen whether we will be better prepared for the next calamities. It was pointed out in the introductory chapter that there are major impediments to effective emergency management policies and programs at the federal, state, and local levels. These impediments include low issue salience, fragmented government responsibility, a general resistance to regulatory and planning efforts, the lack of strong administrative and political constituencieis for emergency management, problems measuring program effectiveness (in the absence of a real disaster), technical problems (mostly related to mitigation programs), and the unevenness of the administrative, political, and fiscal capacities of state and local governments, as well as the diversity of hazards that need to be addressed. Can these impediments be overcome and can we develop programs that will be adequate? It should be noted that many, if not most, of the conferences and workshops on emergency management are now punctuated with calls for attention to "lessons learned" from major disaster events. There is a need to glean lessons from the case studies and disaster experiences to provide foundation for more comprehensive and universal (i.e., all-hazards) emergency management policies and programs.

ALL-HAZARDS PROGRAMS

The arguments for all-hazards programs are logical, rooted in notions of cost-effectiveness and maximum programmatic flexibility. But, the arguments very frequently overlook political, economic, and administrative realities. The realities may change, however, as we learn more about how to address hazards and to respond to disasters.

It is true now that, in the absence of programs designed to address specific hazards or to meet the demands raised by specific emergencies, states and communities make do with what they have. That was the case when fire fighting programs were adapted to needs during the Mount St. Helens eruption in 1980. The principal task of emergency managers, however, was simply to evacuate and secure the immediate area. To the extent that evacuation plans can have utility for fires, volcanic eruptions, as well as floods, hurricanes, and hazardous materials spills, and that warning and communications systems can be used for a variety of disasters, there may be some potential for generic emergency management functions. Indeed, emergency managers are getting more and more knowledgeable about evacuations and warnings as the "lessons learned" elsewhere are disseminated. The problem of too many nonambulatory residents and too few ambulance services was learned from the Florida disaster exercises. The problem of many ill and elderly residents fleeing their homes without taking their medication was also learned in Florida. The problem of many residents electing to remain in unsafe areas to take care of their pets, given that most shelters do not accept pets, is one of the lessons learned in South Carolina's experience with Hurricane Hugo. Problems of routing evacuations along two-lane roads and across narrow bridges and of issuing warnings to minority populations that may not trust government authorities are increasingly being documented. Understanding the processes and their inherent problems is a minimum requirement for developing effective programs. All-hazards programs represent at least a step beyond that.

Other mitigation, preparedness, and response components may continue to be disaster-specific. For example, there is a need for heavy equipment to move debris following earthquakes and structural failures, but little need for such equipment when structures have not fallen. The emergency medical response is often disaster-specific, particularly as regards the need for trauma facilities. Indeed, emergency response may be better served by broadening the training and technical expertise of our emergency services units, as in the hazardous materials training of fire fighters which may be tailored to the kinds of hazardous materials that will most likely be encountered.

The expertise and political wherewithal needed to address hazards and to respond to disasters often exceed the capacities of those who are most directly responsible for those activities. To the extent that communities are generally responsible for their own land-use planning and building codes, the development of comprehensive and effective mitigation programs to reduce the hazard of earthquakes and hurricanes, for example, may be quite difficult without state or federal intervention. Much the same may be true of other emergency management efforts.

The idea of a comprehensive emergency management program, such as the Federal Emergency Management Agency's Integrated Emergency Management System, is also contrary to the programmatic nature of disaster legislative. FEMA has had coordination problems within its own agency due to the disaster-specific nature of its programs. Internal resource allocations are made more difficult because of the compartmentalization. The situation is even more complex given the number of congressional authorization committees involved with FEMA's budget, although the multiplicity of budget hearings may offer some opportunities as well. State and local emergency management agencies likely operate in less complex environments, but their problems in developing comprehensive emergency management programs are no less difficult. Just as FEMA has suffered from the civil defense connection, many state and local emergency management agencies are housed either in civil defense offices and still viewed in those terms or in national guard offices and treated as a secondary (and less important) mission. Moreover, many local agencies are imbedded in government structures that confuse political and administrative authority, rather than make it clear. County governments in the United States, for example, often have multiple elected officials with no clear chief executive officer or chief administrative officer, a number of boards or commissions with their own responsibilities and authority, and several public safety officials who are independently elected, as well as the variety of officials within the county's incorporated areas. In short, responsibility and authority for emergency management may be held by several officials or by none.

The real question may be who should be responsible for the programs? In the chapter on flood policy, Cigler and Burby strongly indicated that states are willing to provide a minimum level of flood management to assure compliance with federal flood insurance guidelines. Much the same may be true of hurricane-related programs in that flood insurance requirements encourage land-use regulation along the coasts and federal expertise is needed to support mitigation and preparedness programs. Indeed, the growing debate over a national earthquake insurance program, or federal underwriting of private insurance and/or reinsurance, centers on the regulation of building codes and land-use. Certainly federal monies and technical expertise have been behind much of the preparation for hurricanes along the Gulf and East coasts. A strong federal role was also indicated in the areas of public health, earthquakes, volcanic hazards, wildfire hazards, and, to a lesser degree, some of the other kinds of disaster, as well as civil defense. At the same time, there are strong indications that state capacities to design, implement, maintain, and operate programs effectively are increasing. The California experience with earthquakes has revealed considerable state and local capacity, although the expense of recovering from the 1989 quake and preparing for the next one may test the limits of all levels of government. The efforts in Florida to prepare for major hurricanes suggest increases in capacity, despite the unanswered questions concerning the adequacy of current programs.

The dilemma of emergency management may be that there is no one agency that has the requisite technical and administrative expertise to perform all the needed functions. While there is some organizational overlap (and some gaps), emergency management involves emergency response agencies, scientific/technical agencies, regulatory (mitigation) agencies, support agencies, coordination agencies or bodies, and responsible officials. The principal challenge for emergency managers, as they increasingly are not housed within emergency response or scientific/technical agencies, is to provide sufficient coordination of involved agencies and officials so that the responsible officials can make the necessary decisions. Resource allocations are done outside of the emergency management agency. Emergency management is a coordination job, not a directive one. Skills and expertise, resources, and political authority have to be brought together to assure effective disaster response. Preparedness, mitigation, and even response programs are negotiated, rather than mandated (unless the political leadership chooses to lend its authority to the process). Hierarchical relationships have to become interpersonal relationships.

All these caveats are not to say that all-hazards programs are impossible. However, such programs may be quite complex and require substantial technical and financial support from federal and state authorities and tremendous political and interpersonal skill on the part of the emergency manager, if local programs are to be successful. What will be necessary in order for communities, states, and the nation to have adequate programs to analyze hazards, assess capabilities, conduct emergency planning, maintain capabilities, respond effectively, and recover from disasters, as the Integrated Emergency Management System model suggests?

We would suggest a coordination mechanism, including those with the technical expertise, the fiscal resources, and administrative capacity, the political acumen, and the responsibility to respond. Such a mechanism would necessarily involve federal, state, and local officials, as well as nonprofit and volunteer organizations and private sector organizations. In that individual and organizational efforts are very much colored by the value systems that guide their design and implementation, care should be taken in choosing participating agencies (Dery, 1984; Pavlak, 1988; Waugh, 1990). Clear lines of responsibility, including legal jurisdiction, need to be defined. The reality of local responsibility and jurisdiction needs to be accommodated. It cannot be assumed that a chain of command will exist, or even that we want it to exist. Tactical decision making has to be a local responsibility during the disaster response, but resource allocations need to be made at the regional or state level. What is being suggested is a decentralized emergency management system (May and Williams, 1986), with all levels of government and all sectors being involved in strategic decisions and with local responders in control of the field operations. It will require some intergovernment flexibility to design and implement the policy and considerable capacity building to help local officials operate the programs. The keys are getting the necessary information to make good decisions, communicating that information to the responsible decision makers, establishing organizational processes that will facilitate learning and effective action, and creating structures that will provide stability in an uncertain environment (Comfort, 1988).

THE IMPERATIVE TO ACT

Indeed, there is an imperative to act. We can expect major hurricanes along the Gulf coast and emergency managers are assessing the vulnerabilities of cities and towns from southern Texas to New England. While Hurricane Gilbert wreaked havoc in the Caribbean in 1988 and American disaster plans were being reviewed in the event that the storm turned northward, the impact of a force 4 or 5 storm making landfall in a heavily populated area was difficult to imagine until Hurricane Hugo. Hugo's 135 mile-per-hour winds demonstrated what damage could be done to an ill-prepared coastline. It is somewhat encouraging that damage assessments suggest that shoddy construction and poor (or nonexistent) building codes accounted for much of the loss. Stricter codes and land-use regulation can alleviate that problem somewhat. Communication problems, slow federal response, and coordination problems associated with the logistics of delivering aid to small, isolated communities pointed up the inadequacies of the federal and state emergency management systems during the Hugo disaster, as well. Those problems can also be addressed.

Seismologists are warning that the 7.1 Loma Prieta earthquake of October 1989 was not the expected 8.0+ "great quake" and that we can expect major earthquakes in or near some of our other large cities. More specifically, the U.S. Geological Survey warns that earthquakes may well occur in the very near future in Honolulu, Anchorage, Seattle-Tacoma, Los Angeles, San Diego, Salt Lake City, Memphis, St. Louis, Buffalo, Rochester, Boston, and Charleston (Budiansky et al., 1989). Many of these cities have not experienced a major quake in over one hundred years and are quite unprepared to respond to one now. In 1985, FEMA estimated that a 7.6 earthquake in the East would kill as many as 2,500 people and cause $25 billion in damage largely because of inadequate building codes. The 7.1 quake in the Bay area killed a remarkably small number of people, despite occurring during the rush hour. The emergency response, for the most part, appeared quite effective. However, the National Oceanic and Atmospheric Administration estimates that a 8.0 quake in San Francisco during the rush hour could kill as many as 11,000 (Budiansky et al., 1989).

There are some encouraging signs that the warnings are having some effect. A prediction of a major earthquake in December of 1990, along the New Madrid fault and likely affecting a broad area of the central United States, has been issued and is being taken very seriously by public officials. During the summer of 1990, some communities in Illinois were already restricting the scheduling of vacation time by public employees during the latter part of the year.

Museum officials in Memphis, Tennessee, were also discussing the loan of irreplacable exhibits to museums outside of the danger area. The prediction is clearly being heeded in some areas around the fault. A question that arises is what happens if the earthquake does not occur. Will there still be support for preparedness programs?

The potential for large-scale hazardous materials accidents, nuclear facility accidents, plane crashes and other transportation accidents, volcanic activity, floods, epidemics, and widespread wildfire, not to mention nuclear war, is also very real. In many ways, the chapters here have only scratched the surface of the issue. The potential devastation from acid rain (Vittes, 1990), nontransport-related hazardous materials spills, ground water contamination from landfills and fertilizer/pesticide runoff, radiological contamination (e.g., around weapons plants), subsidence, train and ship wrecks, depletion of the ozone layer (and its resultant effects), nuclear and/or biological terrorism (Waugh, 1990), and any number of other disaster types were not dealt with directly. In some measure the choice not to address these hazards was because emergency management policies are not well developed or are very similar to the kinds of programs that address the major disaster types addressed here. Certainly there are programs to prevent avalanches, mitigate the effects of sinkholes, and respond to large highrise fires, but they were judged less compelling. In the case of structural fires, the voluminous literature on fire science and the variety of programs mitigated against including that disaster type in this analysis. Fire fighting, outside of the national forests and parks, is a local responsibility. Also, the large number of volunteer fire departments and growing numbers of professional units exhibit a great variety of program orientations, despite the technical assistance and training available through the National Fire Academy in Emmitsburg, Maryland, and state and local fire training agencies.

Are all-hazards programs a good investment of resources? The answer is yes. But, at this point, all-hazards programs will likely be most effective on a functional level, rather than on a comprehensive level. While emergency management functions continue to be housed in limited purpose agencies, e.g., fire and police departments, and dependent upon disaster-specific program legislation and budgets, a comprehensive, all-hazards perspective is lacking. That picture may change with the increasing professionalization of emergency managers and increasing knowledge about hazard management and disaster response programs, but it will take time.

REFERENCES

Budiansky, Stephen, et al. (1989). "After the Great Quake of '89," U.S. News and World Report (October 30): 28-35.

Comfort, Louise K. (1988). "Designing Policy for Action: The Emergency Management System," in Managing Disaster: Strategies and Policy Perspectives, ed. Louis K. Comfort, pp. 3-21 (Durham, N.C.: Duke University Press).

Dery, David (1984). Problem Definition in Policy Analysis (Lawrence: University Press of Kansas).

Drabek, Thomas E. (1987). The Professional Emergency Manager (Boulder, Colo.: University of Colorado, IBS#44).

May, Peter J., and Walter Williams (1986). Disaster Policy Implementation: Managing Programs under Shared Governance (New York: Plenum).

Pavlak, Thomas J. (1988). "Structuring Problems for Policy Action," in Managing Disaster: Strategies and Policy Perspectives, ed. Louise K. Comfort, pp. 22-36.

Petak, William J. (1985). "Emergency Management: A Challenge for Public Administration," Public Administration Review 45 (January).

Vittes, M. Elliot (1990). "Acid Rain as Disaster Agent," in Cities and Disaster: North American Studies in Emergency Management, eds. Richard T. Sylves and William L. Waugh, Jr (Springfield, Ill.: Charles C. Thomas).

Waugh, William L., Jr. (1990). Terrorism and Emergency Management: Policy and Administration (New York and Basel: Marcel Dekker).

Select Bibliography

Ackerman, C., _Flood Hazard Mitigation_ (Washington, D.C.: National Science Foundation, Engineering and Applied Sciences Division, 1980).

Ahearn, Frederick L., Jr., and Raquel E. Cohen, _Disasters and Mental Health: An Annotated Bibliography_ (Rockville, Md.: U.S. Department of Health and Human Services, National Institute of Mental Health, Center for Mental Health Studies of Emergencies, DDHS Publication No. ADM84-1311, 1984).

Aldrich, Howard, _Organizations and Environments_ (New York: Prentice-Hall, 1979).

Algermissen, S. T., _A Study of Earthquake Losses in the San Francisco Bay Area_ (Washington, D.C.: U.S. Department of Commerce, NOAA, 1972).

___, _A Study of Earthquake Losses in the Los Angeles, California Area_ (Washington, D.C.: U.S. Department of Commerce, NOAA, 1973).

American Friends Service Committee, _In the Wake of Hurricane Camille: An Analysis of the Federal Response_ (Philadelphia: American Friends Service Committee, 1969).

American Nuclear Society, "Special Report: The Ordeal at Three Mile Island," _Nuclear News_ (April 6, 1979): 1-6.

American Red Cross, _Disaster Relief Program_ (Washington, D.C.: American Red Cross, 1975).

___, _Hurricane Action_ (Washington, D.C.: American Red Cross, 1975).

Anderson, William A., Local Civil Defense in Natural Disaster: From Office to Organization (Washington, D.C.: Office of Civil Defense, Disaster Research Center Report No. 7, 1969).

___, Some Observations on a Disaster Subculture (Columbus, Ohio: Ohio State University Disaster Research Center, 1965).

___, "Disaster Warning and Communication in Two Communities," Journal of Communication 19 (1969): 92-104.

Andrews, Richard R., "Seismic Safety Planning in California: An Overview of Recent Initiatives," Proceedings of the Third International Conference on Microzonation 3, 1982, pp. 1503-12.

___, "Lessons from Seismic Safety Planning in California," in Preparing for and Responding to a Damaging Earthquake in the Eastern U.S.: Proceedings of Conference XIV, September 16-18, 1981, Knoxville, Tennessee, ed. W. W. Hays (Reston, Va.: USGS, Open File Report 82-220, 1982).

Applied Technology Council, Tentative Provisions for the Development of Seismic Regulations for Buildings (Washington, D.C.: U.S. Government Printing Office, ATC Publication ATC-3-06, NBS Special Publication 510, NSF Publication 78-8, 1978).

Association of Bay Area Governments, Will Local Government Be Liable for Earthquake Losses? (Berkeley, Calif.: Association of Bay Area Governments, 1979).

Association of Flood Plain Managers, FEMA and the States: A Cooperative Effort in Flood Hazard Mitigation (Madison, Wisc., 1982). (Unpublished)

Atlantic Richfield Company, "What An Emergency Plan Should Cover" (Los Angeles: A. Prud'Homme, 1982).

Ayre, Robert S., Earthquake and Tsunami Hazards in the U.S. (Boulder, Colo.: University of Colorado, IBS Monograph, 1975).

Baker, Earl T., and Tae Gordon McPhie, Land Use Management and Regulation in Hazardous Areas (Boulder, Colo.: University of Colorado, IBS#6, 1975).

Baker, George W., and Dwight W. Chapman, eds., Man and Society in Disaster (New York: Basic, 1962).

Banks, Herman J., and Anne T. Romano, Human Relations for Emergency Response Personnel

(Springfield, Ill.: Charles C. Thomas, 1982).

Barakei, Mohammed el, Model Rules for Disaster Relief Operations (New York: UN Institute for Training and Research Policy and Efficacy Studies No. 8, 1982).

Baram, Michael, Alternatives to Regulation: Managing Risks to Health, Safety and the Environment (Lexington, Mass.: Lexington, 1981).

Barberi, R., and P. Gasparini, "Volcanic Hazards," Bulletin of the International Association of Engineering and Geology 14 (1976): 217-32.

Barton, A., Communities in Disaster (New York: Doubleday, 1970).

Bates, F. L., et al., The Social and Psychological Consequences of a Natural Disaster: A Longitudinal Study of Hurricane Audrey (1957) (Washington, D.C.: National Academy of Sciences, National Research Council, 1963).

Bauman, D., and J. Sims, "Flood Insurance," Economic Geography 54 (1978): 189-96.

Berke, Philip, and Suzanne Wilhite, Local Mitigation Planning Response to Earthquake Hazards: Results of a National Survey, College Station, Texas, Texas A&M University, College of Architecture, Hazard Reduction and Recovery Center (National Science Foundation Grant No. ECE-8421106), May 1988.

Binder, Dennis, "Dam Safety: The Critical Imperative," Land and Water Review 14 (1979): 341-92.

Bloomgren, Patricia A., Strengthening State Floodplain Management (Boulder, Colo.: University of Colorado, Natural Hazards Research and Applications Information Center Special Publication 3, Institute of Behavioral Science, University of Colorado, 1982).

Bolt, Bruce, Earthquakes (New York: W. H. Freeman, 1988).

Bristow, Allen P., Police Disaster Operations (Springfield, Ill: Charles C. Thomas, 1972).

Brown, Barbara J., Disaster Preparedness and the U.N.: Advance Planning for Disaster Relief (Elmsford, N.Y.: Pergamon, 1979).

Building Seismic Safety Council, BSSC Program on Improved Seismic Safety Provisions--Societal Implications: A Community Handbook (Washington, D.C.: Federal Emergency Management Agency, Publication No. 83, June 1985).

____, BSSC Program on Improved Seismic Safety Provisions--Societal Implications: Selected Readings (Washington, D.C.: Federal Emergency Management Agency, Publication No. 84, June 1985).

____, NEHRP Recommended Provisions for the Development of Seismic Regulations for New Buildings, 1985 Edition, Part 1: Provisions, Part 2: Commentary, Part 3: Appendix (Washington, D.C.: Federal Emergency Management Agency, Publications Nos. 17, 18, and 19, February 1986).

____, Guide to Application of the NEHRP RECOMMENDED PROVISIONS in Earthquake-Resistant Building Design (Washington, D.C.: Federal Emergency Management Agency, Publication No. 140, July 1987).

____, Abatement of Seismic Hazards to Lifelines: Proceedings of a Workshop on Development of an Action Plan, Volumes 1-6 (Washington, D.C.: Federal Emergency Management Agency, Publications Nos. 26-31, July 1987).

____, Abatement of Seismic Hazards to Lifelines: An Action Plan (Washington, D.C.: Federal Emergency Management Agency, Publication No. 142, August 1987).

Burby, Raymond J., and Beverly A. Cigler, "Effectiveness of State Assistance Program for Flood Hazard Mitigation," Chapel Hill, N.C.: University of North Carolina, Center for Urban and Regional Studies, 1983. (Unpublished)

Burby, Raymond J., and Steven P. French, Flood Plain Land Use Management: A National Assessment (Boulder, Colo.: Westview, 1985).

Burton, Ian; Robert W. Kates; and, Gilbert F. White, The Environment as Hazard (New York: Oxford University Press, 1978).

California Seismic Safety Commission, Seismic Safety in California: Short History and Current Issues (Sacramento, Calif.: CSSC Publication No. 83-06, January 1983).

____, Model Recovery Program, report of the Recovery and Reconstruction Advisory Committee, Earthquake Preparedness Task Force (Sacramento, Calif.: California Seismic Safety Commission, July 1984).

____, Bay Area Earthquake Study, Earthquake Preparedness in the San Francisco Bay Region: An Inventory and Assessment of Current Programs and Activities and Recommendations for Future Comprehensive

Earthquake Preparedness Projects (Oakland, Calif.: California Seismic Safety Commission, September 1984).

___, Bay Area Earthquake Study, Earthquake Preparedness in the San Francisco Bay Region: Appendices (Oakland, Calif.: California Seismic Safety Commission, 1984).

___, California at Risk: Steps to Earthquake Safety for Local Government (Sacramento, Calif: California Seismic Safety Commission, January 1988).

Carson, William D., Estimating Costs and Benefits for Nonstructural Flood Control Measures (Davis, Calif.: Hydrolic Engineering Center, U.S. Army Corps of Engineers, October 1975).

Charles, Michael T.,and John Choon Kim, eds., Emergency Management: A Casebook (Springfield, Ill.: Charles C. Thomas, 1988).

Chayet, Neil L., Legal Implications of Emergency Care (New York: Appleton-Century-Crofts, 1969).

Cohen, Raquel E., and Frederick L. Ahearn, Jr., Handbook for Mental Health Care of Disaster Victims (Baltimore: Johns Hopkins University Press, 1980).

Comfort, Louise K., ed., Managing Disasters: Strategies and Policy Perspectives (Durham, N.C.: Duke University Press, 1988).

Cornell, James, The Great International Disaster Book (New York: Scribner, 1976).

Council of State Governments, Comprehensive Emergency Preparedness Planning in State Government (Lexington, Ky.: Council of State Governments, 1976).

___, The States and Natural Hazards (Lexington, Ky.: Council of State Governments, 1979).

Cuny, Frederick C., Disasters and Development (New York: Oxford University Press, 1983).

Dacy, Douglas, and Howard Kunreuther, Economics of Natural Disasters: Implications for Federal Policy (New York: Free, 1979).

Davis, Ian, ed., Disasters and the Small Dwelling (New York: Pergamon, 1981).

Degenkolb, H. J., Associates, The Whittier Narrows Earthquake, October 1, 1987 (San Francisco, Calif.: Degenkolb Associates, n.d.).

Douty, Christopher M., The Economics of Localized Disasters: The 1906 San Francisco Catastrophe (New York: Arno, 1977).

Drabek, Thomas E., et al., Managing Multiorganizational Emergency Responses

(Boulder, Colo.: University of Colorado, IBS#6, 1981).

___, The Professional Emergency Manager (Boulder, Colo.: University of Colorado, IBS#44, 1987).

Drabek, Thomas E., Alvin H. Mushkatel, and Thomas S. Kilijanik, Earthquake Mitigation Policy: The Experience of Two States (Boulder, Colorado: University of Colorado, IBS#37, 1983).

___, Disaster in Aisle 13: A Case Study of the Coliseum Explosion at the Indiana State Fairgrounds,October 31, 1963 (Columbus, Ohio: Ohio State University, College of Administrative Science, Monograph D-1, 1968).

Dynes, Russell R., Organized Behavior in Disaster (Lexington, Mass.: Lexington, 1970).

Executive Office of the President, The National Earthquake Hazards Reduction Program (Washington, D.C.: Executive Office of the President, 1978).

Farberow, Norman L., and Norma S. Gordon, Manual for Child Health Workers in Major Disasters (Rockville, Md.: U.S. Department of Health and Human Services, National Institute of Mental Health, Disaster Assistance and Emergency Mental Health, DHHS Publication No. ADM81-1070, 1981).

Faster, Harold D., Disaster Planning: Preservation of Life and Property (New York: Springer-Verlag, 1980).

Federal Emergency Management Agency, Civil Defense and the Public: An Overview of Public Attitudes Studies (Washington, D.C.: Federal Emergency Management Agency, MP-62, September 1979).

___, An Assessment of the Consequences and Preparations for a Catastrophic California Earthquake: Findings and Actions Taken (Washington, D.C.: Federal Emergency Management Agency, M&R-2, November 1980).

___, Questions and Answers on Crisis Relocation (Washington, D.C.: Federal Emergency Management Agency, P&P-4, October 1980).

___, Early Progress to Implement Federal Guidelines for Dam Safety (Washington, D.C.: Federal Emergency Management Agency, M&R-1, 1980).

___, Flood Hazard Mitigation: Handbook of Common Procedures (Washington, D.C.: Federal Emergency Management Agency, FEMA-14, 1981).

___, Dam Safety Research: Current, Planned, Future (Washington, D.C.: Federal Emergency Management Agency, FEMA-21, 1982).

___, National Emergency Training Center, Office of Programs and Academics, Senior Executive Policy Center, Managing the Disaster Response--A Search for Theory: Conference Report (Washington, D.C.: Federal Emergency Management Agency, February 1984).

___, State and Local Earthquake Hazards Reduction: Implementation of FEMA Funding and Support (Washington, D.C.: Federal Emergency Management Agency, CPG 2-18, August 1985).

___, A Unified National Program for Floodplain Management (Washington, D.C.: Federal Emergency Management Agency, FEMA-100, March 1986).

___, Disaster Assistance Programs--Making Mitigation Work: A Handbook for State Officials (Washington, D.C.: Federal Emergency Management Agency, DAP 12, June 1986).

___, Plan for Federal Response to a Catastrophic Earthquake (Washington, D.C.: Federal Emergency Management Agency, April 15, 1987).

___, NEHRP Expert Review Committee, The National Earthquake Hazards Reduction Program: Commentary and Recommendations of the Expert Review Committee (Washington, D.C.: Federal Emergency Management Agency, 1987).

___, U.S. Fire Academy, The CEO's Disaster Survival Kit: A Common-Sense Guide for Local Government Chief Executive Officers (Washington, D.C.: U.S. Government Printing Office, FA-81, October 1988).

___, National Earthquake Hazards Reduction Program: Fiscal Year 1989 Activities (Washington, D.C.: U.S. Government Printing Office, 1989).

Feigenbaum, Edward D., and Mark L. Ford, Emergency Management in the States (Lexington, Ky.: Council of State Governments, 1984).

Foster, Harold D., Disaster Planning: The Preservation of Life and Property (New York: Springer-Verlag, 1980).

Friesema, H. Paul, ed., Aftermath: Communities After Natural Disasters (Beverly Hills, Calif.: Sage, 1979).

Fuller, Myron L., The New Madrid Earthquake (Washington, D.C.: U.S. Government Printing Office, 1912; reprinted by U.S. Geological Survey, 1988).

Geipel, Robert (trans. Philip Wagner), Disaster and Reconstruction: The Friuli, Italy, Earthquakes of 1976 (Boston: Allen and Unwin, 1982).

George, James E., Law and Emergency Care (St. Louis, Mo.: Mosby, 1980).

Glantz, Michael H., ed., The Politics of Natural Disaster: The Case of the Sahel Drought (New York: Praeger, 1976).

Gleser, Goldine C., Bonnie L. Green, and Caroline Winget, eds., Prolonged Psychosocial Effects of Disaster: A Study of Buffalo Creek (New York: Academic, 1981).

Goldstein, Arnold S., EMS and the Law: A Legal Handbook for EMS Personnel (Bowie, Md.: R.J. Brady, 1983).

Green, Stephen, International Disaster Relief: Toward a Responsive System (New York: McGraw-Hill, 1977).

Gregg, Michael B., ed., The Public Health Consequences of Disasters, 1989 (Atlanta, Ga.: U.S. Department of Health and Human Services, Public Health Service, Centers for Disease Control, September 1989).

Griggs, Gary, and John A. Gilchrist, Geological Hazards, Resources and Environmental Planning, 2d Ed. (New York: Wadsworth, 1983).

Grigsby, Gordon, Tornado Watch (Columbus, Ohio: Ohio State University Press, 1977).

Grosser, George H., Henry Wechsler, and Milton Greenblatt, eds., The Threat of Impending Disaster: Contributions to the Psychology of Stress (Cambridge, Mass.: MIT Press, 1964).

Gruntfest, Eve, Flash Flood/Dam Failure Warning System Survey, report prepared for the U.S. Bureau of Reclamation, December 1987. (unpublished)

Haas, J. Eugene, Robert W. Kates, and Martyn J. Bowden, eds., Reconstruction Following Disaster (Cambridge, Mass.: MIT Press, 1977).

Hance, Billie Jo, Caron Chess, and Peter M. Sandman, Improving Dialogue with Communities: A Risk Communication Manual for Government, report from Cook College, Rutgers University, N.J. Agricultural Experiment Station, Environmental Communication Research Program, New Brunswick, N.J. (Trenton, N.J.: New Jersey Department of Environmental Protection, 1988).

Hartsough, Don M., and Diane Garaventa Myers, Disaster Work and Mental Health: Prevention and

Control of Stress among Workers (Rockville, Md.: U.S. Department of Health and Human Services, National Institute of Mental Health, Center for Mental Health Studies of Emergencies, DHHS Publication No. ADM85-1422, 1985).

Hayes, Walter W., *Facing Geological and Hydrological Hazards: Earth-Science Considerations*, Professional Paper No. 240B (Alexandria, Va.: USGS Distribution Branch, 1981).

Healy, Richard J., *Emergency and Disaster Planning* (New York: Wiley, 1969).

Herman, Roger E., "The Role of Public Works in Emergency Management," *Public Works* (April 1984): 72-3, 104-5.

Hoetmer, Gerald J., "Emergency Management," *Baseline Data Reports* 15 (Washington, D.C.: International City Management Association, April 1983).

Hoyt, William G., and Walter B. Langbein, *Floods* (Princeton, N.J.: Princeton University Press, 1955).

Hutchinson, Sally A., *Survival Practices of Rescue Workers: Hidden Dimensions of Watchful Readiness* (Washington, D.C.: University Press of America, 1983).

ICMA and FEMA, "How Prepared Is Your Community for Its Next Emergency: A Manager's Checklist," *Local Government Emergency Management: A Practitioners' Workbook*, Handbook Series No. 3 (International City Management Association and Federal Emergency Management Agency, 1980).

Interagency Hazard Mitigation Team, *Hurricane Hugo*, team report for Hurricane Hugo, FEMA-843-DR-SC, October 1989.

Jelenko, Carl, III, and Charles F. Frey, eds., *EMS: An Overview* (Bowie, Md.: R. J. Brady, 1976).

Kennedy, Will C., *The Police Department in Natural Disaster Operations* (Washington, D.C.: Office of Civil Defense, 1969).

Kreps, Gary A., "Sociological Inquiry and Disaster Relief," *Annual Review of Sociology* 10 (1984): 309-30.

Kunreuther, Howard, *Disaster Insurance Protection: Public Policy Lessons* (New York: Wiley, 1978).

___, *Recovery from Natural Disasters: Insurance or Federal Aid?* (Washington, D.C.: American Enterprise Institute, Evaluative Studies #12, 1973).

Leaning, Jennifer, and Langley Keyes, eds., _The Counterfeit Ark: Crisis Relocation for Nuclear War_ (Cambridge, Mass.: Ballinger, 1984).

Leonard, Vivian A., _Police Pre-Disaster Preparation_ (Springfield, Ill.: Charles C. Thomas, 1973).

Lucas, Rex A., _Men in Crisis: A Study of Mine Disaster_ (New York: Basic, 1969).

Lystad, Mary, ed., _Innovations in Mental Health Services to Disaster Victims_ (Rockville, Md.: U.S. Department of Health and Human Services, National Institute of Mental Health, Center for Mental Health Studies of Emergencies, DHHS Publication No. ADM86-1390, 1985).

Maass, Arthur, _Muddy Waters: The Army Engineers and the Nation's Waters_ (Cambridge, Mass.: Harvard University Press, 1951).

MacAlister-Smith, Peter, _International Humanitarian Assistance: Disaster Relief Actions in International Law and Organization_ (Boston: M. Nijhoff, 1985).

Marston, Sallie A., ed., _Terminal Disasters: Computer Applications in Emergency Management_ (Boulder, Colo.: University of Colorado, IBS#39, 1986).

May, Peter J., _Recovering from Catastrophes: Federal Disaster Relief Policy and Politics_ (Westport, Conn.: Greenwood, 1985).

May, Peter J., and Walter Williams, _Disaster Policy Implementation: Managing Programs under Shared Governance_ (New York: Plenum, 1986).

Medvedev, Zhores A. (trans. George Saunders), _Nuclear Disaster in the Urals_ (New York: Norton, 1979).

Meehan, Richard L., _The Atom and the Fault: Experts, Earthquakes, and Nuclear Power_ (Cambridge, Mass.: MIT Press, 1984).

Meltsner, Arnold J., "Public Support for Seismic Safety: Where Is It in California," _Mass Emergencies_ 3 (1978): 167-84.

Mileti, Dennis, Thomas E. Drabek, and J. Eugene Haas, _Human Systems in Extreme Environments: A Sociological Perspective_ (Boulder, Colo.: University of Colorado, Institute of Behavioral Science Monograph, 1975).

Morone, Joseph G., and Edward J. Woodhouse, _Averting Catastrope: Strategies for Regulating Risky Technologies_ (Berkeley, Calif.: University of California Press, 1986).

Murphy, Leonard M., Environmental Research Labs, San Fernando, California, Earthquake of February 9, 1971 (Washington, D.C.: U.S. Government Printing Office, 1973).

National Fire Academy, Community Fire Defenses: Challenges and Solutions (Washington, D.C.: U.S. Government Printing Office, NFA-SM-CFD, Febuary 13, 1984).

___, Fire Risk Analysis: A Systems Approach (Washington, D.C.: U.S. Government Printing Office, NFA-SM-FRA:SA, February 13, 1984).

National Governors' Association, Emergency Mitigation: Strategies for Disaster Prevention and Reduction (Washington, D.C.: National Governors' Association, 1980).

___, "Lessons Learned-The FEMA/States Cooperative Agreement," Emergency Management Bulletin (Washington, D.C.: National Governors' Association, May 1982).

___, Comprehensive Emergency Management Bulletin (Washington, D.C.: National Governors' Association, April 1982).

___, Domestic Terrorism (Washington, D.C.: National Governors' Association, Emergency Preparedness Project, Center for Policy Research, State Emergency Management Series, 1978).

National Institute of Mental Health, Training Manual for Human Service Workers in Major Disasters (Rockville, Md.: U.S. Department of Health and Human Services, National Institute of Mental Health, DHHS Publication No. ADM83-538, 1978, 1983).

___, Role Stressors and Supports for Emergency Workers, proceedings from a 1984 workshop sponsored by the National Institute of Mental Health and the Federal Emergency Management Agency (Rockville, Md.: U.S. Department of Health and Human Services, National Institute of Mental Health, DHHS Publication No. ADM85-1408, 1985).

National Research Council, Committee on the Safety of Nonfederal Dams, Safety of Nonfederal Dams: A Review of the Federal Role (Washington, D.C.: Federal Emergency Management Agency, FEMA-31, November 1982).

___, Commission of Engineering and Technical Systems, Advisory Board of the Built Environment, Multiple Hazard Mitigation (Washington, D.C.: National Academy, 1983).

____, Committee on the Safety of Existing Dams, Safety of Existing Dams: Evaluation and Improvement (Washington, D.C.: National Academy, 1983).

____, Earthquake Prediction and Public Policy (Washington, D.C.: National Academy, 1975).

____, Reducing Disasters' Toll: The United States Decade for Natural Disaster Reduction (Washington, D.C.: National Academy, 1989).

____, Estimating Losses from Future Earthquakes: Panel Report (A Non-Technical Summary) (Washington, D.C.: Federal Emergency Management Agency, FEMA-176, June 1989).

National Research Council, U.S. National Academy of Sciences, and U.S. National Academy of Engineering, Confronting Natural Disasters: An International Decade for Natural Hazard Reduction (Washington, D.C.: National Academy, 1987.

National Science Foundation, A Report on Flood Hazard Mitigation (Washington, D.C.: National Science Foundation, 1980).

National Seismic Policy Conference, Conference Proceedings for meeting of November 1-3, 1983, Seattle, Wash. (Olympia, Wash.: Department of Emergency Services, March 1984).

OECD, Nuclear Third Party Liability and Insurance: Status and Prospects (Paris: OECD, 1985).

Pan American Health Organization, A Guide to Emergency Health Management After Natural Disasters (Washington, D.C.: Pan American Health Organization, 1981).

____, Environmental Health Management After Natural Disasters (Washington, D.C.: Pan American Health Organization, 1982).

____, Medical Supply Management after Natural Disaster (Washington, D.C.: Pan American Health Organization, No. 438, 1983).

Parad, Howard J., H. L. P. Resnik, and Libbie G. Parad, eds., Emergency and Disaster Management: A Mental Health Sourcebook (Bowie, Md.: Charles, 1976).

Penick, James, Jr., The New Madrid Earthquakes of 1811-1812 (Columbia, Mo.: University of Missouri Press, 1976, 1981).

Perry, Ronald W., The Social Psychology of Civil Defense (Lexington, Mass.: Lexington, 1982).

Perry, Ronald W., and Alvin H. Mushkatel, Disaster Management: Warning, Response and Community Relocation (Westport, Conn.: Quorum/Greenwood, 1984).

Petak, William J., and Arthur A. Atkisson, <u>Natural Hazard Risk Assessment and Public Policy: Anticipating the Unexpected</u> (New York: Springer-Verlag, 1982).

Platt, Rutherford H., "The National Flood Insurance Program: Some Midstream Perspectives," <u>Journal of the American Institute of Planners</u> 42 (1976): 303-13.

___, <u>Options to Improve the Federal Nonstructural Response to Floods</u>, report prepared for the President's Committee on Water Policy (Washington, D.C.: U.S. Water Resources Council, 1979).

___, M. Mullen, and J.A. Kusler, <u>Intergovernmental Management of Floodplains</u> (Boulder, Colo.: University of Colorado, IBS#30, 1980).

Quarantelli, E. L., and Russell R. Dynes, "Response to Social Crisis and Disaster," <u>Annual Review of Sociology</u> 3 (1977): 23-49.

___, <u>Disasters: Theory and Research</u> (Beverly Hills, Calif.: Sage, 1978).

___, <u>Organizational Behavior in Disasters and Implications for Disaster Planning</u> (Emmitsburg, Md.: Federal Emergency Management Agency, National Emergency Training Center, Monograph Series, 1984).

Real, Charles R., <u>A Review of Probabilistic Long-Term Forecasts for Major Earthquakes in the San Francisco Bay Region</u> (Oakland, Calif.: California Seismic Safety Commission, Bay Area Earthquake Study, July 1984).

Rossi, Peter, James D. Wright, and Eleanor Weber-Burdin, <u>Natural Hazards and Public Choice: The State and Local Politics of Hazard Mitigation</u> (New York: Academic, 1982).

Rossi, Peter, et al., <u>Victims of the Environment: Loss from Natural Hazards in the U.S., 1970-1980</u> (New York: Plenum, 1983).

Rosenthal, Uriel, Michael T. Charles, and Paul 't Hart, eds., <u>Coping with Crises: The Management of Disasters, Riots, and Terrorism</u> (Springfield, Ill.: Charles C. Thomas, 1989).

Russell, Clifford S., "Losses from Natural Hazards," <u>Land Economics</u> 46 (1970): 383-93.

Savage, P. E. A., <u>Disasters: Hospital Planning</u> (New York: Pergamon, 1979).

Settle, Allen K., <u>Emergency Management in Public Administration Education</u> (Emmitsburg, Md.: Federal Emergency Management Agency, National Emergency Training Center Monograph Series, 1985).

Simpson, Robert H., and Herbert Riehl, The Hurricane and Its Impact (Baton Rouge: Louisiana State University Press, 1981).

Skeet, Muriel, Manual for Disaster Relief Work (New York: Churchill Livingstone, 1977).

Smithsonian Institute, Directory of Disaster-Related Technology (Washington, D.C.: U.S. Government Printing Office, 1975).

Sowder, Barbara J., Disasters and Mental Health: Selected Contemporary Perspectives (Rockville, Md.: U.S. Department of Health and Human Services, National Institute of Mental Health, DHHS Publication No. ADM85-1421, 1985).

State/Federal Hazard Mitigation Survey Team, Hazard Mitigation Opportunities for California, team report fo the Loma Prieta Earthquake, October 17, 1989, FEMA-845-DR-CA, January 1990.

Stephens, Lynn H., and Stephen J. Green, eds, Disaster Assistance, Appraisal, Reform, and New Approaches (New York: New York University Press, 1979).

Stern, Gerald H., The Buffalo Creek Disaster (New York: Random House, 1976).

Svenson, Arthur G., Earthquakes, Earth Scientists, and Seismic Safety Planning in California (Lanham, Md.: University Press of America, 1984).

Sylves, Richard, and William L. Waugh, Jr., eds., Cities and Disaster: North American Studies in Emergency Management (Springfield, Ill.: Charles C. Thomas Publishers, 1990).

Taylor, James B., Louis A. Zurcher, and William H. Key, Tornado: A Community Responds to Disaster (Seattle, Wash.: University of Washington Press, 1970).

Tennessee Valley Authority, Evaluation of the Use of National High-Altitude Photography in Measuring the Extent and Type of Floodplain Development (Knoxville, Tenn.: Tennessee Valley Authority, TVA/ONRED/AWR-86/29, December 1985).

Tierney, Kathleen J., A Primer for Preparedness for Acute Chemical Emergencies (Columbus, Ohio: Ohio State University, Disaster Research Center, 1980).

___, Report on the Coalinga Earthquake of May 2, 1983 (Sacramento, Calif: California Seismic Safety Commission, No. SSC 85-01, September 1985).

Turner, Barry A., <u>Man-Made Disaster</u> (New York: Crane
    Russak, 1978).
Turner, Ralph H., Joanne M. Nigg, and Denise Heller
    Paz, <u>Waiting for Disaster: Earthquake Watch
    in California</u> (Berkeley, Calif.: University
    of California Press, 1986).
UNESCO, <u>The Assessment and Mitigation of Earthquake
    Risk</u>, intergovernmental conference on the
    assessment and mitigation of earthquake
    risk, Paris, 1976 (Paris: UNESCO, 1978).
United Nations, Office of the U.N. Disaster Relief Co-
    Ordinator, <u>Earthquake Prediction and
    Mitigation of Earthquake Losses</u>, <u>Volumes 1-
    2</u>, proceedings of the UNDRO/USSR/UNESCO/UNDP
    training seminar, Dushanbe, U.S.S.R.,
    October 8-14, 1986 (Geneva, Switzerland:
    United Nations Office of Disaster Relief,
    1987).
U.S. Agency for International Development, Office of
    U.S. Foreign Disaster Assistance, <u>Disaster
    History: Significant Data on Major Disasters
    Worldwide, 1900-Present</u> (Washington, D.C.:
    U.S. Agency for International Development,
    July 1989).
U.S. Comptroller General, U.S. General Accounting
    Office, <u>States Can Be Better Prepared to
    Respond to Disasters</u> (Washington, D.C.: U.S.
    General Accounting Office, CED-80-60, March
    31, 1980).
____, <u>National Flood Insurance: Marginal Impact on
    Flood Plain Development, Administrative
    Improvements Needed</u> (Washington, D.C.: U.S.
    General Accounting Office, CED-82-105,
    August 16, 1982).
____, <u>Management of the Federal Emergency Management
    Agency: A System Being Developed</u>
    (Washington, D.C.: U.S. General Accounting
    Office, GGD-83-9, January 6, 1983).
____, <u>Stronger Direction Needed for the National
    Earthquake Program</u> (Washington, D.C.: U.S.
    General Accounting Office, RCED-83-103, July
    26, 1983).
____, <u>Consolidation of Federal Assistance Resources
    Will Enhance the Federal-State Emergency
    Management Effort</u> (Washington, D.C.: U.S.
    General Accounting Office, GGD-83-92, August
    30, 1983).
____, <u>The Federal Emergency Management Agency's Plan
    for Revitalizing U.S. Civil Defense: A
    Review of Three Major Plan Components</u>
    (Washington, D.C.: U.S. Government Printing
    Office, NSIAD-84-11, April 16, 1984).

___, Probabilistic Risk Assessment: An Emerging Aid to Nuclear Power Plant Safety Regulation (Washington, D.C.: U.S. Government Printing Office, GAO/RCED-85-11, June 19, 1985).

___, Health Risk Analysis: Technical Adequacy in Three Selected Cases (Washington, D.C.: U.S. Government Printing Office, GAO/PEMD-87-14, September 1987).

___, Federal Fire Management: Evaluation of Changes Made after Yellowstone, statement of James Duffus III, director, Natural Resources Management Issues, before the Environment, Energy, and Natural Resources Subcommittee, Committee on Government Operations, U.S. House of Representatives, GAO/T-RCED-90-84, May 24, 1990.

___, Preliminary Information on the Federal Government's Response to Recent Natural Disasters, testimony of John M. Ols, Director, Housing and Community Development Issues, before the Subcommittee on Investigations and Oversigh, Committee on Public Works, U.S. House of Representatives, GAO/T-RCED-90-75, May 1, 1990.

U.S. Congress, House of Representatives, A Unified National Program for Managing Flood Losses, report of the Task Force on Federal Flood Control Policy, 89th Congress, 2d Session, 1966, H.Doc. 465.

___, Committee on Public Works and Transportation, Federal Disaster Relief Program, report by the Subcommittee on Investigations and Review, 1978.

___, Committee on Government Operations, FEMA Oversight: Will U.S. Nuclear Attack Evacuation Plans Work? hearing before the Subcommittee on Environment, Energy, and Natural Resources, 97th Congress, 2d Session, 1982.

___, Committee on Science and Technology, Information Technology for Emergency Management, report prepared by the Congressional Research Service for the Subcommittee on Investigations and Oversight, 98th Congress, 2d Session, October 9, 1984.

___, Joint Committee on Defense Production, Civil Preparedness and Industrial Mobilization, report by the Committee, 95th Congress, 1st Session, 1977.

___, Office of Technology Assessment, Issues and Options in Flood Hazard Management

(Washington, D.C.: Office of Technology Assessment, OTA-BP-X-3, February 1980).

____, Senate, Committee on Commerce, Science, and Transportation, <u>Reauthorization of National Earthquake Hazards Reduction Act</u>, hearings held by the Subcommittee on Science, Technology, and Space, 96th Congress, 2d Session, 1980.

____, Committee on Foreign Relations, <u>U.S. and Soviet Civil Defense Program</u>, hearings held by the Subcommittee on Arms Control, Oceans, International Operations and Environment, 97th Congress, 2d Session, 1982.

____, Committee on Commerce, Science, and Transportation, <u>Earthquake Hazards Reduction Act Reauthorization</u>, 98th Congress, 1st Session, 1983.

____, Committee on Environment and Public Works, <u>Omnibus Water Resources Legislation</u>, hearings held by the Subcommittee on Water Resources, 98th Congress, 1st Session, 1983.

U.S. Department of Housing and Urban Development, <u>Evaluation of the Economic, Social, and Environmental Effects of Floodplain Regulations</u> (Washington, D.C.: Federal Emergency Management Agency, FIA-8, March 1981).

U.S. Environmental Protection Agency, <u>Review of Emergency Systems</u>, report to Congress on Sectin 305(b) Title III, Superfund Amendments and Reauthorization Act of 1986 (Washington, D.C.: U.S. Government Printing Office, June 1988).

U.S. Environmental Protection Agency/United Nations Environment Programme, <u>Effects of Changes in Stratospheric Ozone and Global Climate</u>, report of the international conference on health and environmental effects of ozone modification and climate change, <u>Volume 1: Overview</u>, <u>Volume 2: Stratospheric Ozone</u>, <u>Volume 3: Climate Change</u>, <u>Volume 4: Sea Level Rise</u> (Washington, D.C.: U.S. Environmental Protection Agency, October 1986).

U.S. Geological Survey, <u>A Study of Earthquake Losses in the Puget Sound, Washington Area</u> (Reston, Va.: U.S. Geological Survey, 1975).

____, <u>A Study of Earthquake Losses in the Salt Lake City, Utah Area</u> (Reston, Va.: U.S. Geological Survey, 1976).

____, <u>Proceedings of Conference XV: A Workshop on "Preparing for and Responding to a Damaging</u>

Earthquake in the Eastern United States,"
Knoxville, Tennessee, September 16-18, 1981
(Reston, Va.: U.S. Geological Survey, Open
File Report 82-220, 1982).

___, Proceedings of Conference XX: A Workshop on "The
1886 Charleston, South Carolina, Earthquake
and Its Implications for Today," Charleston,
S.C., May 23-26, 1983 (Reston, Va.: U.S.
Geological Survey, Open File Report 83-843).

___, Proceedings of the Symposium on "The New Madrid
Seismic Zone", Reston, Va., November 26,
1984 (Reston, Va.: U.S. Geological Survey,
Open File Report 84-770, 1984).

___, Primer on Improving the State of Earthquake
Hazards Mitigation and Preparedness (Reston,
Va.: U.S. Geological Survey, Open File
Report 84-772, 1984).

___, National Earthquake Hazards Reduction Program:
Overview (Alexandria, Va.: U.S. Geological
Survey, Circular 918, 1984).

___, National Earthquake Hazards Reduction Program:
Fiscal Year 1983 (Alexandria, Va.: U.S.
Geological Survey, Circular 919, 1984).

___, The Loma Prieta Earthquake of October 17, 1989:
What Happened, What is Expected, What Can Be
Done (Washington, D.C.: U.S. Government
Printing Office, November 1989, Revised
January 1990).

___, Lessons Learned from the Loma Prieta, California,
Earthquake of October 17, 1989 (Washington,
D.C.: U.S. Government Print Office, U.S.
Geological Survey Circular 1045, November
1989).

Volcano: The Eruption of Mount St. Helens (Longview,
Wash.: Longview, 1980).

Waugh, William L., Jr., Terrorism and Emergency
Management: Policy and Administration (New
York and Basel: Marcel Dekker, 1990).

___, "Integrating the Policy Models of Terrorism and
Emergency Management," Policy Studies Review
(Fall 1986).

___, International Terrorism: How Nations Respond to
Terrorists (Chapel Hill, N.C.: Documentary
Publications, 1982).

Western, Karl A., Epidemiological Surveillance After
Natural Disaster (Washington, D.C.: Pan
American Health Organization, 1982).

White, Gilbert F., ed., Natural Hazards: Local,
National, Global (New York: Oxford
University Press, 1974).

Wolensky, Robert P., Power, Policy, and Disaster: The
Political-Organizational Impact of a Major

Flood (Stevens Point, Wisc.: Unversity of Wisconsin-Stevens Point, Center for the Small City, 1984)(Final Report, National Science Foundation Grant No. CEE 8113529).

Wood, William C., _Insuring Nuclear Power: Liability, Safety and Economic Efficiency_ (Greenwich, Conn.: JAI, 1982).

Wright, James D., and Peter H. Rossi, eds., _Social Science and Natural Hazards_ (Cambridge, Mass.: Abt, 1981).

___, ed., _After the Clean-Up: Long Range Effects of Natural Disasters_ (Beverly Hills, Calif.: Sage, 1979).

Zucherman, Edward, _The Day after World War III: The U.S. Government's Plans for Surviving a Nuclear War_ (New York: Viking, 1984).

Emergency Management
Organizations and Information
Sources

American Association of Avalanche Professionals
P.O. Box 510904
Salt Lake City, UT 84151

American Meteorological Society
45 Beacon Street
Boston, MA 02108   617/227-2425

American Planning Association
1313 East Sixtieth Street
Chicago, IL 60637   312/955-9100

American Public Works Association
Council on Emergency Management
1313 East Sixtieth Street
Chicago, IL 60637   312/667-2200

American Red Cross
Office of Disaster Assistance
18th and E Streets, N.W.
Washington, DC 20006   202/639-3393

Section on Emergency Management
American Society for Public Administration
c/o Editor, Emergency Management Dispatch
School of Public Administration and Urban Studies
Georgia State University
Atlanta, GA 30302-4018   404/651-3350

Association of Dam Safety Officials
P.O. Box 55270
Lexington, KY 40555   606/257-5140

Association of State Floodplain Managers
P.O. Box 7921
Madison, WI 53707   608/266-1926

Association of State Wetlands Managers
P.O. Box 2463
Berne, NY 12023   518/872-1804

Bay Area Regional Earthquake Preparedness Project
Metrocenter
101 8th Street, Suite 152
Oakland, CA 94607   415/540-2713

Building Seismic Safety Council
1015 15th Street, N.W., Suite 700
Washington, DC 20005   202/347-5710

California Seismic Safety Commission
1900 K Street, Suite 100
Sacramento, CA 95814   916/322-4917

California Specialized Training Institute
California Office of Emergency Services
P.O. Box 8104
San Luis Obispo, CA 93403   805/549-3344

Central U.S. Earthquake Consortium
2610 East Holmes Road
Memphis, TN 38118   901/398-9054

Chemical Manufacturers Association
Chemical Awareness and Emergency Response Program
2501 M Street, N.W.
Washington, DC 20037   202/887-1150

Earthquake Engineering Research Institute
6431 Fairmount Avenue, Suite 7
El Cerrito, CA 94530   415/525-3668

Environmental and Societal Impacts Group
National Center for Atmospheric Research
P.O. Box 3000
Boulder, CO 80307   303/497-1619

Hazard Management Group
Oak Ridge National Laboratory-Energy Division
P.O. Box 2008
Oak Ridge, TN 37831   615/576-2716

Insurance Information Institute
110 Williams Street
New York, NY 10038   212/669-9200

International Association of Fire Chiefs
1329 18th Street, N.W.
Washington, DC 20036   202/833-3420

International City Managers Association
1120 G Street, N.W.
Washington, DC 20005   202/626-4634

International Tsunami Information Center
Box 50027
Honolulu, HI 96850-4993   808/541-1658

National Association of Urban Flood Management
Agencies
1225 Eye Street, N.W., Suite 300
Washington, DC 20005   202/682-3761

National Coordinating Council on Emergency Management
7297 Lee Highway, Suite N
Falls Church, VA 22042   703/533-7672

National Emergency Managers Association
c/o Georgia Emergency Management Agency
P.O. Box 18055
Atlanta, GA 30316   404/624-7000

National EMS Clearinghouse
Council of State Governments
P.O. Box 11910
Iron Works Pike
Lexington, KY 40578   606/252-2291

National Governors Association
444 North Capitol Street
Washington, DC 20001   202/624-5389

Adapted from the compilation of the Natural Hazards
Research and Information Center at the University of
Colorado.

Index

Agency for Toxic Substances and Disease Registry
(ATSDR), 256, 258, 263-4, 269-70
Alcohol, Drug Abuse, and Mental Health Administration
(ADAMHA), 263-4, 267. See also Centers for
Disease Control
American Red Cross, 75, 116, 122, 118, 248
Andrus, Cecil, 152, 214
Aviation disasters, 1, 4, 9, 180, 219-32, 294, 301

Becton, Julius, 210, 287
Boise Interagency Fire Center (BIFC), 131, 133-4, 137-
8, 141
Bridge failures, 235-7, 239, 252, 296
Building codes, 2, 12, 14, 19, 33, 36-37, 43-44, 62,
68, 71, 85, 87, 89, 234, 239-40, 242, 244-6,
250-1, 253, 297, 298, 300
Bureau of Indian Affairs (BIA), 133, 139
Bureau of Land Management (BLM), 37, 131, 133-6, 139,
141
Bureau of Reclamation, 83, 156, 162
Business loans, 31, 71. See also Small Business
Administration

Centers for Disease Control, 38, 55, 255-8, 263-8;
Center for Environmental Health (CEH), 55,
57; Center for Environmental Health and
Injury Control (CEHIC), 257; Division of
Environmental Hazards and Health Effects
(DEHHE), 256; Division of Environmental
Health Laboratory Sciences (DEHLS), 256-7;
Emergency Response Coordinating Group, 256;

About the Editors and Contributors

Caffilene Allen received her Master of Public Administration and Master of Science in Community Counseling degrees from Georgia State University. From 1980 to 1987, she was employed by the Centers for Disease Control (CDC) and, from 1987 to 1989, at the Agency for Toxic Substances and Disease Registry, a federal public health agency with lead responsibilities for emergency response. She is currently a program analyst with CDC's Center for Infectious Diseases.

Joan B. Aron is a senior policy analyst at the U.S. Nuclear Regulatory Commission and an adjunct professor of public policy at the Center for Public Administration and Policy, Virginia Polytechnic Institute and State University. She is the author of numerous articles and book reviews about nuclear energy decision making. She was formerly an associate professor at the Graduate School of Public Administration, New York University, specializing in the governance of the New York metropolitan region.

Margaret Baty is associate vice chancellor at Embry-Riddle Aeronautical University in Prescott, Arizona.

Raymond J. Burby is professor of planning at the University of North Carolina at Chapel Hill. He is the author of eleven books, several of which deal with natural hazards, and dozens of articles, chapters, and other publications. Burby completed a five-year term as co-editor of the Journal of the American Planning Association in 1988 and currently serves on the editorial boards of three journals and on the board of directors of the Urban Affairs Association. In addition to natural and chemical hazards, his research has focused on the evaluation of state and local land-use and environmental management policy and on the effects of the physical environment on individual well-being.

Beverly A. Cigler is professor of public policy and administration at Penn State, Harrisburg. She is the author of over fifty journal articles, book chapters, and technical reports on alternative service delivery, growth management, emergency management, local energy policy and implementation, consultants, fiscal stress, and small cities. She currently serves on six editorial boards and is the TOPS essay editor for Public Administration Review. Cigler is a coordinator of the National Small Government Research Network.

John C. Freemuth is assistant professor of political science at Boise State University.

Ronald John Hy is the director of the Division of Governmental Studies and professor of public administration at the University of Arkansas at Little Rock. He is the author of Financial Management for Health Care Administrators (1989), co-author of Research Methods and Statistics (1983), and author of numerous articles, chapters, and reports.

David T. Jervis is assistant professor of political science at Washburn University of Topeka, Kansas. He is the author of several articles on U.S. foreign policy and its implementation.

Diane Moskow-McKenzie is a graduate assistant in the Master of Public Affairs Program at Boise State University.

Thomas J. Pavlak is professor of public administration and director of the Public Administration Institute at Fairleigh Dickinson University. Prior to this appointment he was on the faculty of the Graduate School of Public and International Affairs at the University of Pittsburgh where he had served as director of doctoral studies and director of the Public Management and Policy Program. Pavlak's current research focuses on issues of administrative justice, organizational effectiveness, and performance evaluation. His recent work includes articles on AIDS in the workplace, union members' attitudes toward the grievance procedure, and disaster planning in New York City.

Loran B. Smith is associate professor of political science at Washburn University of Topeka, Kansas. He has authored several articles and monographs on emergency management and state and local economic development efforts.

Richard T. Sylves is professor of political science at the University of Delaware and a past chairperson for the American Society for Public Administration's Section on Emergency Management. He authored The Nuclear Oracles: A Political History of the General Advisory Committee of the U.S. Atomic Energy Commission, 1947-77. His areas of research and publication include emergency management and the policy areas of science and technology, nuclear energy, defense, and environmental protection. He spent 1986/87 as a public service fellow and producer at WHYY TV-12 Philadelphia/Wilmington public television.

Jeanette M. Trauth is a research associate in the Center for Social and Urban Research at the University of Pittsburgh where she is the coordinator of the Risk and Emergency Management Program. She also has a joint appointment with the University's Center for Hazardous Materials Research. During the past nine years, she has authored more than a dozen policy research reports, articles, and conference papers relating to the organizational aspects of managing hazardous materials. Currently, Dr. Trauth has several research grants to develop methods to explain the risks from various health and environmental hazards to the lay audience.

William L. Waugh, Jr., is associate professor of public administration, urban studies, and political science at Georgia State University. He is the author of Terrorism and Emergency Management (1990) and International Terrorism (1982) and the co-editor of Cities and Disaster (1990) and Antiterrorism Policies (1991), as well as the author of numerous articles, chapters, and reports published in the U.S., Canada, and Western Europe. He is chair-elect of the American Society for Public Administration's Section on Emergency Management and editor of Emergency Management Dispatch.

Donald A. Wilhite is associate professor of agricultural climatology at the University of

Nebraska-Lincoln and director of the International Drought Information Center. He also has an adjunct appointment with the National Center for Atmospheric Research. He specializes in studies of the impact of climate on society and societal response to climatic events. He is the author of numerous papers and book chapters on drought management and planning, his primary area of research activity, and is co-editor (with William E. Easterling) of the proceedings of the International Symposium and Workshop on Drought, <u>Planning for Drought: Toward a Reduction of Societal Vulnerability</u> (1987).